RELIGIOUS OTHERING

Perhaps the most disturbing feature of globalization is the emergence of a new tribalism, an attitude expressed in the common phrase, "thank God we're not like them." *Religious Othering: Global Dimensions* explores this political and religious phenomenon.

Why are these new xenophobic movements erupting around the world at this moment in history, and what are the features of religious identity that seem to appeal to them? How do we make sense of the strident forms of religious exclusion that have been a part of the past and re-emerged around the world in recent years? This book brings together research scholars from different fields who have had to answer these questions in their own ground-breaking research on religious-othering movements. Written in an engaging, personal style, these essays share these scholars' attempts to get inside the worldviews of these neo-nationalists through such research approaches as participant observation, empathetic interviews, and close textual reading.

Religious Othering: Global Dimensions is of interest to students and scholars in religious studies and the social sciences. In addition, anyone concerned about the rise of religious extremism in the contemporary world will be fascinated with these journeys into the mindsets of dogmatic and sometimes violent religious groups.

Mark Juergensmeyer is Distinguished Professor Emeritus of Sociology and Global Studies at the University of California, Santa Barbara, and William F. Podlich Distinguished Fellow and Professor of Religious Studies at Claremont McKenna College.

Kathleen Moore is Professor of Religious Studies and Associate Dean of Humanities at the University of California, Santa Barbara.

Dominic Sachsenmaier is Professor of Modern China and Global History and Dean of the Faculty of Humanities, Göttingen University.

RELIGIOUS OTHERING

Global Dimensions

Edited by Mark Juergensmeyer, Kathleen Moore, and Dominic Sachsenmaier

LONDON AND NEW YORK

Cover image: Leonid Eremeychuk/EyeEm/Getty Images

First published 2023
by Routledge
4 Park Square, Milton Park, Abingdon, Oxon OX14 4RN

and by Routledge
605 Third Avenue, New York, NY 10158

Routledge is an imprint of the Taylor & Francis Group, an informa business

British Library Cataloguing-in-Publication Data
A catalogue record for this book is available from the British Library

Library of Congress Cataloging-in-Publication Data
A catalog record has been requested for this book

ISBN: 978-1-032-28069-1 (hbk)
ISBN: 978-1-032-28067-7 (pbk)
ISBN: 978-1-003-29519-8 (ebk)

DOI: 10.4324/b22926

Typeset in Bembo
by Apex CoVantage, LLC

To the memory of our colleagues,
Michael Jerryson and
Christoph Zimmer

CONTENTS

CONTRIBUTORS

James Aho is Emeritus Professor of Sociology at Idaho State University.

Diana Dimitrova is Professor of South Asian Religions in the Institute for Religious Studies at the Université de Montréal.

Flora Ferati-Sachsenmaier is Research Fellow at Max Planck Institute for the Study of Religious and Ethnic Diversity, Göttingen.

Farid Hafez is Visiting Professor of International Studies, Williams College, and a Senior Fellow at Georgetown University's The Bridge Initiative.

Michael Jerryson was Professor of Religious Studies at Youngstown State University.

Mark Juergensmeyer is Distinguished Professor Emeritus of Sociology and Global Studies at the University of California, Santa Barbara, and William F. Podlich Distinguished Fellow and Professor of Religious Studies at Claremont McKenna College.

Kathleen Moore is Professor of Religious Studies and Associate Dean of Humanities at the University of California, Santa Barbara.

Mareike Riedel is Lecturer, Macquarie Law School, Macquarie University, Sydney.

Dominic Sachsenmaier is Professor of Modern China and Global History, and Dean of the Faculty of Humanities at Göttingen University.

Irene Schneider is Professor of Arabic and Islamic Studies at Göttingen University.

Jamel Velji is Associate Professor of Religious Studies, Claremont McKenna College.

Christoph Zimmer was a lecturer and PhD candidate in East Asian Studies at Göttingen University.

INTRODUCTION

"Thank God We're Not Like Them"

Mark Juergensmeyer, Kathleen Moore, and Dominic Sachsenmaier

When people say, "thank God we're not like them," they are perhaps unconsciously revealing an ethnocentric bias that in its extreme form is a kind of religious othering. This phenomenon has spread throughout the world in the first decades of the 21st century and in its political form has led to ethnic cleansing and strident anti-minority hostilities. Increasingly, it is becoming a phenomenon that is shaped by the forces of globalization.

It is global in its scope, though often it is expressed as anti-globalism and as an attempt to reassert the primacy of traditional national cultures. Perhaps the most disturbing feature of the global age is the emergence of a new tribalism, often organized around ethnic and religious identities. The essays in the book explore answers to basic questions about this phenomenon of religious othering: why are these new xenophobic movements erupting around the world at this moment in history, and what are the features of religious identity that seem to appeal to them?

Globalization and Othering

At the end of World War II, the world seemed to be on the verge of a bold new order. About to abandon the great empires, much of the world was turning toward the notion of the secular nation-state. Fundamental to this construct was the idea of secular nationalism – the understanding that peoples in a particular region were to be represented by governments that were free from the taint of any kind of ethnic, religious, or any other social prejudice. Perhaps nothing exemplified this new world order better than the United Nations, created to be a parliament representing nations from every corner of the planet. More than a symbol, the UN was created to be the instrument of international peace.

But the notion of nationalism, even secular nationalism, contained a fatal flaw. It contained within it the assumption that there were natural communities of people

DOI: 10.4324/b22926-1

in particular places who collectively comprised nations (Lie 2004). In Europe, where the idea of the nation-state first took hold in the modern world, these national communities were supposedly demarcated by cultural and social origins. Most French, for example, spoke French; their ancestors were French; and their religion was largely Roman Catholic Christianity. Even secular nationalism contained ethno-religious assumptions about the homogeneity of peoples within a national community.

To some extent, immigrant societies such as the United States were regarded as exceptions. But until relatively recently, the United States was largely a nation that privileged European immigrants along with an African working class, first as slaves and then as less privileged citizens. The country had a unified language, English, and its religion was largely Christian with a smattering of Jews, but they were largely European Jews. So the basic assumptions about nationalism embracing a social and cultural homogeneity applied to the United States as well.

In other parts of the world, the business of carving out nation-states from old empires or other polities was often undertaken by British and other European officials following the two great world wars of the 20th century or by local elites that took over colonial institutions. To a large degree, nation-states in Africa and the Middle East were drawn around ethnic and cultural lines, replicating the European pattern. In South Asia, British India was split apart on religious lines, creating a Muslim Pakistan and a predominantly Hindu India; in the Middle East, the holdings of the Ottoman Empire were chopped into the states of Turkey, Syria, Iraq, Saudi Arabia, Jordan, Lebanon, and Israel. The problem, however, was that few of these states in Africa, Asia, and the Middle East were completely homogeneous, and much of the political conflict in recent years has been due to the simmering ethno-religious tensions created by these artificial demarcations.

All these problems have been compounded by a new development, globalization. Increasingly, in the last decades of the 20th century and the first decades of the 21st century, the global population has been on the move. The easy access to international travel, the instant communications provided through cell phones and social mobility, and the desperate search for safe harbor in areas of social and political unrest have created a situation where increasingly large numbers of people can live everywhere and do. This is a direct challenge to the old notion of a cultural homogeneity of nationhood. Increasingly, most European countries are confronting fellow citizens in their populations who look differently, speak differently, and worship differently. When a large section of Brussels is comprised of Algerian Muslim refugees, even a multi-cultural country like Belgium finds it difficult to cope.

In other parts of Europe, the resentment against the new immigrants and refugees has taken a right-wing political turn. The second decade of the 21st century has witnessed the sudden successes of *Fidesz*, the Hungarian Civic Alliance, headed by Victor Orban; the Polish party, *Prawo i Sprawiedliwość* ("Law and Justice"), founded by Lech and Jaroslaw Kaczyński; and the *Alternative für Deutschland* (AfD) in Germany. Similar parties have appeared elsewhere in Europe, including the Front National in France, the Italian *Fratelli d'Italia* (Brothers of Italy), and right-wing movements in Norway, Sweden, Finland, Denmark, and the Netherlands. Much of the support for the campaign for Brexit in the United Kingdom has come from anti-immigrant right-wing groups.

Across the pond in the United States, the 2016 election of Donald Trump was supported by strident anti-Muslim anti-Jewish White supremacy nationalist movements opposed to anyone in the country whose ancestry could not be traced to Christian European ethnic roots. White xenophobia was not new in America, however. The history of the United States is clouded with White hate movements, most notably the Ku Klux Klan, which reached its zenith in the first half of the 20th century. Later, Black Muslims became a target for hatred. The fact that many African Americans had embraced Islam provided a double reason for many White supremacists to despise them. For a time, the U.S. Federal Bureau of Investigation (the FBI) secretly scrutinized the movement considering them dangerous and possibly treasonous. By the end of the century and the opening decades of the 21st century, White xenophobia surfaced again in new forms, often in vicious ways.

The violence of contemporary right-wing White Supremacist movements in the United States was graphically demonstrated by the ugly protests in Charlottesville, Virginia, in 2018, the massacre of Hispanic immigrants in El Paso, Texas, in 2019, the White Supremacy character of the 6 January 2021 insurrection at the nation's Capitol building, and the Buffalo, New York assault on an Afto-American grocery store on 14 May 2022 that was motivated by the conspiracy theory that minorities intend to replace the dominant White Christian culture. By the beginning of the third decade of the 21st century, White Supremacists had overtaken Muslim extremists as Americans' greatest fear of terrorism on native soil.

This is a significant social phenomenon that deserves scholarly attention, both in the study of particular cases and in attempts to understand the general pattern. From a broader perspective, however, the question is whether and how these specific developments are related to the rise of religious-related neo-nationalism on a worldwide scope.

From Myanmar to Moscow, new movements of religious nationalism have recently emerged. Perhaps the first significant movement of religious nationalism in contemporary experience was the Islamic revolution in Iran in 1978–79 that privileged Shi'a Islam as the organizing principle of the state. Movements such as the Muslim Brotherhood in Egypt that have been in the background for years have risen to new prominence, and in the Egyptian case, the Muslim Brotherhood briefly controlled the reins of power. The rise of the ISIS, the Islamic State, was largely due to disaffected Sunni Arabs in both Iraq and Syria who joined forces in protest against their political marginalization. In Israel, there has been a hardening of nationalist sentiment that privileges Jewish identities, and in India, the Hindu *Bharatiya Janata Party* has been accused of fostering anti-Muslim sentiments and attempting to redefine nationalism along Hindu lines. The rise of Buddhist nationalism in Southeast Asia has led to tragic violence, with thousands of Myanmar Rohingya Muslims persecuted and expelled. In Russia, leaders of the

Orthodox Church openly endorsed the invasion of Ukraine. It seems, therefore, that religion-related neo-nationalism has a global context.

These movements are products of globalization in two ways. The demographic mobility associated with globalization has led to a strident resentment of newcomers and a defensive protection of traditional cultures and societies. Globalization has eroded trust in the secular nation-state and allowed a defensive ethno-nationalism to take root. At the same time, these phenomena are global in another sense. Since they appear around the world at roughly the same time in history, they give credence to the idea that they are themselves aspects of globalization and somehow connected to one another – they are aspects of a global rise of anti-globalism.

At the heart of these political movements are personal fears. Individuals have seen the arrival of newcomers as threatening to their way of life. Accompanying this sense of being culturally assaulted is the cultural pretension that the newcomers are insufficient in many ways – not just culturally and socially but intellectually and morally. The phrase "thank God we're not like them" expresses this feeling that the outliers are a distant "other" to which the traditional society is vastly superior and that this attitude is blessed by God.

Contexts and Historical Dimensions

Globalization and nationalist sentiments shape the dynamics of religious othering today, but they didn't create it. Negative stereotypes about other beliefs are probably as old as religions themselves – we find traces of them in the Bible, the Qur'an, and many other ancient sacred texts. The Roman Empire witnessed systematic religious persecutions, first against Christians who refused to participate in the official state cult and then, starting from the 4th century, by the Christian majority against the adherents of the former official religions. In the 3rd century BCE, the newly founded Qin dynasty embarked on a broad anti-Confucian campaign, burning books and arresting hundreds of scholars. Religious othering was usually an integral part of such violent suppression.

We could easily extend the list of religious violence throughout history. The European Middle Ages would provide us with rich materials, as would the early modern period with all its religious wars, and we could provide many additional examples from the worlds of Buddhism, Islam, and other religions in all corners of the globe. In most cases, religious violence was not primarily motivated by religious beliefs: it was often rooted in social tensions and political conflicts or tied to economic interests. This is also the case today. Religious identities certainly play a strong role in the Israeli–Palestinian conflict, the hostile relationship between Shiite Iran and Sunni Saudi Arabia, or the more recent persecution of the Rohingya in Myanmar, but even these identity struggles cannot be properly understood without taking other factors and forces into the picture. These range from local political interests to geopolitical rivalries, and while religious identities might not be absent from them, much more profane logics are at work when political interest groups and states clash with one another.

At the same time, there is no reason to discard the cultural factors underlying religious violence as marginal or unimportant. Religious conflict or the suppression of minorities in the name of God would hardly be possible without a hardening of religious identities and polarizing forms of religious othering. Othering can not only imply social segregation, legal suppression, and many other practical measures, but it also takes place at a mental level. The construction or intensification of negative stereotypes doesn't necessarily depend on state authorities or other political forces. In many cases, the driving forces involved in religious othering are figures like priests, imams, shamans, monks, and nuns, and they frequently used forms of religious expression ranging from sermons to prayers and chants. They deploy their spiritual authority and sometimes their personal charisma to portray other religious communities as menacing, as a demonic other.

At its very core, religious othering is grounded in negative stereotypes and the systematic buildup of an imagined divide between one's own faith and other creeds. It emphasizes the communalities of one's own group and exaggerates the differences of others. Particularly when it endorses violence, it can portray the religious other not as a tolerable alternative, but as a hostile force that can threaten one's own community. The alleged threat could be aggression from the other side or something much subtler. Religious authorities often mobilize their believers against a religious other that they perceive as already having begun infiltrating their ranks. For example, many forms of Islamic fundamentalism put the Muslim *umma* in opposition to a West that is defined partly as Christian civilization and partly as an empty, secular form of modernity. Many imams related to these fundamentalist branches ring rhetorical alarm bells against members of local society whom the imams think have already sold out their religious integrity to the West. In the Maghreb, Afghanistan, and many other places, girls' schools have been ambushed by Muslim extremists who claim the schools indoctrinate women to lead un-Islamic lives. The first steps to these ambushes occur at a rhetorical level when these schools are described as other – as agents that will lead to the disintegration of local life and religious bonds.

We could add a long list of modern and pre-modern examples that illustrate the same point: othering is often rooted not in profound differences but in the perceived dangers of assimilation. To put it a different way, the proponents of othering can also fight against what they see as the dangers of a growing sameness. The rise of modern anti-Semitism certainly had deep roots in European history, but at the same time, it was also an expression of anger, prejudice, and hatred against the growing assimilation of Jews in late 19th-century France or Germany. A millennium before the rise of modern anti-Semitism, some essentialist Confucian circles threw their weight behind anti-Buddhist campaigns. They weren't worried that Buddhism was too strange to be feasible in their world. On the contrary, they were concerned about Buddhism becoming too influential within the Chinese state and its surrounding scholarly landscapes. Religious othering is often meant to benefit those who fear that they will be losing power and influence from the growing acceptance of pluralism in their own society.

While religious othering is characterized by many historical continuities, its concrete mechanisms have changed over time. It has evolved along with the history of the media. The European Reformation would have hardly been possible without the wide dissemination of pamphlets that had become possible with the newly developed printing press. Through widely circulated texts, Luther and his followers portrayed the Catholic church as an institutional other that had lost touch with the true spirit of the Gospel. And when books started reaching a broader audience in the flourishing book market of China's Late Ming Dynasty (16th to 17th centuries), many spread religious stereotypes within Chinese society. Some Confucian texts blamed the social and political crisis of the time on Buddhist influences; others targeted the growing number of Chinese Christians. When European missionaries and local converts began publishing books in China, they also resorted to religious othering, depicting Taoism, Buddhism, and many Neo-Confucian schools as baseless learnings that had rendered China's overall condition increasingly unstable. Whether in Reformation Europe or Late Ming China, print media changed the cultures of religious othering. Authors trying to speak to an anonymous audience that was flooded with printed materials had to sharpen their tones to be heard.

Similarly, today's new media have a great impact on religious othering. The internet and social media have become important tools for the self-presentation of religious communities, which can go hand in hand with spreading stereotypes about non-believers or other faiths. As so often, the new medium influences the message: the possibility of spreading brief text messages to a large number of people facilitates the circulation of stereotypes of others. Video clips are also a great tool for identity politics – they convey scandalous and dramatic moments like segments of a speech or the mistreatment of people, which can rapidly enrage a large audience and spread like a wildfire. As a general trend, social media make it harder to convey complex, multifaceted arguments and easier to broadcast simplistic images. We can already see how social media shapes the dynamics of religious othering. Religious communication, for example, has become more visual and faster than in the age of print media.

The current media revolution has also changed other important facets of religious life. Religious communities learn from each other faster than ever before, even across boundaries of languages and faith systems. One example is the way that some conservative Islamic groups in Turkey have adopted arguments for de-secularizing the state from Christian fundamentalists in the United States. While the Turkish Islamic right certainly has no interest in the Christian message, they appreciate the ways in which Christian fundamentalists critique modern states as godless institutions. The circulation of ideas, images, and narratives between different creeds does not mean that religions necessarily grow more appreciative or tolerant of one another. Instead, they appropriate aspects of other creeds and use them to fortify the boundaries between "us" and "them" or between believers and unbelievers.

In today's world, religious othering takes place amid an awareness that religions and societies are interconnected, and is often framed as a battle against global entanglements. Yet what many agents actively involved in religious othering usually fail to admit (or even recognize) is that religions around the globe have been tied to a common web of exchanges and have come to share key concepts. Particularly during the 19th and early 20th centuries, global conditions of imperialism and Western hegemony meant that many languages experienced great change, which impacted the conceptual worlds of religions. In fact, the term "religion" is a case in point (Frans Wijsen and von Stuckrad 2016; Nongbri 2013). In the West, the word "religion" was not commonly used until the 18th century as a term connoting a multitude of faith systems, but after the European Enlightenment, the term began to play an important role in European history.

In many languages, including Chinese, Japanese, or Hindi, an equivalent to "religion" simply did not exist prior to the second half of the 19th century. Unlike in Europe, in the intellectual worlds of pre-19th century China and India, this contrast between a this-worldly philosophy that took human reasoning as its point of departure and religion that started from the word of God simply did not exist. Different teachings were not categorically divided, and the main differences between them were not how secular or transcendental they were, but what core texts they used and how closely related they were to the official state examination system.

In China, starting from the late 1800s, an equivalent of the term "religion" (zongjiao – 宗教) began to spread, first in intellectual circles, then more broadly. During the same period, many other concepts – ranging from "individual" to "society" and from "science" to "rationality" were integrated into the Chinese language (Liu 1995). This terminological change was part of a broader transformation that deeply impacted the ways that the main Chinese learnings related to each other and the world at large. There were now debates about whether Buddhism should be regarded as a philosophy or a religion and efforts to present Confucianism (a term coined by Jesuit missionaries during the 17th century) as one of the world's great religious traditions.

Such processes greatly altered religious identities, and they also led to new forms of religions othering. Once it was redefined as a religion with clear boundaries, Confucianism could be isolated from the rest of the Chinese system. Beginning in the early 1900s, radical modernizing movements started blaming Confucianism for China's alleged stagnation. Like other communist movements around the world, Maoism built on these movements and embarked on radical anti-religious campaigns that primarily targeted Confucianism and that culminated in the Cultural Revolution. The forces seeking to remove Confucianism from Chinese society did not act in the name of any God but on the authority of modernity and progress. Similar things can be said about the more recent forms of nationalism in China that aggressively target substantial religious communities, leading to the persecution of many Muslims and Christians. Large numbers of Uyghur people in Xinjiang have been targeted for "reeducation," and efforts have been made to discourage ethnic Muslim practices.

The example of China sheds light on the roles that the modern nation-state can play in religious othering. While some states defined themselves as secular forces and even oppressed religion, others became the sites of religious nationalism. In countries from Orthodox Serbia to Muslim Pakistan, one faith was defined as a national religion and its clergy acquired extensive political influence. This linking of modern notions of peoplehood and national identities with religious identities could put great pressure on those citizens who practiced other religions. It often led to the marginalization of minorities and the construction of other religions as the enemies of the nation. In quite a few cases including the Yugoslav Wars during the 1990s, national othering and religious othering merged, and the new combination proved to be quite explosive.

As we have seen, religious othering has a long history, and states have been involved in religious violence since antiquity. But modern national identities have added new components to religious othering, including fears of global assimilation and the idea that nations ought to be homogenous communities. Both sentiments are a major component of many forms of nationalism in today's world, and they also frame religious identities.

Essays on Religious Othering

The global dimension of this attitude of religious othering is something that this volume explores. It began as the focus of a research hub in global religion at the Orfalea Center for Global and International Studies at the University of California, Santa Barbara. The scholars there were joined by colleagues convened at the University of Göttingen in Germany, who were also concerned about the rise of religious othering as a global phenomenon. In a series of workshops in Santa Barbara and Göttingen, a number of scholars from other institutions and a range of disciplinary backgrounds were brought into the conversation. This volume is the result of this rich intellectual exchange about a topic that increasingly disrupts the social fabric around the world.

In these workshops, scholars were asked to describe and define the process of religious othering. They defined it as those attitudes, assumptions, and positions that connect religious phenomena with individual and collective identity formation in ways that are dismissive, belittling, and dehumanizing. In many cases, othering creates images of a barbaric threat. The term "barbaric" was chosen intentionally since the origins of the word are indicative of many othering processes. The term comes from ancient Greece, where the incomprehensible language of foreigners sounded like so much "bar bar" to the Greek speakers. Hence, the word *barbaroi* was coined for outsiders, a term that has resonated to the present day. It conveys a pejorative perspective on the barbaric others – not only those incapable of speaking one's own language but also those who are rude, crass, and potentially dangerous.

To such basic notions of social exclusion, we attached two other dimensions – religious and global. We are particularly interested in the way that othering is linked with religious identities, and how this process occurs around the world. We try to better understand the attitudes that are becoming increasingly prevalent in new movements of religious nationalism and exclusion that have been linked with religious traditions in various parts of the globe – the notion that the divine has blessed a people in a way that makes them special and privileges them over the others.

This othering attitude implies multiple dimensions of power. The exclusionary rhetoric that occurs between and among rival groups in attempts to gain control of the political center displaces the Other to the periphery. These acts of boundary drawing are specific expressions of power relations. As one of the participants in the workshop pointed out, the very legitimacy of nationalism depends on the power construct of boundary maintenance and often implies that a particular homogenous cultural group is the basis for national identity. In a time of globalization, as was mentioned at the outset of this introductory essay, the fragility of the nation-state invites new attempts to shore up a national identity on the basis of religious and ethnic unity. Those who are not a part of this honored group are marginalized or worse: some are victims of ethnic cleansing. In many cases, those who are the "others" of contemporary stereotyping are seen as existential threats, potentially undermining the very legitimacy and existence of those who see them as threatening outsiders.

The opening essay in this volume by James Aho on "The Big Lie" explores the effect of rhetoric in creating an inside-outside dichotomy that can be quite destructive. Aho is particularly mindful of the use of that technique during the Nazi regime, but it has resurfaced in the neo-nationalism of contemporary political movements, including in Europe and the United States. At the heart of the "big lie" is an imagined construct of a perverse and threatening segment of society that by its nature provides an existential threat to the civic community. In the Nazi era, Jews were the imagined enemy, but they have also in other contexts been Muslims, secularists, liberals, and gays.

In the next essay, "Why Shari'a Matters: Law, Ethics, and the Muslim Other in the United States," Kathleen Moore shows that Muslims have become this imagined enemy in certain quarters of right-wing political life in the United States. This essay describes American Islamophobia with particular reference to the perceived threat of Muslim ethics, *shari'a*. As the author shows, the concept is multifaceted and in no way a danger to American public life, though the conspiratorial exaggeration of its significance is itself an important phenomenon. The essay begins with a focus on the way a Muslim student feels threatened by the hostility she feels from the rising tide of Islamophobia in U.S. society. The essay shows how shari'a matters not only as an example of the stridency of political discourse in the United States but also as an important element in the sense of identity and security of American Muslims in a hostile cultural environment.

In the following essay, "Buddhist Constructions of the Islamic Other," Michael Jerryson shows how even the Buddhist tradition has the capacity to stereotype and marginalize non-Buddhists. Although Buddhism has a reputation for tolerance, the process of othering is inherent in ancient Buddhist texts and exists throughout its history. Islam became a subject of othering in Buddhist encounters along the Sikh Road. The othering of Muslims has expanded tragically in recent years in

Myanmar, Sri Lanka, and other Buddhist-dominated societies, where the attitude toward Rohingya and other Muslim minorities has been ruthless.

Jamel Velji, in his essay on "Consuming Difference: Coffee and the Specter of the Islamic Other," turns our attention to the way that Islam has been characterized – and caricatured – in relation to coffee. Velji explores the historical references to coffee and its Arab origins and focuses on the symbol for a Viennese coffee that celebrates the conquering of the Ottoman army at the gates of Vienna in 1683 along with the arrival of the Arab-based popular drink, coffee, and the coffee-houses that purvey it. Velji is particularly interested in the seemingly innocent icon of a Moorish boy that has become the symbol of both coffee and Christian domination in Europe. Such symbols, Velji suggests, support the attitude of othering that continues in Austria and elsewhere in Europe in the contemporary era.

In his chapter "Anti-Muslim Racism in Austria and Germany," Farid Hafez takes the recent waves of Islamophobia among far-right political parties in Austria and Germany as his point of departure. He subsequently places them into various overlapping historical contexts: in Hafez' eyes, the othering of Muslims as an existential threat to Europe's alleged civilizational achievements has deep roots in the age of colonialism. At the same time, Hafez points toward continuities from the anti-Semitic ideologies that dominated right-wing politics about a century ago to the strong role of anti-Islamic worldviews among the political right today. He maintains that since persistent anti-Semitic sentiments are now subdued in the wider public, they are often vented as anti-Islamism – not only in Austria but also in other parts of the world.

Mareike Riedel's article, "'They are from Mars': The Othering of Jews and Muslims in European Legal Debates," also discusses the complex entanglements between anti-Semitic and anti-Islamic currents in European societies. Her case study analyzes European debates about the legal status of the Jewish *shechita* and the Muslim *dhabiha* – practices of religious slaughter that share many elements in common. As she shows, already during the 19th century, there had been a direct or indirect coalition between animal rights activists and anti-Semitic groupings who were both targeting Jewish butchering techniques. While she stresses that animal protection movements are not necessarily anti-foreign, Riedel points to the remarkable similarities in the current attempts to ban Islamic forms of butchering in Europe. In the present rhetoric in favor of banning religious slaughter in European countries, Riedel identifies many forms of othering of Muslims and Jews as religions that allegedly prefer pre-modern rituals over the well-being of animals.

In her chapter, "Albanian Muslims: Religious Othering and Notions of European Islam," Flora Ferati-Sachsenmaier investigates the religious othering of Albanians as Muslims from the late 19th century until the present. She focuses particularly on corresponding anti-Albanian and anti-Muslim discourses in neighboring Balkan nations that have long been linked with anti-Ottoman, anti-Turkish sentiments. As she shows, such discourses have already played a role in the late 19th century in societies ranging from Serbia to Greece and remained a recurrent theme in the key political struggles of the 20th century. One can still observe them today.

Emphasizing that Albanians have belonged to several religions for centuries, she argues that the reductionist views of Albanians as Muslims run counter to how they themselves understood their relationship between national identity and religious belonging.

While Muslims are often victims of othering, they can use the attitude of othering toward other Muslims. In his article, "Othering in ISIS," Mark Juergensmeyer explains how Sunni Muslim followers of the Islamic State in Iraq and Syria characterized adherents of the Shi'a branch of Islam as demonic beings, as expendable others. He describes his conversations with former ISIS militants who explain how they came to see Shi'a Muslims as embodiments of the devil, deserving of torture and death. The circle of ISIS othering expanded to other religious groups, including especially Americans and Jews, as an examination of the words used to describe the others indicate. Perhaps the most extreme form of ISIS othering was the attitude toward members of an ancient religious community in Iraq, the Yazidis, who the ISIS leadership falsely accused of being devil worshippers. The experience of one Yazidi boy is described from his capture at the age of 11 to being impressed into military service for ISIS five years later when he was finally able to escape.

Muslims can also regard secularists as the other, as Irene Schneider shows in her essay "The Religious and the Secular: Othering in Palestine in 2013." She mainly focuses on the controversies surrounding a draft for a new family law that was introduced in Palestine around the year 2010. At that time, influential parts of local civil society in Palestine fought for a more secular family law that would have strengthened the legal position of women in marriage, divorce, and childcare. Claiming the exclusive right to draft a new Palestinian family law, the Sharia establishment remained strongly opposed to the suggestions advocated by women's movements and other civil society agents. Schneider particularly investigates the othering of women's rights organizations by the Sharia establishment, which emerged as the winner of this political controversy. Conservative religious circles portrayed the advocacy groups fighting for a secular family law as morally inferior and as a danger to the role of the family in all social relations.

The last two chapters in the book deal with othering related to non-Muslim traditions. The othering of Catholic Christians by the Chinese secular state is the subject of the penultimate chapter, "Disrupted Loyalties? 21st Century Sinicization of the Catholic Other," by Christoph Zimmer. In this chapter, Zimmer turns our attention to the Catholic Church in the People's Republic of China that long has been divided into a government-ordained association and an underground church that doesn't accept state intervention in ecclesiastical matters. Zimmer discusses various forms of othering and assimilationist pressures that Catholics as a transnational religious organization have had to face in China, particularly from the mid-1950s onward. For many believers, Zimmer points out, this led to intense conflicts over loyalty between the state and various branches of the church. He argues that an agreement between the Holy See and the Chinese government in 2018 was supposed to mitigate the pressure of state institutions on Catholics. While in the context of this agreement, the Vatican emphasized the civic duties of Chinese

Catholics, Zimmer maintains that both the pressure of othering and the ensuing loyalty conflicts among Catholics have not disappeared.

The final chapter in the book shows that even White Christians in the European and American West can be the subject of othering. In her article on "Religious Othering in Hindi Films," *Diana Dimitrova* shows that Westerners are often shown in stereotypical ways. In her analysis, she refers to her own academic writing on the concept of othering and applies these concepts to Hindi films, especially the way that people of English, Italian, and other Western backgrounds are portrayed. She looks closely at several popular films to describe the ways that in these cases, Indian films adopt a sort of reverse Orientalism – they stereotype and marginalize Occidental figures in an attempt to elevate Indian culture and national identity.

While many of the chapters in this book deal with Islam – either the othering of Muslims or Muslims othering rival religious groups – we do not mean to imply that this phenomenon is unique to one tradition. In the current geo-political context, it is true that Muslims have often been the target of religious bigotry and humiliation. The reasons for this are varied – many of the new refugees have been Muslims, for instance, and thus appear threatening to the traditional social order of the communities to which they have fled. In other cases, it is because of an alleged association with terrorism that leads to an attitude of Islamophobia. This is especially disconcerting considering that many of the Muslims who have fled areas like Iraq and Syria have themselves been victims of violent Muslim movements like al Qaeda and the Islamic State.

In the essays in this book, the authors have examined recent cases where Muslims and other minority groups have been the subject of the hostility and marginalization of othering. They have demonstrated that the project of religious othering has a long history – both regional and global – and is at the same time a present feature of societies around the world in the global era. It is often linked with political agendas and, in many cases, joined with attempts to shore up national identities based on ethnicity and religion. In its extreme form, this can lead to cruel and strident efforts to alienate minority communities and ethnically cleanse national societies. Behind the somewhat innocent phrase, "thank God we're not like them," can often lie a treacherous effort at alienation and humiliation.

In the process of preparing this book for publication, the editors received the tragic news of the deaths of two of the contributors to this volume. Christoph Zimmer, as his essay in this volume shows, was a promising scholar in the field of Chinese history, with a particular interest in the historical interaction of religions. Michael Jerryson in a series of articles and books had established himself as one of the foremost authorities in the field of Buddhist violence, though, as his essay in this volume shows, he also retained a great affection for the tradition. Alas, their articles in this book may be among their last publications. In recognition of their scholarly contributions and warm collegiality, we dedicate this book to their memories.

References

Lie, John. 2004. *Modern Peoplehood*. Cambridge, MA: Harvard University Press.

Liu, Lydia. 1995. *Translingual Practice: Literature, National Culture, and Translated Modernity, China 1900–1937*. Stanford, CA: Stanford University Press.

Nongbri, Brent. 2013. *Before Religion: A History of a Modern Concept*. New Haven: Yale University Press.

Wijsen, Frans, and Kocku von Stuckrad, eds. 2016. *Making Religion: Theory and Practice in the Discursive Study of Religion*. Leiden: Brill.

1

THE BIG LIE

Its Model, Making, and Motive

James Aho

Of the various kinds of deceptive communication, perhaps the most pernicious is the Big Lie (Ger. *Grosseluege*). This is a rhetorical device recommended by Adolf Hitler in his 1925 edition of *Mein Kampf* (vol. 1, chap. 10). In her magisterial political history of totalitarianism, Hannah Arendt describes the Big Lie as a falsehood "so colossal" (Hitler's phrase) that its acceptance requires adherents to embark on "a complete rearrangement of the whole factual texture – the making of another reality" (Arendt 1967, 308–9).

Chief Nazi propagandist, Josef Goebbels, claimed that the first practitioners of the Big Lie were Jews, supposedly working in the Allied *Luegenfabrik* ("lie factory," meaning the modern university, entertainment industry, liberal news media, and government propaganda offices) during World War I. There, they used "their unqualified capacity for falsehood" to encourage their respective populations to mount a "war of extermination" against Germany.[1] Goebbels points out that it was not so much the "intelligence" of the Big Liars of the time that distinguished them but instead their "remarkably stupid thick-headedness." He goes on to argue that the only defense against the Big Lie is for the Aryan man to contrive his own. And so he did. Catastrophe soon followed, particularly for Jews, but variations of Nazism's Big Lie have continued to flourish in far-right discourse. Today, it is broadcast over the air, seen on cable TV, and disseminated in cyberspace throughout Continental Europe, Britain, Russia, and, most notably, the United States.

This chapter reviews the major features of the contemporary (American) Big Lie, focusing on the central importance in it of a diabolic Other. It then discusses the steps involved in this Other's construction. It closes with the question, Why? What is the attraction of the Big Lie to its adherents?

Arendt offers as one explanation of the craving for revenge by those who have been displaced by modernization, or as we would say today, "globalization." She describes the proponents of the Big Lie as "superfluous men" (examples being

DOI: 10.4324/b22926-2

Nazism's *Kleinmenschen*, little men, or William Graham Sumner's "forgotten Americans"), those rendered redundant by technological disruption, the export of manufacturing to where labor is cheap, and/or the import into the home country of low-paid workers. Arendt adopted the phrase "superfluous man" from Maurice Barrès, who used it to characterize the audiences who were flocking to his proto-fascist gatherings in the late 19th century (Ross 2017, 33). (Barrès is the first person known to have used the word "National Socialism" to describe his program [22].) Superfluous man's resentment at being a loser in the march of history, says Arendt, is flattered by the suggestion that in actuality s/he is an exceptional folk. In Nazi mythology, the groveling *Kleinmensch* becomes an *Übermensch*, a blond, blue-eyed superman, upon whose shoulders the fate of Western civilization rests.

Whatever its literary source, Arendt (1967, 147–57) argues that superfluous man and "superfluous capital" – a phrase she attributes to Karl Marx – emerged simultaneously after 1870 with the rise of industrialization, and it began to forge alliances to advance French, British, Slavic, German, and American "pan-nationalist" colonial projects. These projects promised immense profits for capitalists as well as opportunities for preening patriotism to the over-educated and under-employed.

The subtext of Arendt's argument is that the still popular (liberal) narrative about the Big Lie – that those attracted to it are "SIC," Stupid, Isolated, and/or Crazy – is false (for a refined version, see Lipset 1960, 175). Apart from there being little evidence to support it, Arendt claims that this narrative overlooks the discomfiting reality that "failed men" (her phrase) will find it "easier to accept" a Big Lie than the "old truth" of Enlightenment progress, which they see as a "pious banality" that no one takes seriously; or worse, as a justification for wickedness (Arendt 1967, 334). Considerations of empirical accuracy aside, my objection to Arendt is that her explanation doesn't go far enough. I will argue that the Big Lie is founded on an even *bigger* lie, a self-deception that goes to the roots of our being in the world. But before getting to this, let's review the features of the Big Lie itself.

The Model of the Big Lie

The Big Lie boasts four qualities: mystery, simplicity, prophecy, and infallibility. These are features rarely seen in academic social science, with its skepticism of mystification, its preference for complex explanations, its distrust of prophetic pronouncements, and above all its inclination to test hypotheses against objective reality. Audiences for the Big Lie take issue with academic knowledge claims for exactly these reasons and associate them with "pointy-headed elitists," dismissing them from further consideration.

This is not to say that the Big Lie lacks the appurtenances of scholarship. On the contrary, its paper publications are often chock full of footnotes, references, indices, and appendices; the production qualities of its websites and video clips are as sophisticated as anything disseminated by major corporations, governments, or universities. And if need be, the Big Lie can present itself as "scientific." It can don a white lab coat, conduct "archaeological digs," and appear in public amidst beaker-equipped labs. But as Alexander Koyré (1945, 291) points out, the purpose of the Big Lie is not to account for history in accordance with scholarly standards. It is, instead, to *transform* how audiences experience the past, so as to mobilize them for political action. In other words, the Big Lie "is not a light but a weapon." And its so-called "truth" is assessed by means of the vulgar pragmatism of whatever elevates poll numbers, sells books and online ads, or advances party interests. This explains what Arendt (1967, 333) bewails as the Big Lie's "maddening perplexity": not merely that its purveyors are cynics and its audience dupes, but that its "monstrous falsehoods can eventually be established as unquestioned facts . . . and that the difference between truth and falsehood may cease to be objective and become a mere matter of power and cleverness."

Mystery, simplicity, prophecy, and infallibility can, of course, be found in both far-left and far-right oratory. For purposes of brevity, and given that at the present moment, the dominant Euro-American political ideology tends rightward, the following discussion draws exclusively on what I call far-right fantasy (for more, see Aho 2016, 65–81).

Mystery. In "The Grand Inquisitor" (from *The Brothers Karamazov*), Dostoevsky writes that the average person hungers not only for bread but also for mystery. The Big Lie satisfies this craving by positing the existence of a furtive Force that lurks just beneath the surface of everyday life: a foul and loathsome conspiracy, a "breathing together" of a secret cabal whose goal is to rule the world.

This cabal goes by many names: "Freemasonry," "the Hidden Hand," "the Insiders," "Shadow Government," "the Dark Command," "the Deep State," and so on. From the standpoint of the sociology of knowledge, these and related entities represent the secularization or "humanization" of what were anciently understood as spiritual phenomena, encompassed by terms like "fallen angels," "Satan," "demon," and "Devil." Which is to say, that the cabal is comprised of beings in contention with God, but in human form. Secondarily, the names illustrate how in the melting-pot culture of post-World War II America, right-wing rhetoric has been redirected away from the "Jew" toward non-ethnic groupings. The word "Insider," for example, was coined by the John Birch Society, arguably the largest and most influential far-right faction in the United States the 1950s and 1960s. *None Dare Call It Conspiracy* (Allen 1971), the definitive statement of John Birch canon, explicitly renounces any suggestion that that Insiders are Jews (39) (although the surnames he cites to prove the existence of the conspiracy – Warburg, Lehman, Kuhn, Loeb, and Rothschild – belie his protestations). Lately, however, the list of alleged Insiders has been expanded to include the Jews Henry Kissinger, Zbigniew Brezinski, Madeleine Albright, and the considered human demon himself, George Soros, a one-time Holocaust survivor and billionaire financier of liberal-progressive causes.

Whatever its title, the cabal is reputed to meet at sites such as the Jewish Sanhedrin in Geneva, Switzerland; in the grand ballroom of the Bilderberg Hotel in the Netherlands; behind the ivied walls of the Skull and Bones Club at Yale University; inside the headquarters of the United Nations; or intriguingly, in the dank forests of Bohemian Grove in northern California. There, it is said to make burnt offerings to the ancient Semitic fire gods Molech and Dagon, using as effigies of children, if not children themselves. And it devises plans to establish a tyrannical "one-world" order that is to be borderless, unilingual, non-sectarian, brown-skinned, and egalitarian.

"Bread crumbs" of these evil plans have supposedly been left behind by the cabal, to be ferreted out by self-proclaimed "undercover investigators" like those associated with Infowars.com conspiracy theorist, Alex Jones. Or they are exhumed by entirely fictional figures such as Internet celebrity "QAnon." (Supposedly, QAnon is a high-level government official with an exclusive "Q" clearance.) The results of these investigations are aired or published by underground presses for the edification of the masses. Or they are "inadvertently" leaked in pamphlets like *The Protocols of the Learned Elders of Zion*, *The Plot Against Christianity*, or most recently, in the United Nations publication, *Agenda 21*.

Simplicity. Arendt (1967, 458) tells us that "ideological super-sense [is] more adequate to the needs of the human mind than reality itself," with its fortuitousness and complexity. This being the case, the Big Lie "thrives on . . . escape from coincidence into consistency," into a hack historiography free of randomness and accident (352–53). It attributes every personal misfortune and public calamity, real or imagined, to a single overarching cause: The Plot. This includes wars, recessions, plagues, hurricanes, wildfires, earthquakes, the opioid crisis, gun massacres, and more. Even denials of The Plot by liberal academics are considered part of The Plot. Indeed, the more fervent their denials, the stronger the proof. *Why, if it isn't true, are the elites so defensive about it?* Add to this is the fact that what might reasonably be seen as good is invariably adjudged bad: vaccinations (are "disease vectors"), equal rights for minorities ("our nightmare"), public education ("liberal indoctrination"), the Federal Emergency Management Agency ("concentration camps"), national parks ("land-grabs"), universal medical insurance ("socialized medicine"), etc. As a 17th-century Puritan preacher, Cotton Mather, might have said, *The whole world is polluted!* And the reason for this is The Plot. Understandably, when audiences first learn about The Plot, they feel anxiety and dread. But this too is part of The Plot. "They want to make you anxious and afraid," at least according to the popular radio conspiracy theorist, Clyde Lewis.

Prophecy. The Big Lie re-presents the marginalization of superfluous man (as understood earlier) in symbolic terms, as the impending end of the world, of "everything we've grown up with, everything we've known," cried radio talk show host, Rush Limbaugh. If the superfluous man in question is a fundamentalist Christian, then world collapse is pictured in apocalyptic terms as the final days of Revelation. If, on the other hand, s/he is secularized, then it gives itself to consciousness as a specter of Doom. Many conspiracy mongers leave audiences in a state of benumbed hopelessness. At other times, however, they promise revenge, say, in the form of a "storm" that will reverse their unhappy fortunes. Typically, this is prophesied as a "countercoup" that will arrest the "the new castrati" (one of Limbaugh's favorite foils) and try them for treason. In the event that the "evil tyrants" themselves are able to avoid prosecution – a strong likelihood considering that they control the police and the courts – then their presumed locally available stand-ins will be targeted: undocumented immigrants, political refugees, domestic minorities, and sexual deviants.

Infallibility. Alex Jones, the conspiracy theorist, has "challenged" (his term) critics to "disprove" the lineaments of the Big Lie. This, of course, is an empty gesture. First, as Karl Popper (1965) has shown, evidence (of what quality is another matter) can be cited to support virtually any contention. "The world is full of verifications," "It is easy to obtain confirmations . . . if we look for them" (35–37). On the other hand, no amount of information can ever *dis*prove that the bombing of the Murrah Federal Building in Oklahoma City (1995) or the 9/11 terrorist attack, to cite two examples, were "inside jobs," as Jones claims; that the Sandy Hook elementary school massacre in 2005 was "staged" by paid actors to justify government confiscation of firearms; or that Hillary Clinton partook in a child sex-trafficking ring run out of a Washington DC pizzeria (some believe to supply victims for the gruesome rites conducted at Bohemian Grove). Second, in the logic of the Big Lie, an *absence* of concrete evidence about Insiders, Hidden Hands, or Shadow Governments is treated as confirmation of their existence. According to QAnon, it proves that an *even more* "secret society" resides within an already Deep State, an *even more* insidious cell within a state already opaquely "gray." This is to say that one of the most compelling rhetorical features of the Big Lie is its unfalsifiable, irrefutable verity. In the storm-tossed chaos of a crumbling world, the Big Lie grants superfluous man what academic science never can: something firm to hold on to, the solid ground upon which to stand: cognitive certitude. When "all that is solid melts into the air" (Marx), this is priceless.

The Prototypical Cabalist

The central character in the narrative of the Big Lie is the cabalist, a character who has undergone countless name changes since 1798 when John Robison (1967) first exposed it in *Proofs of a Conspiracy against All the Religions and Governments of Europe*. Yet in the course of these name changes, its traits have remained largely intact. This is why Robison's depiction of the machinations of the Illuminati from over two centuries ago continues to be cited by conspiracy theorists as a source book and guide for understanding what is happening right now. Which underscores the observation just made about the irrefutable nature of the Big Lie: far from being an empirical assertion, perhaps it is best to be understood as a psychological "archetype," to quote Carl Jung (1971), a cross-cultural symbolic complex that arises whenever there is great social tension.

To begin with, the cabalist is invariably depicted as having loathsome intentions, dirty thoughts, and a sordid soul. S/he is said to wear a black gown (like the Jesuits of old or the "black-robed Mormans" [sic] of more recent vintage) or (like the Jewish bankers of our day) black suits. S/he parades around in a black face mask wearing black eye shades, rides black helicopters and black limousines with black-tinted windows, and is often seen in the company of a black cat.

Second, their hands are always described as soiled, sinister, or what amounts to the same thing, "leftist." This is in contrast to the rectal, righteous right-wing. The left hand was once known as the "kackhand" that was used for wiping rather than for eating or greeting. "Kack" in turn can be traced to the ancient Sanskrit noun for shit, *kakka*, "caw-caw," the language of the crow. The crow is the preeminent totem of the Hindu Dalit or Untouchable, a status group considered so filthy that its very shadow or glance is said to be contaminating (Dundes 1997, 10–24). Predictably, the crow is also the basis of the derisive title "Jim Crow," as applied to African–Americans during the post-Reconstruction era.

Third is the legend that the cabalist originates from the "bowels of the underworld," from the "dregs" (Ger. *Dreck* = feces) of society, from the muck, mud, or *Merde* (Fr.), or to quote President Donald Trump, from "shithole countries" in Africa and Central America. In the neo-Nazi fable, "mud people" – Jews, native peoples, blacks, and Hispanics – all are held up in negative contrast to "spirit folk," those whose white skins signify their "delightsomeness" to the Lord, and hence their selection for eternal salvation. A related term is "gook," an offensive tag still occasionally applied by Americans to Asians. "Gook" originally was invoked to describe the Japanese in World War II; nowadays, it is used routinely to defame the Vietnamese.

Fourth, the cabalist is mythologized as residing in decrepit gothic castles or drafty hotels, in gloomy temples, slimy sewers, or "rat-holes" (cf. one-time Iraqi president Saddam Hussein's capture in one during the Second Iraqi war [2003–2010]). S/he inhabits "fenian swamps," like the 19th-century Irish "monsters" so feared by the English; in fog-enshrouded redwood forests such as Bohemian Grove; or in "rat and rodent infested" cites (like Baltimore, Maryland), where "no human being would want to live," according to President Trump.

In sum, the cabalist is trash, rubbish. Hence, its garbage-eating bestiary (Keen 1986). Not only the crow and the rat (*Siehen der Jud!* [Behold the Jew!]) but also other garbage dwellers such as "snakes in the grass," vermin (worms), and raccoons (or "coons," another scornful label for African Americans). There are goats (who represent Satan-worshipers), dogs (homosexuals), cockroaches, and pigs. In the present medicalized era, there are also human "cancers," "disease vectors," and "bacilli." Nazi iconographers adapted from Martin Luther a particularly repellent creature to represent "feces-eaters like Jews," the *Schweinehund* or swine-dog (Brown 1970, 225).

The Making of the Big Lie and Its Arch-Demon

Social scientists today commonly acknowledge that the objective world, the world that exists for us, the only world that can exist for us, this world with all its objects, derives its whole sense and being from ourselves, through oral and written communications, extemporaneous and routinized, verbal and physical, private and public (Berger and Luckmann 1967).[2] Yet even for those intimately familiar with this insight, one component of the world continues to be experienced "naïvely":

the enemy. This is especially evident for proponents of the Big Lie. The malign qualities of their pet adversaries – communists, immigrants, liberals, Jews, Muslims, gays, etc. – are taken-for-granted as inherently given. The following comments are intended to destabilize this conviction or to use the more familiar word, to "deconstruct" (Ger. *destrukt*) it. This involves two steps: first, summarizing how enemies are actually fabricated, and second, inquiring into what lies behind the enterprise of enemy production.

The construction of enemies entails four distinguishable, if not entirely separable, tools: labeling, myth-making, embedment, and sacrifice (Aho 2006).

Labeling. "Labeling" refers to the affixing of a pejorative tag onto a person or group, one who differs from an in-group in some discernibly unacceptable way (Becker 1963). It often takes the form of a nasty-sounding one or two-syllable expectoration like "mick," "nip," "zip," "spic," "chink," "dink," "Hun," "wop," "cunt," "fag," "slope," "kike," "cuck," etc., which needs little further clarification. When more abstract disparagements are at issue, however, as in the cases of "criminal," "madman," or "terrorist," labelers may also be called on to rationalize it by staging what Harold Garfinkel (1956) calls a "public degradation ceremony": an inquisition, a trial, an official hearing, a "court of love," or public confession. Here, the label's suitability is tested and its validity is certified.

Defamatory labels accomplish three things at once. First, like all taxonomic categories, they enable audiences to make sense of the chaos of auditory, olfactory, and visual stimuli with which they are inundated moment by moment. Or to express it more frankly, they transmogrify human beings with all their vagaries and contradictions into "things" – in the case before us, things to be terrified of and loathed. Second, defamatory labels serve as short-hand ad hominem arguments. That is, insofar as the person or group in question is a swine, a pinko, a slut, or a bacterium, then whatever comes out of their mouths is ipso facto idiotic, craven, sick, or nuts. In other words, it is invalid and unworthy of serious attention. This takes us to a label's third and most telling achievement: they don't just describe; they *pre*scribe. They cognitively prepare audiences to act "appropriately." After all, what should we do with human "waste," if not "liquidate" it and "expulse" it? With human "garbage" or "trash"? With two-legged "rats"? Or with "cancers in our midst"? In Nazi Germany, the answer was Cleansing! Ethnic cleansing! *Judenreinmachen*: cleanse the homeland of Jews! As for "fags," one American editorial expressed the recommendation this way: "What we demand and . . . what we expect" is "immediate and systematic cauterization." This, until "the whole situation is cleared up, and the premises thoroughly cleansed and disinfected" (Gerasi 1966, 3–4).

Myth-making. Human beings are intelligent; they demand more than just slanderous labels to violate each another – even when those labels have been authenticated by means of formal rites. We also need stories about why the labeled are as they are reputed to be. Nowadays, such tales comprise a combination of pop-theology (their iniquity grows from a conscious decision to disobey God's commandments); pop-biology (their evil is due to a "demon seed" they have either inherited genetically or acquired through infection); pop-psychology (they have been abusively raised or brain-washed into a "culture of death"); and/or pop-sociology (whatever moral compass they once may have had, has been undermined by rapid social change and "anomie," leaving them without a "moral compass"). Typically, these narratives are verified anecdotally by reference to atrocity tales. Among other things, these portray the desecration of the orifices of women and children in, say, "rape rooms" (as claimed by President George H. W. Bush about Saddam Hussein, prior to the first Gulf War [1990–91]).

When Donald Trump announced his candidacy for the presidency in 2015, the first thing he said about Mexican immigrants was, "They are rapists." In doing so, consciously or not, he drew on a timeless icon of in-group peril. According to Mary Douglas (1966), the female body symbolizes an in-group's gateways and vulnerabilities. This is one reason why the most vociferous advocates of erecting "a big, beautiful wall" to keep Mexican "invaders" out of America, also champion campaigns to protect the purity of "our" women from them. This, by policing the invasion route par excellence, their vaginas; among other ways, by imposing on them draconian anti-abortion and birth control measures.

Other sites of in-group exposure that are routinely subjected to police monitoring are the mouth (as in the kosher diet of orthodox Judaism); the eye (the attack point of the so-called "modern addiction," pornography); and the ear (the alleged target of the "devil's anthem," rock 'n roll or jazz, two colloquial references to sex).[3]

Embedment. Once composed, defamatory labels and myths must next be implanted and embedded, in the hearts and minds of the upcoming generation. Because children are not physically present when slanderous labels are coined or when atrocity tales are devised, they remain unaware of their artificiality. Instead, they receive them innocently, as common sense, what everyone always already knows about them. In approximate order of influence, beginning with the most important, the major agents of embedment are parents, peers, propagandists, pundits, preachers, and professors. How, exactly, political libel is passed on to children – whether through the content of specific lesson plans, by the example of role models, or by the style in which these lessons are conveyed, and whether by means of rote memorization or play-acting, or all of these at once – is a matter of endless debate that need not be addressed here.

Sacrifice. The culminating step in demonization is punishment (from Lat. *poena* = pain, thus the administration of pain). This is when those blamed for a misfortune are called to atone for it. The crucial fact to bear in mind about sacrifice is that to be *blamed* for something is not the same as being its *cause*. To be blamed, say, for low cotton prices, and to be lynched as a result, as happened hundreds of times from 1882 to 1930 in the American Deep South (Tolnay and Beck 1990) or, during the late Middle Ages, to suffer a pogrom for allegedly "poisoning wells," as happened to Jews, means only that one is held to "respond to," be responsible for, it. Causality, in contrast, refers to the bio-psycho-social-cultural conditions that occur prior to an event, and with which they are highly associated, even after other preconditions are controlled for or held constant. To be sure, those held responsible for acting murderously have sometimes done so in fact. But at other times, those called to account for a public calamity or a private sorrow merely have a different skin color, nose or eye shape, physiognomy, language, faith, ideology, appetite, or desire than an in-group; they may have played no role in their causality.

The Motive of the Big Lie

From the standpoint of the protagonist, an enemy is always *diablo*, a devil (from the Greek *dia* = away from + *bolos* = that which is thrown). That is, its qualities are what the protagonist "throws away" from itself. And what it casts off is a truth it cannot bear to embrace, a truth about its "own-most (Ger. *eigenst*) possibility" (Heidegger 1962, 24), namely, that it is in decay and moving inexorably toward the end. By flinging its existential tenuousness and fragility outward onto a "sin-carrier," the protagonist participates in a delusion. This delusion is the "bigger lie" spoken of at the outset of this chapter. And it explains why, the more emphatic its "death-denial" (Becker 1973; Solomon, Greenberg, and Pyszczynski 2015), the more vicious its slanders; the more extravagant its scatological fables; the more insistent it is on passing these on to youngsters; the bloodier its sacrificial rites; and the more relief it feels upon witnessing the enemy's destruction (as applied to war-making, see Underhill-Cady 2001).

The technical term for casting one's own-most possibility onto an Other is "negative transference." Sometimes, it is done with full awareness of what is at stake. This is true of "political plague-mongers," as Ernest Becker (1975) calls them: preachers, propagandists, and pundits. As for the masses, however, negative transference is typically unconscious. Here, instead of seeing themselves (accurately) as co-producers of *diaboli*, they misperceive themselves as innocent victims. Mythologist James Frazer (1951, 306, 342, 599) illustrates this in his discussion of the so-called "savage mind," by which he means a way of thinking unencumbered by the insights of critical sociology.

In ancient Greece, for example, a stable of slaves and degraded individuals was drawn upon during the spring equinox or amidst public *krises*, such as famines, plagues, or pestilence. These served as *katharma* (or *pharmaka*), human toxins whose ceremonial elimination (*kathairo*) was believed to have curative powers. Like medicines taken to relieve dyspepsia, in other words – "*pharmakon*" is the root of the English "pharmaceutical," "cathartic" is derived from the Greek "*katharma*" – legend has it that upon witnessing the toxin's death, the community would experience euphoric *katharsis* (Girard 1977, 286–90). As it was paraded through the public square prior to execution, the *pharmakon's* genitals were whipped with fig branches to render them impotent and harmless (98, 288).

A comparable rite is Yom Kippur (Lev. 16: 29–34), the Day of Atonement, which name comes from "*kippurim*," the victim offered up for sacrifice in ancient Babylonia. Originally, in Yom Kippur, the high priest ritually transferred the sins and adversities of Israel onto the head of a goat or bull, "Azazel," who was then led outside the gates of the village to wander in exile, carrying with it the community's misfortunes.

St. Paul elaborates on this logic, writing that it proves how nothing can be purified without the shedding of blood (Heb. 9: 16–23); he likens the redemptive efficacy of blood sacrifice to a last will and testament, which does not become legally actionable until the death of a testator. But then he adds that rites such as the two just described are "useless," because they are only "reflections" of truth, not Truth itself (Heb. 10: 1). For this reason, he says, God has replaced the escape goat of Yom Kippur with a more "perfect sacrifice": the unblemished "Lamb of God," Jesus Christ (cf. Heb. 9: 14). Christ's death cancels not only the debts of a tiny, exclusive tribe but also those of the entire human race; furthermore, it occurs only once in history, not annually.

Had it been implemented in everyday life, the Christian narrative might well have rendered ceremonies of human riddance unnecessary or at least tempered their ferocity. It hardly needs to be said, however, that things have not turned out this way. Under the influence of Zoroastrianism, with which Israel came into contact during the Babylonian Exile [ca. 599 BCE], Azazel the goat began evolving into Satan: a hairy, horned, cloven-hoofed goat-*man*, head of the so-called "fallen angels" (Pagels 1995). In Genesis 6: 1–4, Azazel-Satan is said to have "lusted" after the "daughters of men" and through them brought forth a race of giants: the "Sons of Darkness" (1 Enoch 6–8; cf. Jubilees 5). This fable was subsequently absorbed into Jewish, Christian, and Muslim mythologies. The Sons of Darkness are the Antagonists against whom the "Sons of Light" are prophesied to struggle and defeat in the End Times.

The first indication of Christianity's appropriation of the transformed Azazel is already evident in Paul's epistle to the Hebrews. Here, Paul's promise that Christ's sacrifice "perfects all whom he is sanctifying" is followed with a dire warning: unless, that is, the person in question "deliberately sins." In that case, there is no redemption, but "only the dreadful prospect of judgement and of the raging fire that is to burn rebels" (Heb. 10: 14). Like the brambles and thistles of the field, sinners shall "end by being burnt" (Heb. 6: 6), with "far severer punishment" to come later (Heb. 10: 14).

It isn't necessary to recount the parade apostates, heretics, and nonbelievers upon whom the title "Sons of Darkness" has been bestowed over time. It is enough to say that they become repositories of every imaginable crime, from sexual perversity and cannibalism to child murder and vampirism. There is the "International Jew," for example, "left-hand" of Christianity (Ruether 1979), and the Satan-worshipping witch. There is the "Christian crusader" of enduring Muslim legend, and the "Great Satan" itself, modern America. And, of course, there is always the jihadi terrorist. It is enough to repeat Pascal's contention (based on his experience of the 30-Years War [1618–1648], which pitted the New Model armies of Protestant Europe against the Catholic League): "Men never do evil so completely and cheerfully as when they do it for religious conviction." To repeat, this is because

"Sons of Darkness" stands for what is refused, what every Jew, Christian, and Muslim fears most, hates, and flees from, their existential fragility and precariousness.

Those upon whom the projective strobe of Jew, Christian, and/or Muslim fall are subject to God's most terrifying commandment: the ban (Heb. *herem*. From the Babylonian *hrm*): "As regards the towns of those peoples which . . . God gives you as your own inheritance," goes the commandment, "you must not spare the life of any living thing. You shall utterly destroy them" (Deut. 20: 16; 13: 13–19; 17–17). Failure to carry out this injunction, the passage continues, is itself punishable by death. The category "those peoples" originally referred to the natives of the land as "promised" Jews by their tribal God, Yahweh. To legitimize their extirpation, the scribe and prophet Ezra (who flourished in the 5th century BCE) associated them with the most revolting impurity he could envision, *nidda*: the menstruant and her blood (Ezra 9: 11). And he characterizes the Promised Land as having been made "unclean because of the foulness (*niddat*) of the natives . . . and of the abomination with which their impurities have infected it from end to end," which, as just indicated, means that it must be cleansed by fire.

Conclusion

Give thanks that the Jewish, Christian, and Muslim *ethoi* of extermination have been compelled to adapt to the conditions of modernity in the approximate order of their arrival in history. Crucial among these conditions is that synagogues, churches, and mosques be administered separately from corporations (where they exist) that claim monopolies over the legitimate means of violence in their respective territories. One result of this has been that the "savage mind" (see earlier) of the Abrahamic faiths has found itself institutionally restrained from acting out its worst instincts. Predictably, it has balked, in one place reviling the separation of church and state as a "liberal lie"; in another, as an "infringement on our liberty," a loser's appeal to "women of both sexes," or as "an affront to our dignity." Or, to borrow from our earlier discussion, it is seen as one more step in the diabolic Plot to "satanify" the world.

Nor has the institutional splitting off of sacred affairs from matters of state come without its own price. For if the 20th century taught us anything, it is that the only thing worse than violence perpetrated in the name of God is violence undertaken without it. When Martin Luther demanded that the Church free itself from its corrupting entanglements with the state, he also inadvertently liberated states to pursue their naked power interests, unencumbered by any moral scruple whatsoever (Luther 1974, 102–3, 130). The outcome has been "pure war" (Virilio 1983), machine-generated mega-death (Wyschogrod 1985).

Yet, there is no going back. A globalizing world beckons us to acknowledge that the Them whom we earlier mistook as wholly different from us, is in large measure a fabrication of our own troubled imagination. It is our own selves "seen as through a glass, darkly" (1 Cor. 13: 12). To become aware of this is, of course, is a wounding. And it does little to protect us from those who continue to insist on transferring their personal rubbish onto us. Furthermore, even when there is little risk to us in eating our own shadow, it does nothing to address our existential problematic, the fact of our ultimate groundlessness and mortality. Nevertheless, it may cause us to momentarily hesitate before mindlessly embarking, one more time, on a futile quest to "kill death." The point is that the conviction of our innocence is an illusion, a cognitive privilege accorded exclusively to the ignorant. The Big Lie doesn't so much expose the truth about history; it reveals how insistent we are in remaining unconscious.

Notes

1 Nazism and its contemporary derivatives hold that the most important product of the Jewish Lie Factory is "Spinozism" (a derogatory term, named after the Dutch Jew, Baruch Spinoza [1632–1677]). Today, it is reviled as liberal Enlightenment philosophy, which maintains (1) that there is an objective reality, (2) that this reality is accessible to every human being by means of reason, and (3) that reason is predicated on individual civil, political, and social rights.
2 This is a sociological rendering of phenomenologist Edmund Husserl's (1977, 26) observation that every object in my life world derives its existence "from me myself, from me as the transcendent Ego."
3 The reverse is also true: in-groups are known to rape vanquished females and males to put the final stamp of approbation on their conquests. Or in a perverse form of "excremental assault" (DePres 1984), they will force the vanquished to "eat shit": drink from filled toilets, clean latrines without hand tools, and/or demand that they eat from bowls soiled by non-scheduled latrine breaks, a particular torment for dysentery sufferers.

References

Aho, J. 2006. "The Danse Macabre." *Sociological Spectrum* 26: 1–17.
———. 2016. *Far-Right Fantasy*. New York and London: Routledge.
Allen, G. 1971. *None Dare Call It Conspiracy*. Seal Beach, CA: Concord Press.
Arendt, H. 1967. *The Origins of Totalitarianism*. Cleveland and New York: World Pub. Co.
Becker, E. 1973. *The Denial of Death*. New York: Free Press.
———. 1975. *Escape From Evil*. New York: Free Press.
Becker, H. 1963. *The Outsiders*. Glencoe, IL: Free Press.
Berger, P., and T. Luckmann. 1967. *The Social Construction of Reality*. New York, NY: Doubleday-Anchor.
Brown, N. 1970. *Life Against Death*. Middletown, CT: Wesleyan University Press.
DePres. 1984. *The Survivors: An Anatomy of the Death Camps*. New York, NY: Columbia University Press.
Douglas, M. 1966. *Purity and Danger*. London: Routledge and Kegan Paul.
Dundes, A. 1997. *Two Tales of Crow and Sparrow*. Lanham, MD: Rowan & Littlefield.
Frazer, J. 1951. *The Golden Bough*, abridged ed. New York, NY: Palgrave Macmillan.
Garfinkel, H. 1956. "Conditions of Successful Degradation Ceremonies." *American Journal of Sociology* 61: 420–24.
Gerasi, J. 1966. *The Boys of Boise*. New York, NY: Palgrave Macmillan.
Girard, R. 1977. *Violence and the Sacred*. Translated by P Gregory. Baltimore, MD: Johns Hopkins University Press.
Heidegger, M. 1962. *Being and Time*. Translated from German by J. Macquarrie and E. Robinson. New York, NY: Harper & Row.
Husserl, E. 1977. *Cartesian Meditations*. Translated from German by D Cairns. The Hague, Netherlands: Martinus Nijhoff.

Jung, C. 1971. "The Concept of the Collective Unconscious." In *The Portable Jung*, edited by J. Campbell. New York, NY: Viking.
Keen, S. 1986. *Faces of the Enemy*. San Francisco, CA: Harper & Row.
Koyré, A. 1945. "The Political Function of the Modern Lie." *Contemporary Jewish Record* 7 (June): 290–300.
Lipset, S. M. 1960. "'Fascism' – Left, Right, and Center." In *Political Man*, edited by S. M. Lipset. Garden City, NY: Doubleday-Anchor.
Luther, M. 1974. *Luther: Selected Political Writings*. Edited by J. M. Porter. Philadelphia, PA: Fortress Press.
Pagels, E. 1995. *The Origin of Satan*. New York, NY: Random House.
Popper, K. 1965. "Science: Conjectures and Refutations." In *Conjectures and Refutations*, edited by K. Popper. London: Routledge and Kegan Paul.
Robison, J. 1967 [1798]. *Proofs of A Conspiracy*. Boston, MA: Western Islands.
Ross, A. R. 2017. *Against the Fascist Creep*. Chico & Oakland, CA: AK Press.
Ruether, R. 1979. *Faith and Fratricide: The Theological Roots of Anti-Semitism*. New York, NY: Seabury.
Solomon, S., J. Greenberg, and T. Pyszczynski. 2015. *Worm at the Core*. New York, NY: Random House.
Tolnay, S., and E. M. Beck. 1990. "The Killing Fields of the Deep South." *American Sociological Review* 55: 526–39.
Underhill-Cady, J. 2001. *Death and the Statesman*. New York, NY: Palgrave Macmillan.
Virilio, P. 1983. *Pure War*. New York, NY: Foreign Agent Series.
Wyschogrod, E. 1985. *Spirit in Ashes: Hegel, Heidegger, and Man-Made Mass Death*. New Haven, CT: Yale University Press.

2

WHY SHARI'A MATTERS

Law, Ethics, and the Muslim Other in the United States

Kathleen Moore

> You know, I just hope that Americans overall get a better understanding of what shari'a law even is, so that they're not as paranoid every time they see a Muslim. Like, that'd be beautiful. Because even after the Chapel Hill shooting, all the girls I know that wear the hijab were so scared to leave the house, and, like, even I felt so paranoid when I left the house that day. I felt like everyone was looking at me even if they hadn't heard about it. Like, I don't want everyone to feel scared, especially when you're not really doing anything wrong. Like, it's kind of not fair that you have to live like that in America, of all places.[1]

Marwa was in her late teens when I interviewed her, completing her coursework at the local community college. On a late afternoon in the spring of 2015, we shared a pot of tea in a halal Thai restaurant east of Los Angeles. After we talked about her upcoming wedding and her plans to transfer to Berkeley in the Fall, our conversation turned to events in the news. She had many important reflections on the complicated politics of the presidential primaries then underway, and what it meant for her everyday living. In a reflective tone, she shared how the brutal murders of three Muslim college students – 3,000 miles away, in Chapel Hill, North Carolina – made her feel vulnerable, unable to leave her house without feeling "paranoid." Marwa felt conspicuous and believed that her friends who, like her, wore a headscarf, felt the same way. A series of dangers associated with being Muslim in the current climate made her an easy target. Visual markers of faith – like a headscarf or a beard – play a role in how Muslims are treated, and it is not surprising that women like Marwa fear for their own personal safety.

My interview with Marwa was one of over a hundred conducted with Muslims across California as part of a research project between 2014 and 2017. In this essay, I draw from those semi-structured interviews in order to explore some important

DOI: 10.4324/b22926-3

implications of a system of Islamophobia at work in the United States in the first decades of the 21st century. In this historic moment, imagery of a "creeping shari'a" has been used rhetorically with the intent of generating fear that a repressive Islamic theocracy might be imposed on an unsuspecting American public. This has rendered Muslims and Islam into a specifically *legal* threat to governance of the self and the polity. This brief analysis looks at how Muslims across California have responded to the portrayal of shari'a as anti-American, and how they understand and experience shari'a in the context of virulent attacks on it and on Islam and Muslims more generally. In the following sections, I explore the meanings that Californian Muslims like Marwa give to and the intentions they derive from shari'a when dominant public discourses represent it as a cause for alarm in American life. I attempt to show that shari'a matters not only because anti-Muslim discourse makes the word cogent and visible to non-Muslims and a catalyst for the perceived threat of Islamic practice in the United States. It also matters for the development of American Muslims' sense of security and identity in midst of an ethos rooted in the fear of Muslims and Islam as un-American. The first section provides an overview of the literature in the field of Islamophobia studies, the second section explores the digital texture of Islamophobic discourse, and the final section considers some of the gendered aspects of the religious othering of Muslims in the United States in the first decades of the 21st century.

American Islamophobia Studies

There is a vast literature, including an academic journal, dedicated to the topic of Islamophobia, and the term itself has been defined in a number of ways. Scholars have labeled the fear, anger, or hostility toward Islam as "Islamophobia" or "anti-Muslim racism" (Shryock 2010; Bravo Lopez 2011; Ernst 2013; Cheng 2015; Green 2015; Considine 2017; Love 2017; Mondon and Winter 2017; Beydoun 2018; Evolvi 2018). While "Islam" and "Muslim" are religious signifiers, a notion of race is at work as well (Selod 2015). Even before the founding of the American republic, deeply ingrained anxieties have driven anti-Muslim sentiment and the fundamental salience of religion continues to construct racial categories and boundaries in American society (Haney Lopez 1995; Holt 1995; Moore 1995; Gualtieri 2001; Chan-Malik 2018). The archetype may have morphed over the years, from swashbuckling Turk to oil-rich Arab sheikh and bomb-carrying fanatic, but the mark of inherent un-Americanness has remained the same throughout American history. It has been revisited in every generation and underwrites the racial knowledge that Muslims, in the thrall of fanaticism, violence, and misogyny, are a threat to the civilized West. Post-9/11 expressions of anti-Muslim hostility are heirs to this legacy (Marr 2006; Fluhman 2008; Spellberg 2014).

Within this growing body of literature is a subset that has investigated the processes that many scholars regard as the racialization of American Muslim identity (e.g., Bayoumi 2006; Cainkar 2008; Garner and Selod 2015; Selod 2015; Considine 2017; Love 2017; Chan-Malik 2018; Kaufman 2019). This othering of

Muslims reflects a centuries-long history of racism against minoritized ethnic and religious groups in the United States (Gotanda 2011; Selod and Embrick 2013; Sheehi 2018). Racialization has been defined as a racial formation project where categories are constantly created, occupied, transformed, and deployed within specific cultural, political, social, and economic contexts. But anti-Muslim hate departs from other forms of racism in its unusual preoccupation with the law. Virulent opposition to mosque-building in the United States and anxieties about "creeping shari'a" portray Muslim Americans as supporters of terrorism and link Muslim "foreignness" with a threat to the U.S. legal system (Mitchell and Toner 2016; Wright 2016; Esposito and Delong-Bas 2018). For instance, in a 2009 Senate Foreign Relations Committee hearing, then Yale Law School Dean Harold Koh's views on transnationalism nearly derailed his confirmation as a legal adviser to the U.S. State Department because his detractors distorted his position on shari'a as foreign law.[2] The hatred of shari'a is associated with a fear that any accommodation of Islam – particularly by state and federal legal systems – poses a threat to democratic values, the separation of church and state, and the rule of law. Thus, people's understandings or misunderstandings of shari'a as a foreign and threatening legal system render Islam into a visible religious and legal problem.

In 2010, Oklahoma voters passed a referendum by a 70% majority to amend the state constitution to forbid the consideration of shari'a in state courts. The measure was struck down eventually in a federal appeals court, but anti-Muslim activists continued to promulgate, state by state, similar bills of legislation that would "ban" shari'a across the country. By the end of 2011, more than half of the states had introduced such a bill onto their legislative agenda, and by 2020, only a handful of states had not considered this legislation.[3] What was this "ban the shari'a" movement meant to address? No one was bringing shari'a before the state or federal bench. In other words, no litigants had asked American judges to make an official ruling that would adopt or enforce something called "shariah law." Even the main architect of the anti-shari'a bills admitted that the legislative purpose was "heuristic," to stoke suspicion rather than actually ban shari'a (Elliot 2011; Mitchell and Toner 2016; Elsheikh, Sisemore, and Ramirez Lee 2017). In many states, shari'a was not explicitly banned, but foreign and international laws were, due to the unconstitutionality of passing a law specifically targeting Islam. Critics of the anti-shari'a movement called it inflammatory and said its most tangible impact was the spread of an alarmist message that aimed at broadly categorizing all Muslims as un-American (Massoud and Moore 2020).

All of this polemicizing begs the question, What is shari'a, anyway? In Arabic, the word shari'a literally means a path, understood to lead toward a water spring, which signifies purity and cleansing. By Muslim theologians and jurists, it is taken to mean God's divinely revealed law (Afsaruddin 2014; Ahmed 2016; Ahmad 2017). Over time, it has come to be understood as the moral, ethical, and behavioral principles, derived from the Qur'an and the traditions of the Prophet Muhammad, that Muslim jurists use to interpret specific legal rules. While often presented in the West only in relation to corporal punishments (*huduud*) and misogyny, for scholars of Islam, shari'a is the foundation of a broad range of legal rulings over the centuries. For many Muslims living in the United States, the word shari'a historically had not been a major part of an everyday vocabulary; it has been the purview of classically trained Muslim scholars, not the concern of a "lay" person. But in a national space that is increasingly dominated by negative opinions about shari'a, Muslims began to take a fresh look at shari'a and give it a new utility by consciously inverting it from a foreign discourse into an asset for daily living. So how have American Muslims responded to this perception of Islam and shari'a as anti-American? Some, whose speech has been chilled by these debates, are much more reluctant to discuss publicly the importance of religious law and ethics. Others, particularly Muslim scholars and Islamic civic groups, have openly discussed shari'a and its place in American law and society, identifying points of convergence with democratic values (e.g., Jackson 2011; Howe 2018). The internal diversity of their views typically goes ignored in the polarizing context of partisan, anti-shari'a politics that relies instead on tropes that depict Islam and Muslims as anti-modern and inherently incompatible with American political liberalism.

Thus, while proving to be a convenient shorthand, the term shari'a contains a problematic reductionism for a much more complex set of phenomena. A growing awareness of the elasticity of the word is apparent in how American Muslims responded to the perception of shari'a as contrary to American liberal values. In our California-based study, many of the Muslims we met often first heard of shari'a – as a term, much less a theological principle – from a variety of sources, including family members, sermons, private study, media, or in schools and classrooms domestically or overseas. Younger people consistently reported that they first heard the term shari'a from negative news accounts of Islam or Muslims, particularly after 9/11.[4] According to Saad, a male graduate student of South Asian descent in Southern California, "after September 11th it became more meaningful, because people – non-Muslims, especially – started having these negative views . . . about 'creeping shari'a'."[5] A Latina Muslim in her 60s in Los Angeles concurred, "Basically, this word came out not only for me but for the entire Latino community after 9/11."[6] One Muslim in the U.S. military said that he heard about shari'a first from other soldiers "who wanted to kill ragheads." He lamented that he, too, "bought it" because, in his words, "I didn't know what I was talking about, either."[7] The term shari'a was linked to their self-consciousness of being perceived as a legal "other" produced by the experience of racism and bigotry.

At certain moments, some of the California Muslims we met reproduced the binary between "good" and "bad" interpretations of shari'a that is embedded in public discourse. In a cultural milieu of Islamophobia built on negative media representations of Islam, many of the Muslims we met were trying to live ethical lives where what is "ethical" is situated – by implicit and explicit intentions of the individuals themselves – within a broader moral horizon. Like many Americans, some people we met viewed shari'a through the lens of national security and counterterrorism – shari'a as a threat to public order – reinforced by myriad journalists, academics, and pundits. Some of our interviewees, for instance, referred to a limited kind of shari'a practiced "over there," in countries that enforce draconian codes of criminal law, gender segregation, or inheritance. These references were often the premise for a meaningful distinction implying that their own beliefs and practices are more moderate or logical than the "bad" interpretation associated with (*fill in the blank*, ISIS, al-Qaeda, Salafi) behavior. These contrasting tropes of "good" versus "bad" shari'a, or unruly versus humane Muslims, are not surprising since they are part of the effects of Islamophobia. As with other forms of racism, Islamophobia is enacted through state power and its dominant culture. The people we met were not immune to these processes or to media representations of Islam as a problematically legalistic religion.

Anti-shari'a discourse flattens the complexity of law and ethics. Although the people we interviewed said they generally do not use the word "shari'a" in their daily living, they spoke of more specific practices that are guided by shari'a principles, like eating clean foods (*halal* or *zabiha*), dressing modestly, and avoiding forbidden (*haram*) behavior such as littering, stealing, or cheating on a spouse. Corporal punishment, or *huduud* – punishment imposed for acts of adultery, theft, and murder – is criminal law often associated with shari'a. Zayd, an imam (prayer leader) born in California with some postgraduate education at Al-Azhar University in Cairo, mused, "You think about shari'a as these corporal punishments, [but] I never thought about it as how I treat my neighbor, or my parents . . . or my prayer . . . or my fasting."[8] "What shari'a is thought of today [is] cutting off the hand, and . . . whipping . . . the adulteress," said an activist, echoing many of our respondents.[9] Even fictional representations of Muslims employ tropes of corporal punishment: "When I was in high school I saw . . . Aladdin, and he steals . . . something, and the guy brings out his big . . . . machete [like] he's ready to chop [Aladdin's] arm. Like, that was my understanding [of] shari'a."[10]

Kamila, a 30-something attorney born and raised in Southern California, offered a comparison between corporal punishment and the kind of punishment sanctioned in California law. She said, "sometimes what the *huduud* prescribes – although it may appear to be harsher than what California prescribes – is often comparable."[11] They are similar, in her opinion, not in the punishment itself but in the evidentiary requirements necessary for extreme punishments. Others argued that influential scholars of Islam sometimes interpret the Arabic word *qata'a* (to cut) metaphorically, to mean the "cutting" of family ties (typically by isolating the thief) rather than any physical cutting off of hands.[12]

Images of shari'a spanned the spectrum as people struggled to define it and explain its relevance. Sousan, for instance, a woman who left Malaysia for the United States in her 20s, said she would not "want to be in a situation like in Saudi Arabia, where you cannot drive." She was also nostalgic for "the Islam" of her childhood in 1960s Malaysia "before all the fanatics [came] in." Initially, Sousan associated shari'a with conservative religious norms – typically around inheritance, marriage, and divorce – as she had learned from her family overseas. But in moving to California and becoming an ethnic and religious minority, her understanding of shari'a broadened into a term encompassing her everyday concerns and practices.

She wrote a letter to the imam of the local mosque to ask where she could buy *halal* (Arabic, permissible) foods. The imam invited her to attend a mosque picnic, where she began to build relationships with others and, over the years, she came to understand shari'a as practices related to prayer, hygiene, hospitality, weddings, and "who's gonna say the final rites for me?" These questions and practices broke the hold that an "unruly versus humane" binary once had on her thinking.[13]

The fear of Islamic practices is neither natural nor innate. It is a learned response or an ideological construct produced at the intersection of several political and intellectual currents. Islam and Islamic practices are a crucial discursive terrain, and the ways that individuals experience them are always produced within and mediated by discursive norms and power relations. A certain digital texture of Islamic practice has arisen through Web 2.0 technology and is transforming how individuals encounter Islamic practices. The rise of online fatwa banks, personal blogs, and individual interpretations of Islamic texts and law disseminated through social media platforms like Facebook, Tumblr, and YouTube have facilitated more emotive and personal forms of religiosity (Sands 2010, 141). At the same time, the internet has also made it easier to spread anti-Muslim hate.

Islamophobia and Media

> I would just see things trending on Twitter and people attacking Muslims with it. Like, "You and your shari'a law." Wait a minute. I was like, "What is my shari'a law?" I wasn't unfamiliar with the word, but I just didn't understand it the way he was saying it.[14]

This brings us back to Marwa, the college student mentioned at the beginning of this essay. She is made to feel the tensions surrounding the indeterminate word, shari'a. She is uncomfortable with the notion that there is a positivist law, an identifiable body of written law "out there" to which these hostile tweets refer. She considers shari'a as guidance for personal transformation, for making herself into what she considers to be a good Muslim, through ordinary actions. In describing how she responds to the tweets she mentions, she says, "Right, meaning you have to be calm, you have to be understanding, you have to be patient, you have to be kind . . . shari'a law kind of keeps you in place. It ensures that you're being the best person you possibly can be." These actions might not be immediately recognizable as "religious" (unlike, for instance, wearing a headscarf), but they are nonetheless an important part of Marwa's ethical subjectivity.

A growing amount of research attempts to document and analyze the rise of Islamophobic content in media and mainstream culture (e.g., Ali et al. 2011; Bail 2015; Beydoun 2018; Gottschalk and Greenberg 2008; Green 2015; Khan, Shah, and Ahmad 2017; McAlister 2005). Called "cyber-Islamophobia" by some scholars, social media has been a significant purveyor of anti-Muslim hate (Chao 2015; Muller and Schwarz [2018] 2020; Jenkins and Williams 2021). Social media spreads messages across multiple social networks, and a range of anti-Muslim organizations produce messages that assert that shari'a is a danger to American democracy, that all Muslims have a religious obligation to follow shari'a, and that Muslims will impose shari'a on the American polity and society. Until recently, a lot of this was ignored or dismissed by mainstream media as being the work of fringe elements pedaling bigotry, and strategies certain anti-Muslim individuals and organizations used to generate anxiety. But in the first years following the 9/11 attacks, the highly emotional anti-Muslim messaging at the periphery of the dominant cultural environment in the United States began to drift toward the mainstream. The "emotional energy" of anti-Muslim organizations began to take hold by 2007, when there were four times as many anti-Muslim organizations producing anti-Muslim hate on social media and elsewhere as there were in 2001 (Bail 2015, 72–3). By 2008, the political influence of these organizations was substantial. In the 2008 presidential election, politicians began to warn about the imminent threat posed by shari'a, and by 2008–2010, these organizations had federal and local contracts to train counter-terrorism agents (Bail 2015, 89).

Many of the Muslims we interviewed had read negative comments on social media, including Twitter feeds and Facebook posts. Like Marwa, many felt that shari'a had something to do with personal betterment. But contradictory media coverage and viral attacks on their religion led them to seek more knowledge of shari'a that would put their own questions to rest. For Selma, hearing and seeing negative images of shari'a in mainstream media motivated her to seek information from sources she could trust: "All that . . . hate when people say, 'Oh, they're imposing shari'a.' That's the only context I've heard it, and I haven't learned about it from an Islamic perspective."[15] Ana said, "if this is Islamic, and [at the same time] it's a bad thing, then that can't be right."[16] Sousan echoed this idea: "I think I am a good Muslim [because] I want to be more knowledgeable. [But] right now if you ask me about shari'a, I don't know anything, except for that little bit . . . that my grandfather taught me."[17]

These expressions of shari'a are gendered. Religious authority is masculine, as men and women look to male relatives (like, "my grandfather") and male classically trained imams and scholars for answers. College-aged students and recent graduates spoke about seeking Islamic legal knowledge by following their favorite imams and scholars on Twitter or YouTube, watching recorded sermons, and reaching out to them to ask questions on social media platforms. Some of our interviewees attended weekly *halaqa*, or study circles, some of which were by and for women to discuss issues specific to women's lives. Women engage in formal or informal study of Islamic topics, including shari'a, for the sake of personal knowledge and ethical living rather than as preparation for any public role.

Contemporary American Islamophobia is also gendered (Hammer 2013; Perry 2014; Jamal 2017). Men and women are not racialized in the same way but in gendered ways. Women's attire (headscarf, hijab, burqa, and chador) is typically characterized as a demonstration of female oppression, and women who wear it in the United States are often questioned about their nationality and their cultural values because the way they dress signifies foreignness and misogyny (Selod 2015, 6). Islamophobic discourses focus on images of Muslim men as more likely to be a threat to national security. But the importance of the civilizational clash thesis and civilizational status hinges on the representation of women's roles and bodies in anti-Muslim rhetoric. The presence of gendered Islamophobia is evident in hate crimes, political rhetoric, and media.

For example, in April 2019, Rep. Ilhan Omar experienced a rise in death threats after President Trump tweeted an allegation that Omar was anti-Semitic.[18] A few months later, in the middle of the summer during his re-election campaign, Trump famously tweeted that a handful of progressive congresswomen of color – who became known as 'the squad' – should "go back and fix the broken and crime infested places from which they came." The next day, Trump tweeted again:

> so interesting to see "Progressive" Democratic Congresswomen, who originally came from countries whose governments are a complete and total catastrophe, the worst, most corrupt and inept anywhere in the world (if they even have a functioning government at all), now loudly and viciously telling the people of the United States, the greatest and most powerful Nation on earth, how our government is to be run.

Three of the four women to whom he refers were born in the United States, but not Omar, who is a naturalized U.S. citizen. Just days before Trump's tweets, Fox News host Tucker Carlson labeled Omar an "ungrateful immigrant," and as a woman of Muslim heritage who wears the headscarf, she became emblematic of the perpetual foreignness about which Trump's supporters were concerned. Omar worried aloud about the safety of Muslim immigrants, saying "when you have a president who clearly thinks someone like me should go back, the message he is sending is not for me, it is for every single person who shares my identity." Her concern is more than plausible since pushing Muslims as a whole outside of the boundaries of national belonging has been a national project for more than two centuries. "Well, there's a lot of talk about the fact that she [Omar] married her brother – I know nothing about it," Trump told news reporters at the peak of the Twitter storm he had created (Qiu 2019). This remark was picked up by the *New York Times* and the *Washington Post*, introducing the rumor to many readers for the first time. The rumor had been circulating since 2016 when Omar ran in a state election in Minnesota. Far-right blogs and internet forums perpetuated an unsubstantiated story that a British citizen who married Omar in 2009 and divorced sometime later was her brother. Omar provided the press with a timeline of her marital story, but no matter how many times she denied the claim as "absolutely false and ridiculous," it continued to circulate. The intimate details of her relationships have been mediated by both far-right blogs (in 2016) and mainstream sources (2019), alleging incest and suggesting that Omar's personal life is morally questionable. Constructed as a religious deviant, in the seemingly endless Western obsession with the Muslim woman's body, Omar's chance for normality, to be considered truly a citizen, is contingent upon her own account of herself. The racialized and gendered dynamics of this discourse ultimately produce the marginalized position of her and women like her (i.e., Muslim women). A newly empowered, aggressive, and virulent form of nativism has surfaced, and anti-Muslim hate has gone mainstream.

Conclusion

> California law is telling you what not to do and, like, this is what you're allowed to do, but if you do this, you're going to go to jail, you're going to – whatever. But shari'a law is telling you, like, small things on how to be a better person, on how to build your character, and on how to, like – it's giving you ways, it's giving you, like – it's giving you advice, basically, on how not to fall into trouble, you know?[19]

Paradoxically, populist invocations of a fear of shari'a led to a renaissance among Muslim Americans in our study about how to create a good society rooted in values. "Religious law has limitations because it's a prescriptive law. But all law is prescriptive. . . . There isn't one particular answer but . . . that complexity is part of what I try to get across," a lawyer told us about how she understood law's elasticity as a result of learning about shari'a.[20] Similarly, when we asked the extent to which her views of the American legal system changed as she learned more about shari'a, a college student said, "at the beginning I thought there was only one [interpretation], and now I think that there's more than one way" to interpret the law.[21] Recognizing multiple, competing interpretations means that learning about the law, including Islamic law, does not provide clear answers. But the effort motivates one to learn more: "the more I study, the more confused I am. But not in a bad way, you know? [I am] interested and motivated."[22]

In this essay, I have tried to show three main points about systemic Islamophobia. First, populist discrimination against Muslims and Islam saturates the American Muslim's everyday experience, and certain depictions of shari'a are instrumental for that project. Second, California Muslims' responses to anti-shari'a populism demonstrate the importance of studying how religious minorities experience and learn particular lessons about the processes of religious othering. Third, the othering of Muslims in the United States emerged in part when people defined shari'a narrowly as criminal law, but shari'a is more often a guide to ethical living. In keeping with the expectations of liberal citizenship, the people we met defined their experiences of shari'a largely as aspects of their private lives, influencing their choices to consume, obey traffic laws, and exercise their own religious authority. Muslims are interpreting, discussing, and operationalizing shari'a in multiple ways. It could be around dietary and alcohol choices (e.g., eating *halal*), consumer purchases, or life rituals (e.g., marriage and burial). The prevailing anti-shari'a discourse, and the racializing project underlying it, has shaped a counter-discourse of agency for

Muslim Americans, which involves a changing legal consciousness characterized by personal analysis of religious norms alongside federal, state, and local laws.

Many of the people we met were already trying to be better people; they did not try to become better people simply because Islam was being vilified. While shari'a may or may not have been the driving force of their ethical deeds – for instance, dressing modestly or acting with temperance – for many who foreground being Muslim as their defining identity, it consciously has become so. Many consciously followed shari'a principles to answer everyday life questions, including around finances, marriage and divorce, dietary restrictions, and how to treat the environment. Our conversations were reflective of the place of shari'a in their lives and the impact of shari'a on their interactions with a dominant, non-Muslim society. Many of the Muslims we met engaged in Islam (and shari'a as a part of Islam) because of what they argued was its flexible and accommodating qualities and its inherent compatibility with a liberal ethos.

This essay has critically examined how Muslims in the United States are being othered by being stripped of protections that should be guaranteed by citizenship. Non-Muslim American interest in shari'a has been triggered by a fear that it constitutes a threat to Americans' shared identity and values. Electoral politics, the far-right, and mainstream media, for instance, continue to warn about the dangers of "creeping shari'a." But there is no empirical evidence to show that shari'a is supplanting civil or criminal law in the United States. Negative portrayals of shari'a have long been associated with terrorism and the most extreme forms of corporal punishment, which was a source of great frustration for Californian Muslims in our study. The blame fell on the media and politicians for having framed a national discourse in ways that misrepresented shari'a in order to elicit Islamophobic sentiment.

These deep-seated stereotypes are at the heart of Edward Said's seminal work on Orientalism, which he defined as a system of thought based on an essentialized construction of the East and West (Said 1978). He theorized that discursive strategies lay behind the West's attempts to fix the identity of the East as a blend of reality and fantasy – an effort to reduce the whole Eastern civilization to an antithetical counterpart to the West. The direct result of these methodical depictions of the "East" is the homogenization of highly diverse communities as intellectually inferior cultures and people incompatible with modernity. Said's identification of power structures that dictated the terms of representing religious otherness based on the center-margin binary is further explored in *Covering Islam*, which Said wrote in response to the media coverage of the Iranian hostage crisis. He wrote,

> [N]egative images of Islam continue to be very much more prevalent than others, and . . . such images correspond not to what Islam "is" . . . but to what prominent sectors of a particular society take it to be. Those sectors have the power and the will to propagate a particular image of Islam, and this image therefore becomes more prevalent, more present, than all the others.

The increased public visibility of Muslims in the West has engendered debates that are deeply connected with who Americans are. The directions I have tried to suggest here lead to research agendas that will study the powerful interests behind systemic Islamophobia and will take into account not just race and gender but also sexual orientation, ethnicity, class, and other crucial identities that might moderate or exacerbate the processes of othering. Future research is needed to examine additional vantage points of the othering of Muslims, and how that has been and can be changed through the law itself. Such projects would draw upon the relationship between religion, law, and popular discourse. Muslims in the United States live and work within "not only an imagined Islam but a contrived America," and both are complicit in inventing various forms of discrimination (Jackson 2011, 96). We can continue to learn from studies that bring to our attention the vulnerability of Muslims to religiously and racially motivated violence.

Notes

1 Interview with Marwa, a female college student in her late teens, U.S. born of Arab background. The interview was conducted in San Bernardino County, east of Los Angeles, in April 2015, as part of a research project called *Shari'a Revoiced* (www.shariarevoiced.org), conducted by Kathleen M. Moore and Mark Fathi Massoud, with funding from the University of California Humanities Research Institute (UCHRI) and the Luce Foundation. Pseudonyms are used to preserve confidentiality.

2 Daniel Pipes, "Harold Koh, Promoter of Shari'a?," www.danielpipes.org/blog/2009/03/harold-koh-promoter-of-sharia. See also Hearing Before the Committee on Foreign Relations, United States Senate, One Hundred Eleventh Congress (April 28, 2009) – to Consider the Nomination of Harold H. Koh to be Legal Advisor to the Department of State, www.congress.gov/111/chrg/shrg65250/CHRG-111shrg65250.htm.

3 California is one of the few states in which anti-shari'a legislation has not been introduced onto the legislative agenda to date. Others are Illinois, Maryland, Massachusetts, Nevada, New York, and Rhode Island. See Elsheikh, Sisemore, and Ramirez Lee 2017; for maps of the spread of anti-Muslim hate across the country, see Elfenbein et al. (2018).

4 Interview 22 with Sherene, Egyptian–American woman born in California, late 30s or early 40s, in Orange County, California, January and April 2014; Interview 39 with Mona, Latina Muslim convert, graduate student in her early 30s, in Los Angeles County, September 2014. With the exception of major public figures and officials, all names have been changed to preserve confidentiality.

5 Interview 53 with Saad, a male graduate student of South Asian background, in Los Angeles County, September 2014.

6 Interview 76 with Dima, a female originally from Mexico, in her 60s, a nurse and leader of a Latinx Muslim organization, in Los Angeles County, April 2015.

7 Interview 66 with Nasir, a male participant, U.S. born of Arab background, in his 20s, in Alameda County, December 2014.

8 Interview with Munir and Zayd, in their late 30s or early 40s, both born in California and of South Asian background, both imams with some training at Al-Azhar University, interviewed in April 2014.

9 Interviews 6–7 with Salim and Asma. Salim, born overseas and immigrated to the United States as a young child, is in his late 40s or early 50s. He has an MBA degree and is a leader in a Muslim advocacy organization. Asma, U.S. born of Arab background, is in her late 20s or early 30s. She works for a Muslim advocacy organization. Interviewed in Los Angeles County in April 2014.

10 Interview with Fardosa, attorney, US born of Afghani background in her late 30s, in Orange County, November 2014.
11 Interview with Kamila, a female attorney and leader in a Muslim civil rights organization, born in California of South Asian background, interviewed in San Francisco County, May 2015.
12 Interview with Hala, a female restaurant owner of Palestinian descent, in her late 50s, in Orange County, April 2014.
13 Interview with Sousan, a community activist and artist of Malaysian background in her mid-50s. She has served on the board of directors of her local mosque. Interviewed in Santa Barbara County, April 2014.
14 Interview with Marwa, a female college student in her late teens, U.S. born of Arab background, in San Bernardino County, April 2015.
15 Interview with Selma, a media professional born in California of Arab background, in her 20s, interviewed in Los Angeles County, October 2015.
16 Interview with Ana, a female graduate student of South Asian background, in her late 20s, interviewed in Los Angeles County in September 2014.
17 Interview with Sousan (see note 13).
18 See "Ilhan Omar: Muslim lawmaker sees rise in death threats after Trump tweet," BBC News, posted 15 April 2019; accessed on 26 April 2021, at www.bbc.com/news/world-us-canada-47938268?ocid=socialflow_twitter.
19 Interview with Marwa, a female college student in her late teens, U.S. born of Arab background, in San Bernardino County, April 2015.
20 Interview with Amal, a female attorney, U.S. born of South Asian background, Los Angeles County, April 2014.
21 Interview with Johara, a female college student in her late teens or early 20s, interviewed in Riverside County, April 2014.
22 Interview with Suhail, a male graduate student born in California of South Asian background, interviewed in Orange County in September 2014.

References

Afsaruddin, Asma. 2014. "Shari'a and Fiqh." In *The Oxford Handbook to American Islam*, edited by Yvonne Y. Haddad and Jane I. Smith, 174–86. New York and Oxford: Oxford University Press.

Ahmad, Ahmad Atif. 2017. *Islamic Law: Cases, Authorities and Worldview*. London: Bloomsbury.

Ahmed, Shahab. 2016. *What Is Islam? The Importance of Being Islamic*. Princeton, NJ: Princeton University Press.

Ali, Wajahat et al., 2011. "Fear, Inc.: The Roots of the Islamophobia Network in America." *Center for American Progress*, August 6, 2011. Accessed May 2, 2021. www.americanprogress.org/issues/religion/reports/2011/08/26/10165/fear-inc/.

Bail, Christopher. 2015. *Terrified: How Fringe Anti-Muslim Organizations Became Mainstream*. Princeton, NJ: Princeton University Press.

Bayoumi, Moustafa. 2006. "Racing Religion." *The Centennial Review* 6 (2): 267–93.

Beydoun, Khaled A. 2018. *American Islamophobia: Understanding the Roots and Rise of Fear*. Oakland, CA: University of California Press.

Bravo Lopez, Fernando. 2011. "Towards a Definition of Islamophobia: Approximations of the Early Twentieth Century." *Ethnic and Racial Studies* 34 (4): 556–73.

Cainkar, Louise. 2008. "Thinking Outside the Box: Arabs and Race in the United States." In *Race and Arab Americans before and after 9/11: From Invisible Citizens to Visible Subjects*, edited by Amaney Jamal and Nadine Naber, 46–80. Syracuse, NY: Syracuse University Press.

Chan-Malik, Sylvia. 2018. *Being Muslim: A Cultural History of Women of Color in American Islam.* New York: NYU Press.
Chao, En-Chieh. 2015. "The-Truth-About-Islam.Com: Ordinary Theories of Racism and Cyber Islamophobia." *Critical Sociology* 41 (1): 57–75.
Cheng, Jennifer E. 2015. "Islamophobia, Muslimophobia or Racism? Parliamentary Discourses on Islam and Muslims in Debates on the Minaret Ban in Switzerland." *Discourse and Society* 26 (5): 562–86.
Considine, Craig. 2017. "The Racialization of Islam in the United States: Islamophobia, Hate Crimes, and "Flying While Brown"." *Religions* 8 (9): 165–84.
Elfenbein, Caleb Iyer. 2021. *Fear in Our Hearts: What Islamophobia Tells Us About America.* New York: New York University Press.
Elliot, Andrea. 2011. "The Man Behind the Anti-Shariah Movement." *The New York Times*, July 30, 2011.
Elsheikh, Elsadig, Basima Sisemore, and Natalia Ramirez Lee. 2017. "Legalizing Othering: The United States of Islamophobia." Report of the Haas Institute, UC Berkeley, September 8, 2017. www.haasinstitute.berkeley.edu/global-justice/islamophobia/legalizing-othering.
Esposito, John L., and Natana J. Delong-Bas. 2018. *Shariah: What Everyone Needs to Know.* Oxford and New York: Oxford University Press.
Ernst, Carl W. 2013. *Islamophobia in America: The Anatomy of Intolerance.* New York: Palgrave Macmillan.
Evolvi, Giulia. 2018. "Hate in a Tweet: Exploring Internet-Based Islamophobic Discourses." *Religions* 9 (10): 307ff. doi:10.3390/rel9100307.
Fluhman, Spencer. 2008. "An 'American Mahomet': Joseph Smith, Muhammad, and the Problem of Prophets in Antebellum America." *Journal of Mormon History* 34 (3): 23–45.
Garner, Steve, and Saher Selod. 2015. "The Racialization of Muslims: Empirical Studies of Islamophobia." *Critical Sociology* 41 (1): 9–19.
Gotanda, Neil. 2011. "The Racialization of Islam in American Law." *The Annals of the American Academy of Political and Social Science* 637 (1): 184–95.
Gottschalk, Peter, and G. Greenberg. 2008. *Islamophobia: Making Muslims the Enemy.* Lanham, MD: Rowman and Littlefield.
Green, Todd. 2015. *The Fear of Islam: An Introduction to Islamophobia in the West.* Minneapolis: Fortress Press.
Gualtieri, Sarah. 2001. "Becoming "White;" Race, Religion, and the Foundations of Syrian/Lebanese Ethnicity in the United States." *Journal of American Ethnic History* 20 (4): 29–58.
Hammer, Juliane. 2013. "Center Stage: Gendered Islamophobia and Muslim Women." In *Islamophobia in America: The Anatomy of Intolerance*, edited by Carl W. Ernst, 109–44. New York: Palgrave Macmillan.
Haney Lopez, Ian. 1995. *White by Law.* New York: NYU Press.
Holt, Thomas C. 1995. "Marking: Race, Race-making, and the Writing of History (Presidential Address Before the American Historical Association, 1994)." *The American Historical Review* 100 (1): 1–17.
Howe, Justine. 2018. *Suburban Islam.* Oxford and New York: Oxford University Press.
Jackson, Sherman A. 2011. "Muslims, Islam(s), Race, and American Islamophobia." In *Islamophobia: The Challenge of Pluralism in the 21st Century*, edited by John L. Esposito and Ibrahim Kalin, 93–107. Oxford and New York: Oxford University Press.
Jamal, Amaney A. 2017. "Trump(ing) on Muslim Women: The Gendered Side of Islamophobia," *Journal of Middle Eastern Women's Studies* 13 (3): 472–75.

Jenkins, Laura Dudley, and Rina Verma Williams. 2021. "Anti-Muslim Religious Communication in India and the United States: A Comparative and Interpretive Analysis." In *Exploring the Public Effects of Religious Communication on Politics,* edited by Brian Calfano. Ann Arbor, MI: University of Michigan Press.

Kaufman, Sarah Beth. 2019. "The Criminalization of Muslims in the United States, 2016." *Qualitative Sociology* 42 (4): 521–42.

Khan, Raja Arslan Ahmed, Mudassar Hussain Shah, and Noor el Bashar Ahmad. 2017. "Securitization of Islam and Muslims Through Social Media: A Content Analysis of Stopislam in Twitter." In *Islamophobia and Racism in the United States*, edited by Erik Love. New York: NYU Press.

Love, Erik. 2017. *Islamophobia and Racism in the United States*. New York: NYU Press.

Marr, Timothy. 2006. *The Cultural Roots of American Islamicism*. Cambridge, UK: Cambridge University Press.

McAlister, Melani. 2005. *Epic Encounters: Culture, Media, and US Interests in the Middle East, 1945–2000.* Berkeley: University of California Press.

Mitchell, Joshua L., and Brendan Toner. 2016. "Exploring the Foundations of US State-level Anti-shari'a Initiatives." *Politics and Religion* 9: 720–43.

Mondon, Aurielien, and Aaron Winter. 2017. "Articulations of Islamophobia: From the Extreme to the Mainstream?" *Ethnic and Racial Studies* 40 (13): 2151–79.

Moore, Kathleen M. 1995. *Al-Mughtaribun: American Law and the Transformation of Muslim Life*. Albany, NY: SUNY Press.

Muller, Karsten, and Carlo Schwarz [2018] 2020. "From Hashtag to Hate Crime: Twitter and Anti-Minority Sentiment." Available at SSRN: https://ssrn.com/abstract=3149103

Perry, Barbara. 2014. "Gendered Islamophobia: Hate Crime Against Muslim Women." *Social Identities* 20 (1): 74–89.

Qiu, Linda. 2019. "Repeating False Claims, and Then Cooking Up a Few of His Own [National Desk]." *The New York Times*, July 19, 2019, Late Edition (East Coast). https://search-proquest-com.proxy.library.ucsb.edu:9443/docview/2259709508?accountid=14522.

Said, Edward. 1978. *Orientalism*. New York: Pantheon Books.

Sands, Kristin Zahra. 2010. "Muslims, Identity, and Multimodal Communication on the Internet." *Contemporary Islam* 4: 139–55.

Selod, Saher. 2015. "Citizenship Denied: The Racialization of Muslim American Men and Women post-9/11." *Critical Sociology* (2015): 1–19. doi:10.1177/0896920513516022.

Selod, Saher, and David G. Embrick. 2013. "Racialization and Muslims: Situating Muslim Experience in Race Scholarship." *Sociology Compass* 7 (8): 644–55.

Sheehi, Stephen. 2018. "Duplicity and Fear: Toward a Race and Class Critique of Islamophobia." In *With Stones in Our Hands: Writings on Muslims, Racism, and Empire*, edited by Sohail Daulatzai and Junaid Rana, 35–55. Minneapolis, MN: University of Minnesota Press.

Shryock, Andrew, ed. 2010. *Islamophobia/Islamophilia: Beyond the Politics of Enemy and Friend.* Bloomington, IN: Indiana University Press.

Spellberg, Denise. 2014. *Thomas Jefferson's Qur'an: Islam and the Founders*. New York: Vintage Books.

Wright, Stephanie. 2016. "From 'Mohammedan Despotism' to 'Creeping Shari'a': Cultural (Re)Production of Islamophobia in the United States." *Islamophobia Studies Journal* 3 (2): 199–213.

3

BUDDHIST CONSTRUCTIONS OF THE MUSLIM OTHER

Michael Jerryson

It was mid-June 1976 and the well-known Thai Buddhist monk Kittiwuttho was in an interview with the liberal magazine *Caturat*. Kittiwuttho had been troubled for a while. Only the year before, Vietnam had fallen to communism. Along Thailand's southeastern border, the Khmer Rouge had killed Cambodia's Buddhist monks and any other intelligentsia who stood in the way of their socialist agenda. Just on the other side of Thailand's northeastern border, Laos had adopted communism. Directly north of Thailand, China had become one of the world's leading communist countries. And to make matters worse, Thai national news had reports about Thai communists amassing in southern Thailand.[1]

While some eminent Thai Buddhist monks like Buddhadasa found components of socialism helpful, Kittiwuttho saw the ideology as a threat to Buddhism. In his interview, Kittiwuttho explained that communists were a danger to the country and that killing communists did not constitute killing a person, "because whoever destroys the nation, the religion, or the monarchy, such *bestial* types (man) are not complete persons. Thus, we must intend not to kill people but to kill the Devil (Māra); this is the duty of all Thai" (Keyes 1978, 153).

During this interview and subsequent talks and sermons, Kittiwuttho drew a distinction between Buddhists and communists. Communists were not only non-Buddhist, but they were also not fully human. They were the Other. In the interview with *Caturat*, Kittiwuttho expounds, "It is just like when we kill a fish to make a stew to place in the alms bowl for a monk. There is certainly demerit in killing the fish, but we place it in the alms bowl of a monk and gain much greater merit" (Keyes 1978, 153). In this instance, Kittiwuttho establishes and justifies communists as the Other through Buddhist imagery and rhetoric.

There are manifold ways for Buddhists to create the Other. Kittiwuttho did it through oppositional ideologies. This is not an anomaly in Buddhism nor in the panoply of religious systems. In her monograph *The Curse of Cain*, Regina Schwartz

DOI: 10.4324/b22926-4

argues that the origin of violence is a person's identity formation – namely, the creation of the Other. She locates the origin of violence in identity formation and finds that "imagining identity as an act of distinguishing and separating from others, of boundary making and line drawing, is the most frequent and fundamental act of violence we commit" (Schwartz 1997, 5). Buddhists have been the Other for a myriad of cultures and traditions, most notably in Brahmanical Hinduism, the Chinese Tang Dynasty, Turkish rulers in India, Shinto in Meiji Japan, and communist rule in Mongolia and Cambodia.[2] However, the reverse is also true: Buddhists have cast people as the Other as well. This Buddhist "Othering" is identifiable across Buddhist traditions. This chapter aims to identify strategies and patterns of Buddhist "Othering" in the *long durée*.

Often, Buddhist presentations of their religion include the claim that there is a particular Buddhist tolerance in early scriptural sources. This positive evaluation of inter-religious hermeneutics identified in canonical texts has been largely unquestioned in the academic study of Buddhism. The stance further cements the image of Buddhism as deeply tolerant toward non-Buddhists. Yet this Buddhist perspective raises two important questions: first, who counts as "Buddhist" and "non-Buddhist"? Second, what does tolerance toward the defined "non-Buddhist Other" mean?

While there are philosophical approaches to Buddhist alterity, there is a lack of work on the sociological approaches to Buddhist otherness.[3] In pursuit of this latter direction, this chapter analyzes the ways in which Buddhists have constructed their religious identity vis-à-vis non-Buddhists, and how Buddhists – at certain points in history – have made Muslims the Other. To provide a framework with methods of Othering, I draw upon the work of the historian of religion Jonathan Z. Smith, who provides an instructive structure to religion and othering.[4] In doing so, it is important to use previous research that identifies patterns in Buddhism's relations to other religions, but as our primary concern is hostility and marginalization of religious others, the model focuses on constructions of Buddhist superiority.

In his chapter "Differential Equations on Constructing the Other" of *Relating Religion*, Smith provides three basic models in which people make the Other. The first model has the Other represented metonymically as the presence or absence of one or more traits. His second model is when the Other stands topographically as the periphery compared to the center. In this model, the Other is often mapped as the wild anomie as opposed to the urban nomos. While both the first and second models assert levels of superiority over the Other, Smith finds the third model the most pernicious and mischievous form of Othering. This is where the Other represents deficient linguistic or intellectual abilities – the bar-bar-bar that becomes the nomenclature for barbarians (Smith 2004, 231). This type of Other becomes depicted as subhuman. The people or communities become – to use a term by the eminent historian of religion Charles Long – *signified* (Long 1995, 1–10).

In addressing the Buddhist approach and application of the Other, this chapter maps out Smith's models in the Buddhist context and examines the third model and its manifestations in the contemporary period.

Three Models

Buddhism was absent from Jonathan Z. Smith's description of the three models. The absence of Buddhism from his work does not mean that Buddhism is exempt from these occurrences. Rather, the religious distinctions found in other religions are also found in Buddhist traditions and should not be taken at face value: who are constructed as "Buddhist" and "non-Buddhist," and on what criteria? "Buddhist" and "non-Buddhist" are in themselves normative terms intended to draw boundaries between a "Self" and "Other." Labeling one's opponents as "non-Buddhist" has a long tradition, and in early Buddhist texts, there are multiple examples of polemics and negative campaigning of the Buddha's opponents. While Buddhist traditions provide examples that fit the first two models, the more prevalent examples come from the third model. Due to time constraints, I will devote this time to exploring this model.

The Linguistic and Intellectual Other

J. Z. Smith notes that the first two models have an us-versus-them dichotomy with implicit superiority; however, these models can provide complex reciprocal relationships. In contrast to these two, he deems the third model quite different: "The third model, where the 'other is represented linguistically and/or intellectually in terms of intelligibility,' admits no such ambivalence" (Smith 2004, 237).

Classification of the world in which we live is a basic human enterprise, and self-identities are constructed by distinguishing ourselves from what we are not. Being "civilized" and not "uncivilized" is thus a specific conception of self. Throughout history, it has been an important part of religious self-understanding to represent "civility" and "civilization" and others as "uncivil," "barbarians," "subhuman," or possibly infants yet to be civilized. Examples of such ideas abound in world history, but it is perhaps less well known that such ideas also flourish in Buddhism, a religion often perceived to be tolerant and inclusive.

In his classic study, the anthropologist Stanley Tambiah notes that Buddhist institutions built by forest monks are often interconnected with state formation. Tambiah writes:

> Starting as little-endowed fraternities, and locating themselves on forest edges on the frontiers of advancing settlements, the forest monks could act as elite carriers of literate civilization and could serve as foci for the collective religious activities and moral sentiments of frontier settlements. It is an alliance of this sort, a paired relationship between founding kings . . . with expansionist ambitions and the ascetically vigorous forest monks at the moving edge of human habitation . . . that domesticated the local cults and incorporated them within a Buddhist hierarchy and cosmos.
>
> *(Tambiah 1984, 69)*

The idea of "civilizing" the non-Buddhist other is also clearly expressed in early Buddhist texts. For example, the early Buddhist sources from Sri Lanka, the

Dīpavaṃsa (4th century CE) and the *Mahāvaṃsa* fifth (century CE) portray the island's inhabitants prior to the advent of Buddhism in terms of demons and beasts that the Buddha tamed, pacified, and civilized through his extraordinary powers.[5] Furthermore, in the so-called *vaṃsa* literature, the Buddha is said to *conquer* the island through harsh means, and the island is seen as belonging to him. There are various versions of the account of the Buddha's first visit to the island. The most dramatic narration of the encounter of the Buddha with the island's non-human inhabitants (demons called *yakkhas*) is found in the *Vaṃsatthappakāsinī* (sometimes called the *Mahāvaṃsaṭīkā*), where the Buddha harasses the non-human beings with 11 different types of afflictions. After the Buddha has assailed them with, among other things, thunderstorms, drought, and hot ashes, the *yakkhas* promise the Buddha the right over the island (Gunawardana n.d., 98).

In the aforementioned *Mahāvaṃsa*, we also find one of the most controversial and radical examples of Buddhist Othering. This text tells of the Buddhist king Duṭṭhagāmaṇi (161–137 BCE), who in order "to bring glory to the doctrine" killed the (Tamil) king Eḷāra together with thousands of men on the battlefield. As he was feeling remorse for the slaughter, eight *arahants* come to comfort him, but the king asks: "How shall there be any comfort for me, O venerable sirs, since by me was caused the slaughter of a great host numbering millions?" The *arahants* reply that

> From this deed arises no hindrance in thy way to heaven. Only one and a half human beings have been slain here by thee, O lord of men. The one had come unto the (three) refuges, the other had taken on himself the five precepts. Unbelievers and men of evil life were the rest, not more to be esteemed than beasts. But as for thee, thou wilt bring glory to the doctrine of the Buddha in manifold ways; therefore cast away care from thy heart, O ruler of men![6]

The text states that non-Buddhists are sub-human, and through a strategy of dehumanizing the opponent, killing for the sake of the *Dhamma* is justified. Interestingly, the text constructs a difference between the practice of taking refuge in the Triple Gem (the Buddha, the Dhamma, and the Sangha) and the taking of the five precepts. One possible interpretation of this distinction is that the authors of the *Mahāvaṃsa* claimed that belief (taking the refuges) was not enough to qualify as fully Buddhist but had to be accompanied with moral practice (taking the five precepts). Steven Jenkins has pointed out the ways in which Buddhist texts are concerned with the moral standing of the victim for the karmic repercussion of the perpetrator (Jenkins 2011). If the victim is of low morale, the killing is considered less bad than if the victim had been of high moral status. However, an interesting exception to this general principle of moral hierarchy is in fact found in the *Mahāvaṃsa* story of Duṭṭhagāmaṇi and Eḷāra: king Eḷāra is considered a just king and king Duṭṭhagāmaṇi erects a monument to his memory. This story questions the absoluteness of the moral hierarchy thesis suggested by Jenkins in that it shows that in some cases, the moral worthiness of the victim was not the only stick by which to judge the auspiciousness or inauspiciousness of a violent action: here what qualifies the action of the perpetrator is the non-Buddhist identity of the victim.

This slight turn of phrase, "not more to be esteemed than beasts," has important connotations, both within the taxonomy of alterity and in Buddhist doctrine. Throughout the centuries, people have dehumanized their opposition as a means to legitimate substandard and harmful treatment. Sam Keen explains in his seminal work *Faces of the Enemy* that part of the process of creating an enemy is to obscure the person's face and not to think about their humanity. He writes, "Traditionally, we have maintained this practice of unthinking by creating dehumanizing stereotypes of the objects of our violence and reserving rational thought for determining the weapons, strategies, and tactics we will use in destroying 'them'" (Keen 1986, 24). Dehumanization interrupts our cognitive process of feeling affinity toward another or our capacity to relate to her/him. Turning to the Pāli canon, we find that negative campaigning against non-Buddhist Others is frequent, and some texts even portray *brahmins* as *inferior* to dogs (Freiberger 2011, 185). But the labeling of people as animals has deeper religious significance.

To conclude, using Smith's model of Othering, Buddhism like the ancient Semitic religions studied by Smith contains processes of Othering. However, following the Buddhist doctrinal notion of impermanence suggests that one aspect that distinguishes Buddhism is that condemnations of the "Other" are never eternal.

Buddhist Constructions of the Muslim Other

When exactly was the "Muslim Other" constructed as an object and in need of Buddhist theorizing? Smith points out that difference is constructed as "alien" when the Other is perceived as challenging "a complex and intact world-view." "Muslim Otherness" is thus *not* the result of an inherent or fixed Buddhist theory of Otherness or of Islam but is rather contingent upon political and social realities. It is not a constant religious syntax of violent radical difference. As Islam is a thousand years younger than Buddhism, Buddhist texts explicitly discussing Islam and Muslims are "late" texts. The social and political circumstances for the Buddhist–Muslim encounter vary, but it is clear that some of these Buddhist texts construct negative and sometimes dehumanizing images of Muslims. Buddhists have labeled Muslims as barbarians and also animals.

Johan Elverskog provides powerful examples in *Buddhism and Islam on the Silk Road*. In his review of the *Kālacakra Tantra*, Elverskog notes how Buddhist author/s identify the Muslim as uncivilized and in need of the Buddhist doctrine: "The barbarians observe the demonic dharma; they are proponents of a Creator, a soul, and are free of casteism" (Elverskog 2010, 100–1). Much of this negative depiction occurs through articulations of Islamic dietary preferences, which Buddhist scriptures depict as both primitive and inane: "[The barbarians] kill camels, horses, and cattle, and briefly cook their flesh together with blood. They cook beef and amniotic fluid with butter and spice, rice mixed together with vegetables, and forest fruit, all at once on the fire. Men eat that, O king, and drink bird eggs, in the place of the demon [barbarians]" (Elverskog 2010, 252).

Here, the authors of the *Kālacakra Tantra* make use of the classical means of othering linguistically. The Sanskrit term *barbara* is synonymous with a fool or loon and relates to the Greek *barbaros*. Both the Sanskrit and Greek terms derive from the imbecilic stammering of those who cannot speak the in-group's language; those who stumble with their words, resulting in a "buh, buh, buh." In this passage, barbarian is the translation of the Sanskrit term *mleccha*. The term *mleccha* derives from the verbal root *mlech*, which means to speak indistinctly. Similar to *barbara*, the nominal case refers to a person who cannot speak Sanskrit. This person is a foreigner and an outcaste Other. For the author/s of the *Kālacakra Tanta*, Muslims are barbarians, their diet primitive and unfit for civilized society.

Within Buddhist scriptures, there is the consistent admonishment that one should not harm or injure (*ahimsā*) a sentient being. Yet there are categories within this admonishment that demarcates Other sentient life from the rest. The harming of a human is the worst crime; slightly less is to harm a supranatural being. The least offensive is to harm an animal (Horner 1983, 1, 1992, 146–47). When Kittiwuttho calls communists "bestial," and the enlightened monks tell the Sinhalese king the millions are not more esteemed than beasts, this is not merely a process of dehumanization. It is a process of Othering the value of their lives. The latter is especially prevalent in the contemporary period in which perceived transnational threats lead Buddhists to label Muslims as fish, dogs, and other animals.

Buddhist textual depictions of Muslims as inhuman often follow from a perceived threat of Islam. In contemporary India's conflict-ridden Kashmir, Ravina Aggarwal notes the tensions between the Buddhists and Muslims. From 1989 to 1992, the Ladakh Buddhist Association advanced a social boycott in response to the perception that Islam threatened the survival of the Buddhist community. Aggarwal writes, "Those involved in the Boycott increasingly used the derogatory term *phyi-pa* (outsiders) for Muslims to differentiate Islamic culture from 'indigenous' Buddhist culture. The image of endangered cultural purity was liberally used" (Aggarwal 2004, 75). As primitive outsiders, Muslims tainted the purity of Buddhism. In the village of Mingchanyul, villagers conflicted over two religious events: the annual Buddhist festival of *sngo-lha* and the annual solemn, mourning public demonstrations for Shias, Muharram. Aggarwal reports that the Muslim-to-Buddhist convert, "Stanzin was more critical of the situation than the other youth. He kept referring to the Muslims as phyi-pa (outsiders) and to their customs as *go-log* (inverted)" (Aggarwal 2004, 89).

Most – if not all – Buddhist fears of Islam and Muslims ultimately evolve around two key themes: the destruction of Buddhism and the triumph of Islam. Thus, anti-Muslim discourses are tied to larger concerns about "Islamization" of Buddhist majority societies and subsequent eradication of Buddhism, expressed in what the Burmese scholar Nyi Nyi Kyaw has coined a "myth of deracination." Today, Buddhists often point to the extinction of Buddhism in India in the 12th century CE – symbolized by the Turkish destruction of the Buddhist monastic university of

Nalanda – as a proof for their fear of Islam today. Exactly when the destruction of Nalanda became the symbol of the decline of Buddhism in India is not certain, but it is clear from British colonial archaeological excavations and colonial historiography that the expansion of Islam in South Asia did not coincide with Buddhism's demise.

Knowledge of India's past became accessible to colonial subjects throughout the Empire, including Sri Lanka (then Ceylon) and Myanmar (then Burma). In the late 19th and early 20th century, it was picked up by Buddhist revivalists and modernist reformers such as Anagarika Dharmapala to champion the Sinhala Buddhist cause. In a letter written in 1922, Dharmapala positions Islam as the cause of Buddhism's decline in South Asia. He states, "The vestiges of Buddhism were destroyed by this inhuman, barbarous race. Thousands of bhikkhus were killed, temples were destroyed, libraries were burned and Buddhism dies in India" (Guruge 1965, 207). For Dharmapala, the decline of Buddhism in India, then, is no less the result of Islamic expansionism. He explains, "The Mohammaden, an alien people by Shylockian method, became prosperous like the Jews." It is noteworthy that the point of reference for Dharmapala's anti-Muslim sentiments is not local Buddhist–Muslim interactions but in fact European (Shakespeare and the Jews). Thus, one aspect of today´s Buddhist Islamophobia can be traced back to European anti-Semitism: European anti-Semitic ideas about the greedy and prosperous Jew were transferred onto local Muslims in Ceylon. This conflation of anti-Semitism and Islamophobia has a long history in Europe[7] and was later exported throughout the British Empire – including Ceylon – informing Buddhist reformers like Dharmapala.[8] As research on Buddhist modernism has shown, the dark side of Buddhist anti-colonial revivalism was the exclusion of not only Christianity (as the colonial religion) but also other non-Buddhist religions, such as Hinduism and Islam.

The Distant and Beastly Other

Smith challenges the reader to question how different difference has to be in order to constitute "Otherness." Under what circumstances and to whom are such distinctions of interest? The point Smith wishes to make is that distinctions are made sharpest between close neighbors – the proximate Other. While this point seems to fit well with Muslims and other Abrahamic traditions or early Buddhism and its competition with *brahmins* or Jain groups, it does not fit with Buddhist–Muslim relations. On the one hand, it is plausible to argue that internal discipline and intra-Buddhist distinctions are more important to the state than "Distant Others"; traditionally, Theravada Buddhist states have not been concerned with the regulation of Muslim religious practice. Thus, it is the discipline of the Buddhist Self and not the distant Other that is of primary concern. On the other hand, there is a perception that the "Muslim Distant Other" is coming closer, constituting an existential threat to Buddhism.

In contemporary Chiang Mai, Thailand, Brooke Schedneck observes Buddhist monks engaged in a program called Monk Chat at popular tourist temples.

Drawing on Pattana Kitiarsa's taxonomy of Siamese Occidentalism (Kitiarsa 2010, 57–74), she finds that these monks describe Westerners, Chinese, and Muslims in very distinctive ways. White Westerners are the "beneficial" Other. Schedneck explains that monks see their Western presence as "possibilities of English conversational practice, but also prestige to a temple community in which foreigners would travel to and be interested to visit" (Schedneck 2018, 1888–1916, 1902). The monks see Chinese tourists as the "familiar" Other. As opposed to the Westerners, who might have little to know familiarity with Buddhism and Thailand, Chinese tourists generally have some knowledge. Yet, the monks treat Muslims as the most "distant" Other. According to the monks, Muslims display less interest in Buddhism than the Christian Westerners. Some of these monks and other Thai Buddhists see Muslims as a threat to their country and Buddhism (Schedneck 2018, 1888–1916). Furthermore, there is a perception among Buddhists in Thailand, as well as in Myanmar, that Buddhist monks are not allowed into mosques.

It is not just Muslim tourists who are the "distant" Other. Even Thai Muslims endure the perception of being "distant." In southern Thailand, Thai Malay Muslims are doubly displaced from the normative identity due to their Malay ethnicity and Muslim identity (Jerryson 2011, 143–77). When this displacement is coupled with perceived threats to normativity, the caricature becomes more pronounced. It gravitates from the "distant" other to the beastly other.

Contemporary Buddhist Othering of Muslims

Often times, Buddhist caricatures of an intellectual Other spawn from conceptions of existential threat. In the 1970s, communism had a widespread regional influence throughout Southeast Asia. This spread and its violent confrontations with Buddhist societies provoked Buddhists. In the 21st century, communism has receded in Southeast Asia. In its wake, another existential threat has loomed: Islam. The largest populated Muslim country in the world is Indonesia. Neighboring Thailand's border is Malaysia, an Islamic state. Buddhists did not collectively perceive Islam or Muslims as a threat until there were global examples that connected Muslim identity with violence against non-Muslims.

Fueled by new forms of communication, worldwide concerns over the rise of global jihadism, and the subsequent securitization of Islam, local Muslims in Buddhist societies are increasingly portrayed as a threat to national security. Muslim associations are seen as representatives of international terrorist networks and local agents of Islamic global imperialism. Leading monks have called mosques "enemy bases," and they have identified the *niqab* as a direct threat to the state and its territory. The BBS, for example, has published posters that show Sri Lanka as a *niqab*-dressed woman with evil-red eyes, symbolically identifying the *niqab* as a direct security threat to the state and its territory.

In Burmese Buddhist discourse, but increasingly also in BBS understanding, the Rakhine state in Myanmar, which borders the populous Muslim state of Bangladesh, is glossed as a "frontier state" between what is seen as two distinguishable and separate worlds of Buddhism and Islam. This is the home of the Muslim Rohingya population, which is denied citizenship in Myanmar and for those who have fled to Bangladesh, also face dire living conditions there. In contemporary anti-Muslim discourse, the Rohingyas are seen as filthy, as hyperfertile and underdeveloped, and – according to the famous Rakhine Buddhist nationalist Aye Chan – as "virus" (Zan and Chan 2005).

Another aspect of the alleged 'Islamization' of Buddhist women in Myanmar relates to Buddhist–Muslim marriages and the idea that Muslim males force their Buddhist spouses to become Muslim. "Love Jihad" refers to a claimed Islamist conspiracy whereby Muslim men trick non-Muslim women into marriage as a means to spread Islam. Love jihad is a tool for "Islamization" of Buddhist women by their Muslim husbands. From this perspective, mixed marriages are conceptualized as a means of conversion and thus represent a danger to the very survival of Buddhism.

Such fears were prominent in BBS discourses but nowhere were the fears of the Muslim Male Other as widespread as in Myanmar during the first phase of political liberalization (2011–2016). In a now-famous BBC interview in 2013, Aung San Suu Kyi, after a tough interview on the violence in Rakhine, was recorded as saying: "Why didn´t anyone tell me I was going to be interviewed by a Muslim?" This outburst, as well as the controversy following the publication of the quote in 2016, is telling of the new sensibilities when it comes to Muslim–Buddhist relations in Myanmar. Why would the religious identity of the reporter matter to the Nobel Peace Laureate? The 2012 communal violence in Rakhine, the western state of Myanmar bordering Bangladesh, drew the world's attention to the lack of state protection of certain Muslim minority communities in Buddhist majority states today. Violence spread from Rakhine to other parts of Myanmar in 2013 and 2014, mostly affecting Muslim communities. In addition, anti-Muslim hate speech was prominent on social media.

Such fears – and the political use of them – created the political space necessary to get passed four laws to "protect race and religion." These laws were created by Buddhist monks in order to stop the "Islamization" of Myanmar and are used to trump Buddhist family law over Islamic family law (Crouch 2016). The laws sent a strong signal to Myanmar citizens that inter-religious marriages (particularly between Buddhism women and Muslim males) were regarded with suspicion, and moreover, that (Buddhist) conversion (to Islam) had to be under strict state supervision. It remains uncertain to what extent the laws are applicable to non-citizens like the Rohingya population. What remains clear is that the laws received great support among local Buddhism women in Rakhine who saw the laws as necessary against Muslim sexual aggression (Walton, McKay, and Kyi 2015).

Since 2012, Myanmar has been plagued with riots and communal attacks, many of which Buddhists turn on their Muslim neighbors. During his trip to document the plight of the Rohingya in Myanmar, the journalist Nicholas Kristof met with Buddhists and asked them about their perspectives. In one powerful interaction, Kristof asked a young Burmese Buddhist what he would do if he met a Muslim. With a shy smile, the boy replied, "I'd kill him."[9] This vehemence is intimately connected to the juridical and political Othering of Myanmar's Muslims.

Conclusion

Relations and boundaries between "Buddhist Self" and "non-Buddhist Other" in early Buddhist texts are bargained from a Buddhist *minority* position. Reading texts from a historical critical point of view, therefore, it is important to ask under what conditions are understandings of the Other articulated. As discussed more in detail under Smith's third category of the "Linguistic and Intellectual Other," it is possible that the degrees to which "othering" processes are "soft" rhetorical devices in religious polemics to convince others to the Self's religion, or when "othering" processes are strong and violent, are contingent upon majority–minority relations and political contexts.

Little attention has been paid to Buddhist anti-Muslim sentiments as a discursive field that is both local and global. A close look at anti-Muslim conspiracies reveals that such discourses operate at different levels, serving various interests and concerns: some discourses relate to local business competition, while others portray Muslims and Islam as a security threat to the state. Furthermore, Buddhist activists in South and Southeast Asia use discourses, signs, and symbols that first came into use in European, Indian, or North American settings, indicating global flows of Islamophobic ideas and objects. This is a disconcerting aspect of globalization, and the hope is that this chapter and this book will stimulate others to explore further its significance.

Notes

1 This chapter draws material from Jerryson and Frydenlund (2020).
2 For examples of European and Islamic ways to Other Buddhism and Buddhists, see Lopez (2013). For Islamic caricatures of Buddhists and Buddhism, see Elverskog (2010).
3 One of the notable contributions to this underdeveloped discourse is Perry Schmidt-Leukel's expansive edited volume (2012).
4 The differentiation and Othering *per se* is not necessarily hostile and violent. For example, as Inden reminds us, Orientalism (as a form of Othering) can be both negative and positive.
5 *Mhv.*, verses 3–4. *Mvh.* builds upon the earlier *Dpv.*, which builds on the now lost *Sīhalaṭṭhakathā-Mahāvaṃsa*, which was part of the Mahāvihāra Canon, written down in the first century BCE (Walters 2000, 107).
6 *Mhv.* (transl.) XXV 109–111.
7 For example, Muslims were identified with the legendary "Red Jews."
8 Anagarika Dharmapala was under strong European and North American influence: through British schooling system in Ceylon, as well as through contact with Madam Blavatsky and Henry Steel Olcott of the Theosophical Society.
9 Nicholas Kristof, "21st Century Concentration Camps," *New York Times*, June 16, 2014, www.youtube.com/watch?v=hqMSfT9eI6o.

References

Aggarwal, Ravina. 2004. *Beyond Lines of Control: Performance and Politics on the Disputed Borders of Ladakh, India*. Durham: Duke University Press.

Crouch, Melissa. 2016. "Personal Law and Colonial Legacy: State-Religion Relations and Islamic Law in Myanmar." In *Islam and the State in Myanmar: Muslim-Buddhist Relations and the Politics of Belonging*, edited by Melissa Crouch. New York: Oxford University Press.

Elverskog, Johan. 2010. *Buddhism and Islam on the Silk Road*. Philadelphia: University of Pennsylvania Press.

Freiberger, Oluver. 2011. "How the Buddha Dealt with Non-Buddhists." In *Religion and Identity in South Asia and Beyond: Essays in Honor of Patrick Olivelle*, edited by Steven Lindquist. London: Anthem Press, 185–195.

Gunawardana, R. A. L. H. Undated. *The Kinsmen of the Buddha: Myth as Political Character in the Ancient and Early Medieval Kingdoms of Sri Lanka*. Colombo: Social Scientists' Association.

Guruge, Ananda, ed. 1965. *Return to Righteousness: A Collection of Speeches, Essays and Letters of the Anagarika Dharmapala*. Colombo: Department of Government Printing.

Horner, Isaline Blew, trans. 1983. *The Book of the Discipline (Vinaya-Pitaka): Vol. III (Suttavibhanga)* 1942. Oxford, U.K.: Pali Text Society.

———. 1992. *The Book of the Discipline (Vinaya-Pitaka): Vol. I (Suttavibhanga)* 1938. Oxford, UK: Pali Text Society.

Jenkins, Stephen. 2011. "On the Auspiciousness of Compassionate Violence." *Journal of the International Association of Buddhist Studies* 33 (1–2): 299–331.

Jerryson, Michael. 2011. *Buddhist Fury: Religion and Violence in Southern Thailand*. New York: Oxford University Press.

Jerryson, Michael, and Iselin Frydenlund. 2020. "Buddhists, Muslims and the Construction of Difference." In *Buddhist-Muslim Relations in a Theravada World*, edited by Iselin Frydenlund and Michael Jerryson. New York: Palgrave Macmillan.

Keen, Sam. 1986. *Faces of the Enemy: Reflections of the Hostile Imagination*. New York: HarperCollins Publishers Inc.

Keyes, Charles. 1978. "Political Crisis and Militant Buddhism." In *Religion and Legitimation of Power in Thailand, Laos, and Burma*, edited by Bardwell L. Smith, 147–64. Chambersburg, PA: ANIMA Books.

Kitiarsa, Pattana. 2010. "An Ambiguous Intimacy: *Farang as Siamese Occidentalism*." In *The Ambiguous Allure of the West: Traces of the Colonial in Thailand*, edited by Rachel V. Harrison and Peter A. Jackson, 57–74. Hong Kong: Hong Kong University Press.

Kristof, Nicholas. 2014. "21st Century Concentration Camps." *New York Times*, June 16, 2014. www.youtube.com/watch?v=hqMSfT9eI6o.

Long, Charles H. 1995. *Significations: Signs, Symbols, and Images in the Interpretation of Religion*. Aurora, CO: The Davies Group.

Lopez, Donald S. 2013. *From Stone to Flesh: A Short History of the Buddha*. Chicago: University of Chicago Press.

Schedneck, Brooke. 2018. "Religious Others, Tourism, and Missionization: Buddhist 'Monks Chats' in Northern Thailand." *Modern Asian Studies* 52 (6): 1888–1916.

Schmidt-Leukel, Perry. 2012. *Buddhism and Religious Diversity*. London: Routledge.

Schwartz, Regina. 1997. *The Curse of Cain: The Violent Legacy of Monotheism*. Chicago: University of Chicago Press.

Smith, Jonathan Z. 2004. *Relating Religion: Essays in the Study of Religion*. Chicago: University of Chicago Press.

Tambiah, Stanley. 1984. *The Buddhist Saints of the Forest and the Cult of the Amulets: A Study in Charisma, Hagiography, Sectarianism, and Millennial Buddhism*. Cambridge: Cambridge University Press.

Walton, Matthew, M. McKay, and D. K. Mar Mar Kyi. 2015. "Women and Myanmar's 'Religious Protection Laws'." *The Review of Faith & International Affairs* 13 (4): 36–49.

Zan, U. Shwe, and Aye Chan. 2005. *Influx Viruses: The Illegal Muslims in Arakan*. Yangon: Burma Library. www.burmalibrary.org/docs21/Aye-Chan-2015-08-Influx_Viruses-The_Illegal_Muslims_in_Arakan-en-red.pdf.

4

CONSUMING DIFFERENCE

Coffee and the Specter of the Islamic Other

Jamel Velji

As a scholar of Islamic Studies and Religious Studies, I am struck by a stubbornly persistent trend in the study of Islam to valorize two elements of what is perceived to be "Islamic" over many others.[1] These are problematic emphases that scholars have highlighted long ago: the study of subjects in the "premodern" (or "classical") time period, i.e., before the fall of Baghdad in 1258 as Islam's "golden age," and the study of these phenomena through the prism of Arabic philology. These two longstanding disciplinary conventions result from the ways in which Islam has been studied in the Western academy.[2] There is a tacit logic behind these scholarly conventions that encodes an othering into the study of Islam – and, by extension, helps to define the contours of what is "Islamic" in relation to what is 'Western.'[3] This logic is that the classical period of Islamic civilization is only a precursor to Western ascendancy,[4] and the study of Arabic, though spoken as a mother tongue by only 15% of the world's Muslims, can provide the truest insight into what is Islamic (Kumar 2012). Among the manifold effects of this disciplinary emphasis is a kind of freezing of Muslim agency through Muslims' associations with the premodern, as well as a privileging of the Arabic-speaking Muslim as an embodiment of the "authentic" vision of the tradition. Shahzad Bashir has recently argued that the subsuming of Islamic history to a Western timeline has, in fact, been at the heart of these and other disciplinary problems in the study of Islamic history.[5]

I bring up this legacy of the Western specter of Islam as enshrined in the disciplinary horizon of Islamic Studies to highlight how a parallel problem exists in the production of knowledge about Muslim contributions to Western culture. More specifically, this chapter illustrates how the legacy of the history of coffee – a beverage popularized and domesticated by Muslims – also illuminates the specter of the other, here the Islamic other. Just as Islamic Studies' disciplinary frameworks tend to ossify certain Western perceptions of Muslims, I illustrate how some popular

DOI: 10.4324/b22926-5

books on the history of coffee, as well as an example from coffee advertising, illustrate a deep unease with Islam and Muslims' foundational roles in coffee culture.

First, a brief history of coffee. According to Ralph Hattox's survey of the sources, by around the middle of the 15th century "a potion made from some stimulating vegetable matter seems to have gained popularity among the adherents of certain Sufi orders in the Yemen" (Hattox 1988, 22–23). By the late 15th century, the drink is made not from parts of the coffee plant but from elements of the bean itself. Sources attribute this transformation in coffee brewing to the scholar and Sufi Muhammad al-Dhabhani, who dies around 1470 (Hattox 1988, 23). Coffee is first widely used in Yemen and is most closely associated with Sufi orders (Hattox 1988, 22–23); it rapidly spreads to the Hijaz (or Western Saudi Arabia, including Mecca and Medina) and then to Cairo. In the early 16th century, coffee is a hotly contested substance in both Mecca and Cairo. In 1511, there are attempts to prohibit coffee in Mecca. In 1525 or 1526, a jurist orders the closing of Meccan coffeehouses because of concerns that these houses were encouraging unsavory social behaviors. In the following year, that same jurist dies, and coffeehouses reopen. In 1534 or 1535, a preacher in Cairo rails against coffee, starting a riot in which coffeehouses are attacked but soon after a judge decides in their favor (Hattox 1988, 29–45). Coffee then enters Europe toward the second half of the 17th century – among the first cafes in Europe are the coffeehouse in Oxford, England (1650); the Procope in Paris (1686); and café Florian in Venice (1720).

There is much more to say about coffee's history. Hattox, for instance, recounts the details of the legal debates arguing for coffee's permissibility in the Islamic tradition. He also discusses the nature of some of the earliest coffeehouses dotting the landscapes of the Levant, Mecca, and Cairo. There is also a fascinating question of origins: coffee is thought to have come from Ethiopia, but recent scholarship on the beverage has actually found that while coffee grows wild in Ethiopia, it was not drunk as a beverage there until Muslims popularized drinking the extract from the bean in the 16th century (Schaefer 2001, 26ff.). And there is, of course, the question of how coffee spread through Europe and the Americas – stories that involve the mass enslavement of peoples; the reshaping of coffee's Islamic and Ethiopian pasts; fears over coffee's stimulating properties; and coffeehouses that served as places for social reform and the plotting of revolutions.[6]

Returning to the presentation of coffee's Islamic heritage, I turn now to two popular books presenting the history of coffee – one explicitly on coffee's history, focusing on a global history of coffee, and another focusing on the history of stimulants. Mark Pendergrast's widely circulated and widely acclaimed *Uncommon Grounds, The History of Coffee and How it Transforms our World*, a global history of coffee, distills the rich Islamic heritage of coffee to one and half pages in a book that is almost 400 pages long. In the section "coffee goes Arab," he casually states about coffee's migration from Ethiopia to the Yemen:

> The Arabs took to the stimulating drink. (According to legend, Mohammed proclaimed that under the invigorating influence of coffee he could

> "unhorse forty men and possess forty women.") They began cultivating the trees, complete with irrigation ditches, in the nearby mountains, calling it *qahwa*, an Arab word for wine – from which the name *coffee* derives.
>
> *(Pendergrast 2010, 5–6)*

The next section of the text addresses debates about coffee's permissibility in Islam and then details coffee's arrival in the West.

In this brief selection, there are three ways in which Pendergrast's portrayal of the history of coffee illustrates, intentionally or unintentionally, a vision of Islam as other. These three visions are accomplished through the reproduction of a medieval polemic about the foundational figure of the tradition, the Prophet Muhammad, being both lascivious and violent, and here is how each of these mechanisms of othering works in turn.

First, the presentation of Muhammad as violent and lascivious stands in tacit contrast to the founder of Christianity, who is considered peaceful and celibate. Second, note how the inclusion of the Prophet of Islam in this narrative makes unusual strength and unusual lasciviousness inherent to the nature of the Arabs as well as Muslims, perhaps signaling an underlying and enduring fear of the Muslim/Arab other (note how the logic of this trope also fashions Christian men as the normative standard by which others can be judged). This legend, I should mention, is not found in any of the Islamic sources I have seen, but the trope about the Prophet having unusual sexual powers is standard fare in medieval Christian anti-Muslim polemics. The specific trope of the Prophet having the sexual powers of 40 men is actually part of the *Risalat al-Kindi*, a widely read polemical text circulated in medieval Europe.[7]

Third, and perhaps most interestingly, the reproduction of this polemic linking Muhammad, coffee, and excessive strength somehow becomes an explanation, by extension, for the ascendancy of Islamic civilization, a subject that some had difficulty accounting for. The logic here is that Arabs were able to gain the strength to build a civilization precisely because their Prophet drank coffee (!) Note how this account also impinges on the theological veracity of Muhammad's prophecy – and by extension, Islam itself, rendering both somehow illogical and reduced to the influence of a substance. In other words, Islam and its messenger are not perceived as legitimate religious or political forces, in tacit comparison, once again, to the rational and theologically supreme force of Christianity.

The force of this polemic hinges upon the anachronistic inclusion of the Prophet of Islam in a vignette about coffee, a substance discovered more than 800 years after his death. This account also serves as a kind of polemical inversion of the genre of literature known as *hadith*, the sayings and actions of the Prophet. Pendergrast's anachronistic re-telling of coffee's origins is narratively successful because of the stubbornly persistent perception of the place of Muslims in the history of the West – the idea that Islamic civilization was a temporary holding place for and precursor to European ascendancy. This logic locates Islamic civilizational contributions such as the fountain pen, the hospital, algebra, eye surgery, and now coffee squarely in the historical past, effacing individual microhistories of these contributions, and geographically distant from the "West." It also locates the "West" (read: Christianity) as something normative, rational, and theologically superior. So, ironically, Muslims themselves – who actually domesticated coffee – become cast as the other, as simultaneously the substance becomes extracted from its civilizational context. This, then, is how Pendergrast's derogatory comments about the Prophet of Islam in a history of a commodity that becomes popular more than 800 years after his death can become entirely normative even today.[8]

The other book that I wish to discuss is Wolfgang Schivelbusch's *Tastes of Paradise*, a history of spices and intoxicants. In his discussion on coffee, Schivelbusch writes:

> It is difficult to determine precisely when coffee was introduced to Arabic culture. According to legend, Mohammed was cured of narcolepsy with coffee . . . in the Islamic world, too, it became a popular beverage relatively late, certainly no earlier than the fifteenth century.
>
> Although the dating may be vague, the *logic* [italics original] of coffee drinking for Arabic-Islamic civilization is incontestable. As a nonalcoholic, nonintoxicating, indeed even sobering and mentally stimulating drink, it seemed to be tailor-made for a culture that forbade alcohol consumption and gave birth to modern mathematics. Arabic culture is dominated by abstraction more than any other culture in human history. Coffee has rightly been called the wine of Islam.
>
> *(Schivelbusch 1992, 17)*

The logic of inserting the Prophet of Islam in this vignette serves a similar purpose as in the Pendergrast account: coffee serves as the elixir that makes the Prophet (and by extension Islam) successful. The Prophet's narcolepsy once again becomes a foil to the "normative" prophet who functions without any substances, the prophet of Christianity. And finally, note how this account's description of Muhammad as a narcoleptic hearkens back to widely circulated tropes about Oriental indolence.

Schivelbusch's account also states that there is an explanation of why certain cultures drink certain beverages. Here the logic seems to be that Arab civilization seems to be formal, austere, and abstract – in contrast to all other civilizations. This explanation once again rests on a logic of tacit contrast: that European culture is creative and engaged with the present. The logic also rests on striking misperceptions and anachronisms that help to freeze Arab civilization in contrast to providing fluidity to European civilization. Perhaps the most obvious stereotype includes the contrast between alcohol and coffee, though in reality Muslims have and have had a multiplicity of perspectives on alcohol. Schivelbusch's assertion about the essentialization of culture illuminates the conflation between Islamic and Arab, while also reifying through its opposition to the conflation of European and Christian.

While the two widely distributed texts earlier illuminate in popular materials the retelling of coffee's Islamic origins, it is also fascinating to see how coffee's Islamic heritage can be (re-) presented visually. I wish to now turn to the iconography of a major European coffee company, Julius Meinl, to illustrate how the Muslim heritage of coffee is represented in the brand's iconography.

Meinl began as a spice shop in Vienna in 1862 and in 1913 became the most significant coffee and tea importer in central Europe.[9] In 1924, Meinl used the first iteration of the logo that is today synonymous with their brand: the Meinl Mohr, a logo that looks like a boy wearing a tasseled fez.[10]

On a previous version of their website, Meinl illustrates how the logo has changed over the years.[11] Among the ten versions of the logo reproduced there, the one at the far left of the page – presumably the earliest version of it – portrays a dark-skinned boy with somewhat exaggerated lips wearing a red fez drinking coffee out of a tipped bowl. The current iteration of the logo has dispensed with the boy's skin color, as well as his consuming coffee. This iteration of the logo is entirely red, and his facial features look delicate and boyish. In their description of the evolutionary trajectory of the logo, the company states that the logo has been updated with the aim of evoking a European cherub of the sort found in a certain style of Austrian architecture. Versions of this icon appear ubiquitously on merchandise associated with the company, from coffee cups to sugar packets, from storefronts to packages of tea.

I wish to show how this icon that is supposed to somehow represent the Muslim heritage associated with coffee serves to ironically distort this heritage. Let me now illustrate how this works. First, and most obviously, note how this process of updating the icon is in fact synonymous with its Westernization. The coffee boy becomes divested of his distinctively "Moorish" features to evolve into something that is much lighter in hue, acquiring distinctly European features in the process.

At the same time, the various historical iterations of the Mohr tell a story about the homogenization of the other. Among the ten versions of the icon reproduced on the website, the Mohr is alternately portrayed as black and brown, and one is thus left wondering which people the Mohr is supposed to represent. This indeterminacy is instrumental in helping to efface differences between various groups, portraying them all as the "other," reminiscent of Schivelbusch's timeless account of all people in Arab–Islamic civilization.

Third, Meinl describes today's icon as that which now resembles a cherub of the kind found in a certain style of Austrian architecture.[1]This description of this logo has subsequently been modified. See now https://juliusmeinl.com/us/about-julius-meinl/who-we-are. Accessed 25 May 2022. This angel is not Islamic, nor does it fly free between cultures or between heavens. Rather, the angel is tethered to a specific geographical place and cultural context – the architectural, religio-spiritual landscape of Austria. The Mohr here becomes divested of its humanness through its explicit identification with an otherworldly figure tethered to a distinct time and place – one separate entirely from any Islamic affiliation.

The divestment of the Mohr's humanity is made complete through an examination of Meinl's description of a recent cup redesign. According to this description,

Meinl states that the prominent designer Matteo Thun came up with the new design by drawing the Mohr, inverting him, and making the fez's tassel the cup's handle.[12] In a sketch on Meinl's website, one can see both the icon and the inverted Mohr.[13] The Mohr now becomes completely effaced of its humanity, made literally into one's drinking vessel for the consumer, or maybe even into the drink itself.

One might wonder why I have spent so much time dwelling on the representation of a certain Austrian icon that appears on sugar packets and packages of teas and coffees. There are two reasons: first, because of this icon's historical affiliations and, second, because of this icon's ubiquity, which has a certain power to construct our perception of reality. I will now take each of these two points in turn, illustrating how this icon and its ubiquity only serve to reify the specter of the Islamic other.

First, the history. In narrating the history of the logo, information on the Meinl website states that the icon commemorates the story of coffee's arrival to Vienna.[14] It reproduces the widely circulated legend that a person named Georg Franz Kolschitzky – whom Meinl describes as an imperial official and entrepreneur – found some coffee that the Ottomans had abandoned after the second siege of Vienna in 1683. Kolschitzky then founded Vienna's first coffeehouse, called Blue Bottle. The logo, the description states, is a representation of the story of Kolschitzky's role in bringing coffee to Vienna.

Various elements of European literary and artistic production have celebrated the second siege of Vienna as a watershed moment in the history of Europe, a turning point in which the forces of Christianity finally defeated the Muslim threat that had been looming for more than a century in Christian territory. The reality on the ground, as always, was a bit more complicated. The siege was not just a battle between Muslims and Christians; rather, it occurred among alliances formed across religious lines (the Ottomans were actually aided by Imre Thököly, leader of the Hungarian Protestants).[15] Further, there was a generations-old notion that "the most recent Christian success was the first act of a reversal that would put an end to the monstrosity of the Turkish presence in Europe" (Tolan et al. 2013, 167). This anticipation of ridding Europe of "the infidels" was tethered to a mentality of war that linked battles against "the Turks" to a vision of sacred duty (Tolan et al. 2013, 164–69). This was a sentiment that was propagated by various Christian forces, in particular the papacy (Tolan et al. 2013, 167), and was also shared on the other side by Ottoman leaders, who cast their battles against "Christians" as a form of jihad (Tolan et al. 2013, 178–79). Yet, the siege of Vienna

> was of great psychological importance for the Habsburgs and the whole of Europe. It seemed to western observers that the tide of Ottoman conquest was turning. The literary production of the time reflects the exaggerated expectations of contemporaries that the forces of Christianity would at last triumph after centuries of struggle.
>
> *(Finkel 2006, 288)*

And while this battle was certainly a setback for the Ottomans, it was by no means the end of the empire or of the Ottoman presence in Europe.

The Meinl icon celebrates the defeat of the Ottomans through the description's explicit reference to Kolschitzky, a Pole who, as legend has it, was part of the relief army that was instrumental in breaking the siege of Vienna. Kolschitsky, according to this legend, was a messenger who, having lived among the Turks, was able to travel back and forth through enemy lines, in Turkish uniform, to deliver messages to the Austrian leadership about the arrival of the relief army. These messages were instrumental in bolstering the city's morale, in turn helping Hapsburg forces defeat the Ottomans. Among the spoils that the Ottomans left were bags of unroasted coffee beans. Kolschitsky was one of the only people who knew what to do with these beans. He then apparently acquired a license to open Vienna's first coffee shop, Blue Bottle,[16] which, incidentally, is also the name of a contemporary American coffee shop named in Kolschitsky's honor.[17]

The memory of Kolschitsky's role in bringing coffee to Europe is commemorated throughout Viennese café culture, despite the fact that Vienna's first coffeehouse was opened by an Armenian named Johannes Diodato (Baghdiantz-McCabe 2008, 195–96). Kolschiky's presence is ubiquitous in the city; at Kolshitygasse, the street named after him, one finds a monument to Kolschitsky, dressed in Turkish uniform, pouring coffee with his right hand, with a shield and weapons behind him. The monument is an exquisite testament to and celebration of the final military defeat of the Muslim threat. By extension, it is also a celebration of Europe remaining Christian and of coffee becoming a domesticated European (Christian) product.[18]

But why might the Mohr be the icon that Meinl has chosen to represent their brand? Why not Kolschitsky? The Mohr (in English, "Moor") is a word synonymous with Muslim (Arjana 2014, 67), and here it seems as though early iconography of the Meinl Mohr alternates between the portrayal of the coffee boy as black and brown. There is a rich history of European painting and literary output depicting the black Turk, sometimes synonymous with the Moor, as connected to the devil (Arjana 2014, 67); indeed, "[d]uring the Renaissance, the black Muslim continued to occupy a place in the Christian imaginary as a nefarious figure and enemy of Christendom" (Arjana 2014, 67). What I find fascinating about the Meinl Mohr is how this icon has become a representation of a victory over a threat that is still present but has become attenuated. This attenuation is represented through Mohr's sexual immaturity – he is still only a boy – and his foreignness is partially "humanized" through the acquisition of European angelic features. He thus represents the victory of fully mature Christendom over an emasculated, subservient, and immature Islam. This moment in history – and this asymmetrical power dynamic – becomes reified through this icon. The asymmetrical power dynamic is further commemorated through the branding of the icon on various consumable objects. The Islamic threat thus becomes perpetually visible and perpetually domesticated through the act of ingesting the Mohr – here the Mohr as the (black/brown) coffee that is drunk, the inverted fez in its container.[19]

The Meinl Mohr is ubiquitous in the Viennese cityscape. The Mohr is imprinted on umbrellas at Meinl shops; he lights up the sky from atop a Meinl building close to the Vienna opera house; he is on the commercial-grade grinder at major cafes such as Café Museum; and he is imprinted on virtually everything at the giant Meinl store am Graben, including on child-size shopping carts at that store, where one can also purchase miniature Meinl Mohrs. This symbol of European/Christian conquest and the domestication of spoils – as well as Meinl's discursive economic custodianship over those spoils – suffuses the Viennese cityscape. Viennese café culture is also inexorably linked to the city's identity, and Julius Meinl claims to be an intrinsic aspect of the Viennese café tradition.[20]

This symbol, and all it represents, is not only restricted to the Viennese cityscape or other locations in which Julius Meinl has cafes. Rather, it is set into motion globally through Meinl's relationship with Austrian Airlines. Austrian is the country's largest carrier, with about 120 destinations worldwide.[21] The carrier links Vienna with destinations such as Cairo, Marrakesh, Los Angeles, Tokyo, Shanghai, and Cape Town and has a particularly strong presence in Central Europe.[22] Regardless of whether one is flying the relatively short distance from Vienna to Prague or Copenhagen, or traveling further afield to Bangkok or Washington, DC, one will likely encounter the Meinl Mohr on one of these flights. At least before catering service was modified due to the pandemic, all Austrian's flights served Julius Meinl coffee,[23] and the Meinl Mohr could be found on accompanying sugar packets. With Austrian Airlines making the Meinl Mohr globally locative, the memory of Austria's victory in the siege is perpetually commemorated, and Vienna becomes the global epicenter from which this message emanates. As this symbol conflating coffee, defeat of the Muslims, and European ascendancy is continuously distributed throughout the world daily, the symbol and what it conveys "creat[es] an effect we recognize as reality, by organizing the world endlessly to represent it" (Mitchell 2000, 17). The global distribution of this icon reifies a particular vision of reality that marginalizes the Muslim through its ceaseless representation.

At this point, one might wonder what might be able to counter the specter of the Islamic other. What could combat the negative images of Muslims that have been constructed and made pervasive through the deployment of anachronistic vignettes, generalizations about the nature of entire societies, or the global distribution of particular images? Apart from re-thinking the discipline of Islamic Studies, which many scholars are currently doing, I propose that telling more nuanced stories of global coffee cultures – both Muslim and non-Muslim – would do a great deal to unsettle our understanding of the "other." In celebrating these stories, we can begin to see that what brings us together around our daily brew is far more complicated than what we might think – like the tasting notes on bags of specialty coffee such as Blue Bottle.

I wish to thank Mark Juergensmeyer, Kathleen Moore, and Dominic Sachsenmaier for inviting me to participate in workshops on the issue of religious othering at UC Santa Barbara and the University of Göttingen. I am grateful for their feedback, as well as the feedback of the other workshop participants, on various iterations of this chapter. I also wish to thank Chloe Martinez for her helpful comments. This chapter is dedicated to Michael Sells.

Notes

1 How to define what is "Islamic" is an ongoing discussion in the field, parallel to debates about how to define "religion" in Religious Studies. See, for instance, Ernst and Martin (2010), and Ahmed (2017).
2 See Kumar (2012). Using Lockman and others, Kumar identifies these two trends as key features of Orientalism (Kumar 2012, 28–32). See also Lockman (2010). For more on the study of philology and the study of religion, see Masuzawa (2005, 147–206); Lockman (2010, 68 ff.), and Ernst (2003, 18–24).
3 In articulating Western perceptions of Muslims, Maxime Rodson observed that this scholarship created "*homo islamicus* (Latin for "Islamic man")," which "referred to the perception that the Muslim constituted a distinct type of human being, essentially different from 'Western man'" (Lockman 2010, 74).
4 This, in turn, is related to the idea that civilizations somehow enter a period of decline after their flourishing (Kumar 2012, 30–31).
5 Bashir writes:

> This reification of time is the source of a number of fundamental problems in the modern academic conceptualization of Islam. It is connected to familiar plotlines such as: overemphasis on the Arab Middle East; unending concern with the period of the origins of Islam, followed by a classical age, and supposed decline; the tendency to see evolution of ideas and practices as part of a predetermined or natural cycle of some sort that can be understood without reference to material circumstances; and undervaluation of the role of human agency in creating "time" within Islamic social, cultural, and religious contexts. These problems are quite well known and although they have been addressed on a discrete basis, the fact that they relate to investment in a single chronology has received little attention.
>
> Bashir (2014, 521)

6 The extent of this literature is outlined in the two-volume bibliography, Coffee, a Bibliography: A Guide to the Literature on Coffee. Produced by Richard von Hünersdorff and Holger G. Hasenkamp; introduction by Ralph S. Hattox. See also the still standard reference work on coffee by William H. Ukers, *All About Coffee*, New York: The Tea and Coffee Trade Journal Company, 1922.
7 See, for instance, Tolan (2002, 62, 67). In *Saracens,* Tolan outlines the main themes of the *Risalat al-Kindi* as well as other influential polemics.
8 There is a growing body of excellent scholarship highlighting negative perceptions of Islam and their global repercussions. For the medieval period and beyond, see works by Tolan. See also Qureshi and Sells (2003), Lockman (2010), and Abu-Lughod (2013).
9 Julius Meinl History, YouTube www.youtube.com/watch?v=mAEJ5a_-rhs (1:38), accessed 25 May 2022.
10 Julius Meinl History, YouTube www.youtube.com/watch?v=mAEJ5a_-rhs (1:50), accessed 25 May 2022.
11 www.meinlcoffee.com/us/about-us/brand-values/, accessed 1 February 2022. This evolutionary trajectory of the icon has now been removed from the website.
12 https://shop.meinl.com/default/thun, accessed 25 May 2022.
13 https://shop.meinl.com/default/thun, accessed 25 May 2022.
14 https://juliusmeinl.com/About-Julius-Meinl/Who-We-Are, accessed 25 May 2022.
15 See, for instance, Finkel (2006, 283ff), Wheatcroft (2008, 108ff). I am grateful to Heather Ferguson for pointing me to these sources.
16 This account of the Kolschitsky legend is taken from Ukers (1922, 45–48).
17 https://bluebottlecoffee.com/our-story, accessed 25 May 2022.
18 A scholarly project documents online how the Viennese cityscape is suffused with monuments commemorating victory over the Ottomans during the siege of Vienna, and how these monuments have been galvanized to shape sentiments against various constituencies. See: www.oeaw.ac.at/en/tuerkengedaechtnis/home, accessed 25 May 2022.

19 Depiction and consumption of the Moor appears in other culinary traditions in Austria, including the dessert called "Mohr im Hemd," or Mohr in White Shirt," a chocolate pudding with cream. My thanks to Andreas Zanella and Farid Hafez for providing important background information about this and other culinary traditions.
20 https://juliusmeinl.com/About-Julius-Meinl/Who-We-Are, accessed 25 May 2022.
21 https://www.austrianairlines.ag/en/corporate-profile/about-austrian/, accessed 25 May 2022. See also https://www.flightconnections.com/route-map-austrian-os, accessed 25 May 2022.
22 Ibid.
23 Personal communication with Austrian airlines spokesperson, 20 September 2019.

References

Abu-Lughod, Lila. 2013. *Do Muslim Women Need Saving?* Cambridge, MA: Harvard University Press.

Ahmed, Shahab. 2017. *What Is Islam? The Importance of Being Islamic.* Princeton: Princeton University Press.

Arjana, Sophia Rose. 2014. *Muslims in the Western Imagination.* Oxford: Oxford University Press.

Baghdiantz-McCabe, Ina. 2008. *Orientalism in Early Modern France: Eurasian Trade, Exoticism, and the Ancien Régime.* Oxford: Berg.

Bashir, Shahzad. 2014. "On Islamic Time: Rethinking Chronology in the Historiography of Muslim Societies." *History and Theory* 53 (December 2014), 519–44, 521.

Ernst, Carl W. 2003. *Following Muhammad: Rethinking Islam in the Contemporary World.* Chapel Hill: University of North Carolina Press.

Ernst, Carl W., and Richard Martin, eds. *2010. Rethinking Islamic Studies: From Orientalism to Cosmopolitanism.* Columbia, SC: University of South Carolina Press.

Finkel, Caroline. 2006. *Osman's Dream: The Story of the Ottoman Empire 1300–1923.* London: John Murray.

Hattox, Ralph S. 1988. *Coffee and Coffeehouses: The Origins of a Social Beverage in the Medieval Near East.* Seattle: University of Washington Press.

Kumar, Deepa. 2012. *Islamophobia and the Politics of Empire: Twenty Years After 9/11.* Chicago: Haymarket Books.

Lockman, Zachary. 2010. *Contending Visions of the Middle East: The History and Politics of Orientalism.* New York: Cambridge.

Masuzawa, Tomoko. 2005. *The Invention of World Religions, Or, How European Universalism Was Preserved in the Language of Pluralism.* Chicago: University of Chicago Press.

Mitchell, Timothy. 2000. "The Stage of Modernity." In Questions of Modernity, edited by Timothy Mitchell. Minneapolis: University of Minnesota Press.

Pendergrast, Mark. 2010. *Uncommon Grounds: The History of Coffee and How It Transformed Our World.* New York: Basic Books.

Qureshi, Emran, and Michael A. Sells, eds. 2003. *The New Crusades: Constructing the Muslim Enemy.* New York: Columbia University Press.

Schaefer, Charles G. H. 2001. "Coffee Unobserved: Consumption and Commoditization of Coffee in Ethiopia before the Eighteenth Century." In *Le Commerce du café avant l'ère des Plantations Colonials*, edited by Michael Tuchscherer. Cairo: Institut français d'archéologie orientale.

Schivelbusch, Wolfgang. 1992. *Tastes of Paradise: A Social History of Spices, Stimulants, and Intoxicants.* Translated by David Jacobson. New York: Vintage Books.

Tolan, John Victor. 2002. *Saracens: Islam in the Medieval European Imagination.* New York, NY: Columbia University Press.

Tolan, John Victor, Gilles Veinstein, Henry Laurens, and John L. Esposito. 2013. *Europe and the Islamic World: A History*. Translated by Jane Marie Todd. Princeton, NJ: Princeton University Press.
Ukers. William H. 1922. *All About Coffee*. New York: The Tea and Coffee Trade Journal Company.
Wheatcroft, Andrew. 2008. *The Enemy at the Gate: Habsburgs, Ottomans and the Battle for Europe*. London: Bodley Head.

5

FROM COLONIALISM TO NAZISM TO COLOR-BLINDNESS

Understanding Anti-Muslim Racism in Austria and Germany

Farid Hafez

Introduction

Austria and Germany are especially interesting to examine with regard to the rise of nationalism and racism. They were the most important empires in World War I and World War II, and the Third Reich was constructed on the knowledge, political ashes, and the nationalist and racist aspirations of political camps from the two countries. The Holocaust, which marked the industrial extinction of Jewish life in the Third Reich is a reminder of the destructive forces of racism. Austria and Germany not only share an important episode as central parts of the Third Reich but are also even more interesting to compare when it comes to political parties' reproduction of racist ideologies post-World War II.

The two diverge most sharply when it comes to the post-war popularity of the political far-right. Austria has a long history of a successful far-right political party, the Freedom Party of Austria (FPÖ, *Freiheitlichen Partei Österreichs*), which has had growing electoral support since 1986. The FPÖ governed as a major coalition partner from 2000 to 2005/7 and then again from 2017 to 2019 (Hafez and Heinisch 2019). Germany has only recently become home to a relatively successful far-right political party, the Alternative for Germany (AfD, *Alternative für Deutschland*), established in April 2013 (Lees 2018). But does this late arrival of a successful far-right political party on the federal level really indicate a difference in Islamophobia's role as one of the most potent contemporary racist imaginaries in both countries? Rather than reducing racism to the political far-right, this chapter discusses the relevance of Islamophobia against the backdrop of a broader history of racism in both countries. The main argument of this chapter is that contemporary Islamophobia is best understood not through the role of nominal far-right political parties but at the backdrop of a long history of racism.

DOI: 10.4324/b22926-6

When it comes to racism, including anti-Jewish and anti-Muslim racism, the two countries share important traits: first, in both, one encounters a denial of the existence of racism in general, which is related to the historical and scholarly neglect of racism in Austria (Sauer 2012) and Germany (El-Tayeb 1999) from the colonial period to the present. In a European context, of course, the countries do not stand alone in this respect. Fatima El-Tayeb argues that generally Europe largely

> continues to imagine itself as an autonomous entity . . . untouched by "race matters" . . . a colorblind continent in which difference is marked along lines of nationality and ethnicized. Others are routinely ascribed a position outside the nation, allowing the externalization and thus silencing of a debate on the legacy of racism and colonialism.
>
> *(El-Tayeb 2008, 658)*

She further claims that this is achieved by excluding colonialism, which allows for the externalization of its postcolonial populations, from the list of key events that have shaped contemporary Europe (El-Tayeb 2008, 658). This, among other factors, makes the Muslim, alongside the African migrant, who is Europe's external other, embody the position of a religious and cultural opponent to Christianity and enlightened Europe. Second, the history of German *völkisch* anti-Semitism, which led to the annihilation of six million Jews during the Holocaust, was initially met by a denial of guilt. In Austria, which presented itself as the first victim of the Third Reich for the first decades of its existence after the end of World War II, this denial comes from the highest level of political leadership (Michaels 1996). This later led to a depoliticization of racism. The creation of a culture of commemoration in which völkisch anti-Semitism was framed as a singular phenomenon also took away critical reflection on contemporary racism in Germany. This is what historian Astrid Messerschmidt has termed the post-National Socialism era in Germany (Messerschmidt 2017). In Austria, anti-Semitism was redeployed openly, a fact that became visible during the 1986 Waldheim affair (Wodak 1990) and was later introduced systematically by the far-right FPÖ (Wodak and Pelinka 2002). Third, much scholarship has demonstrated the entanglement between anti-Semitism and Islamophobia. Not only did Edward Said's *Orientalism* (1978) highlight anti-Semitism as the secret sharer of Orientalism, a German literature on both phenomena has grown (Shooman 2014), although many scholars still see anti-Semitism as a singular phenomenon that is separate from racism.

Using this backdrop, this chapter wants to elaborate on the role and meaning of Islamophobia in contemporary Austrian and German discourses. Before discussing this specifically, I will first contextualize Islamophobia in a long history of racial othering, especially in regard to colonialism and anti-Semitism in both countries. I will then put this in a global context, discussing the relevance of Islamophobic ideology for far-right political parties and movements today to discuss how Muslims are otherized in political discourse today.

Old Histories: Colonialism, Racism, Antisemitism, Islamophobia, the "Oriental Other"

Formally speaking, the German Kaiserreich was a late-comer to the project of colonialism, only acquiring colonies in the mid-1880s and formally holding them for only 30 years (Schilling 2015). But Germany moved quickly, and by the late 1890s, it was the fourth largest colonial empire after Britain, France, and the Netherlands (Conrad 2012, 3). But to fully understand German colonialism, we must go beyond the start of colonialism and consider "Germany's early economic entanglement in slavery in the Americas and the genealogies of pre-colonial German intellectuals' participation in the creation and dissemination of racial stereotypes" (Raphael-Hernandez andWiegmink 2017, 427). This entanglement was "utilized by the German Empire to justify its entry into the colonial era, and a variety of German travelers played a crucial role: as so-called explorers, they traveled to different parts of Africa to test economic possibilities for Germany" (Raphael-Hernandez and Wiegmink 2017, 427).

German colonialists believed that their superior civilization would bring backward African societies modernization and progress that would be gratefully accepted by the colonized subjects. Along with technical modernization, the "civilizing mission" also meant implementing a system of education (Conrad 2012, 77). But against this discourse of self-representation of German benevolence, the reality of German colonialism was its special harshness. Only in the German empire was intermarriage prohibited. Only the German colonial wars were built on genocidal strategies of warfare, as seen in the attacks on the Herero and Nama in 1904 (Conrad 2012, 4). The colonial experience also had an impact on German society. Both debates about best colonial practice in the Reichstag, where it was a contested issue and the huge colonial exhibition in 1896 resulted from Germany's colonial practices abroad. The arts and popular culture, trade and migration regimes, and knowledge production, especially anthropology and geography, were deeply connected with the colonial project. Key ideological notions like race (Hamann 2015) that shaped the following years, especially during the Nazi regime, were developed in the era of colonialism (Grosse 2005). More specifically, some scholars have traced the origins of the genocidal politics of the Nazis to the brutal colonial wars in Africa (Zimmerer 2005; Madley 2005; Kühne 2013). Nevertheless, the German public remains ignorant about Germany's history of colonialism, something German historian Jürgen Zimmerer has called the "colonial amnesia of Germans."

The Austrian public is even less critical or informed about the colonial legacy of the Habsburg Monarchy, even though historians speak of the Habsburg Monarchy as "micro-colonialisms" (Feichtinger, Prutsch, and Csáky 2003), "soft colonial" (Prutsch 2003, 36), and a "proximate colony" (Donia 2007, 7). Other authors argue that the Habsburg rule over Bosnia and Hercegovina was to Vienna what rule over Egypt or India was to London or rule over Indochina or Algiers to Paris. Balkan countries were in Europe and inhabited by white people but were nonetheless regarded as barbarian and populated by semi-oriental people who had to be "civilized" (Ković 2017, 109). Bosnia and Hercegovina, which had been under the control of the Ottoman Empire for four centuries and was thus accounted an "Oriental" province, could easily be framed as European mission land that had to be brought back to its European orbit, with Europe here meaning Western Europe (Okey 2007, vii).

Colonial practitioners such as the de facto governor of Bosnia and Herzegovina Benjamin von Kallay (1839–1903) made the civilizational mission very clear. Kallay once said: "Austria is a great Occidental Empire . . . charged with the mission of carrying civilization to Oriental peoples. Administration is our only politics" (Donia 1981, 14). He also learned from the colonial experiences of other empires, and Maria Todorova has drawn on Edward Said's concept of Orientalism, to create the concept of "Balkanism" (Todorova 2009) to describe the space of a romanticized, exoticized, and demonized Balkan in Western European imaginations. Western Europeans saw the region as a site of transition between East and West, Christianity and Islam, Europe and Non-Europe, and civilization and barbarism. Bosnia and Hercegovina, the only formal colony of the Dual Monarchy with a large Muslim population, is the ideal place to investigate power relations between a Catholic colonizing empire and an otherized Muslim population.

During these colonial encounters, Muslims were primarily colonial subjects, while Jews were the internal Oriental "others." As Ivan Kalmar and Derek Penslar argue in their book *Orientalism and the Jews*, "Orientalist representations of the Jews have always been at the very center of orientalist discourse" (Kalmar and Penslar 2005, xiv), reflecting not only modern Western imperialist discourse but also a politico-theological Christian one. Both Muslims and Jews have long been seen as the "Asiatic Oriental" within Europe, while the Muslim was the "Oriental outsider" (Klug 2014, 452–54). Orientalist relations toward Jews and Muslims, that is, anti-Semitism and Islamophobia, are central to the preservation of a white, Christian identity. Thus, the figure of the "Jew" and that of the "Muslim" can be read as the twin founding pillars of exclusion in the context of white European Christian identity, regularly appearing as "otherized." To give one example, in 1321, Andalusian Jews were charged with well poisoning, having been, it was claimed, incited by Muslims. Similarly, during the Reformation, Jews were portrayed as companions of the devil who had a pact with the Turks (Benz 2011, 176). In modern times, Muslims and Jews were partly equated with one another. For example, the German philosopher Georg Wilhelm Friedrich Hegel taught that there "was a so-called 'Arab' religion, out of which sprang both Judaism and Islam" (Hegel [1833–1836] 1987, 129). As Kalmar points out, in the 19th century, the religious others of Jews and Muslims were grouped together into the racial other of Semites. Both were seen as inherently opposed to European values; however, in 19th-century Europe, Jews, who mainly lived in Europe, were of greater interest to Europeans than were Muslims. Since the "Muslim Oriental" was largely located outside European borders, European political forces including Catholics and German nationalists focused on the "Jewish Oriental," the enemy within. Within the European imaginary, however, both were treated as strangers to European culture, religion, and civilization (Kalmar 2017, 13). As Kalmar and Penslar point out, "the Western image of the Muslim Orient has been formed, and continues to be formed in inextricable conjunction with Western perceptions of the Jewish people" (Kalmar and Penslar 2005, xiii).

So what does the "colonial amnesia of Germans"[1] and the even greater Austrian amnesia mean for the imagination of the otherized today? As mentioned, the cruelties of the Nazi's anti-Semitic program have met a wave of denial in Austria and even in Germany; it takes time to cope with this past. The depoliticization of anti-Semitism, which developed alongside the creation of a culture of commemoration of the Holocaust that frames *völkisch* anti-Semitism as a singular phenomenon unconnected to colonialism and racism, prevents a genuine coming to terms with the past. We can see this in the fact that anti-Semitism is condemned, while Islamophobia has become the "new normal," an accepted form of racism. As scholars like Moshe Zuckermann argue, because anti-Semitism is taboo in Germany and anti-Semites cannot be openly anti-Semitic anymore, Islamophobia becomes an outlet for hidden or latent anti-Semitism (Zuckermann 2012, 16). While there is a lively debate about the potential and limits of comparison between anti-Semitism and Islamophobia (Hafez 2016), most observers argue that "Islamophobia in a political sense is more pressing than anti-Semitism" (Bangstad and Bunzl 2010, 226) today.

Islamophobia: Mainstreaming and Connecting the Global Far-Right

The rise of Islamophobia in Austria and Germany reveals a crisis of Germanness. The question of "does Islam belong to Germany?" is regularly and heatedly debated by the German public, and the same is true in Austria. But "Islamophobia tells us more about the Islamophobe than it tells us about the Muslims/Islam" (Hafez 2018a). The process of othering and the racialization of Muslims can be understood with reference to older forms of racism such as anti-Jewish and anti-Black racism (Hafez 2019b). As Jean-Paul Sartre argued in his Anti-Semite and Jew, "if the Jew did not exist, the anti-Semite would invent him" (Sartre 1948). According to Sartre, anti-Semitism hence tells us little about Jews and Jewry but a lot about anti-Semites. But what does it tell us? In *Orientalism*, Edward Said used a similar psychoanalytical approach to try to understand what the image of the Oriental tells us, arguing that the imagination of the Orient was based on "desires, regressions, investments, and projections" (Said 1978). Importantly, Said not only allows us to see othering as a process of framing the alleged "other" negatively but also opens up the possibility that the process of othering can include negative as well as positive essentialization of self and other. Similarly, the writer and social critic James Baldwin, in a debate with Malcolm X and Martin Luther King in May 1963, re-focused the discussion from the racialized object to the racist subject: "I'm not the n****r here and you invented him, you the white people invented him, then you've got to find out why. And the future of the country depends on that, whether or not it is able to ask that question" (Peck and Baldwin 2017). What this insecurity tells us is that human beings in Austria and Germany, where the rise of Islamophobia is highly spread in the population, have not grappled with their own crisis, and thus why they need the figure of the Muslim. As data reveal, more than half of Germans perceive Islam as a "threat" (Pickel and Yendell 2016, 291). The same is true for Austria, where large majorities see Islam and Muslims as a threat to their lives and three-quarters of respondents disagree with the statement that Islam belongs in Austria (Hafez 2018b, 54). The hegemony of Islamophobia – not only in Austria and Germany, but across Europe – has allowed far-right movements and political parties to mobilize using anti-Muslim claims.

Far-right parties around the globe have always been in contact. But while one of the most successful far-right leaders, Jörg Haider, whose party formed the first coalition government in postwar Europe in 2000, was not allowed to enter Israel, only ten years later, things have changed dramatically. After the "Jerusalem Declaration," the best single documentation of the far-right's shift from antisemitism and toward Islamophobia, signed by the Austrian FPÖ, Belgium's Vlaams Belang, the German Die Freiheit (Freedom Party), and the Sweden Democrats in 2010, a far-right delegation with a Nazi past was invited to Israel by businessmen and members of the Knesset and the Orthodox right-wing party Shas. The alignment was built on a new consensus: Muslims were branded as the new fascists and Nazis, and far-right politicians as the "new Jews." And this new strategy based on shared Islamophobic discourse and campaigning paved the way for the creation of a new unity within the far-right camp not only in Europe but also in the United States and Israel:

> Far-right parties with former historical links to fascism or National Socialism have been attempting to distance themselves from their previous antisemitism by positioning themselves as pro-Israeli, while their reliance on the epistemic essence of racialization has only moved from a Jewish to a Muslim subject. The "Muslim" in the Islamophobic paradigm becomes a shining embodiment of the culturally inferior, yet powerful and threatening "enemy within," who lies in wait to conquer western civilization. This strategy is designed to make the far-right parties appear more attractive to the mainstream since Islamophobic claims are regarded as much less "problematic," and a much more widely held form of racism in western societies, than antisemitism.
>
> *(Hafez 2014b)*

One major turn in this debate is that former nationalist camps that previously never cooperated are now united under the banner of fighting an alleged Islamization. In the past, German nationalism, for instance, was opposed to the Italian version of nationalism, and vice versa, due to historical questions about borders. Now, however, European far-right parties have come together and formed successful political groups under one leadership in the European Parliament. In 2011, the European Alliance for Freedom (EAF) was formed, becoming the

Europe of Nations and Freedom in 2015 and Identity and Democracy (I&D) in 2019. The exchange of ideas and experiences between far-right parties and camps leads to transnational cooperation, both ideologically, in the sense of borrowing discourses from each other, and organizationally, in the sense of building networks that can become more formalized. While the EAF was not able to reach the minimum requirement of having Members of the European Parliament from seven parties represented in the European parliament, the I&D group is today the fourth largest group within the European Parliament and includes the FPÖ and the AfD.

Although the United States has lagged behind Europe, Islamophobia has also become central to the campaigning of far-right activists there,[2] especially after the 2008 dispute over the inconveniently named "Ground Zero mosque," which successfully initiated a nationwide debate (Lean 2012), Islamophobic campaigns were identified as a successful tool for political mobilization and Islamophobic conspiracy theories were adopted as a strategy by Republican politicians who alleged that candidate and later president Barack Obama was a Muslim. With Donald Trump as the 45th president of the United States, this rhetoric became central and was used to mobilize against Muslim congresswomen like Ilhan Omar and Rashida Tlaib, while Trump implemented anti-Muslim policies such as the infamous Muslim Ban (Bridge Initiative Team 2019). Of course, anti-Muslim racism has to be seen in relation to the deeply racist structure that informed the construction of the United States as a white settler colony (Glenn 2015) that especially white Christians have to grapple with (Jones 2020). More currently, this growing Islamophobia has pushed the Republican Party further to the right (Chinoy 2019), and personal links between Republicans and European far-right politicians (Hafez 2014b, 469–67) have increased (Kim Sengupta Diplomatic 2017).

Today, a shared anti-Muslim ideology unites political leaders with a heavy anti-Muslim agenda. The government of India's prime minister, leader of the BJP, Narendra Modi, has stripped four million people, mostly Muslims, of citizenship. It deported Rohingya refugees back to Myanmar. The re-emergence of Hindu nationalism is enforced by an Islamophobic campaign. Modi's ties to RSS – a far-right Hindu nationalist group that works to establish a racially pure Hindu state – are known. While Modi was governor of Gujarat, over a thousand Muslims died during communal riots and a pogrom (Islam 2019). In October 2019, two months after the Indian government's removal of Kashmir's special autonomous status, 23 members of the European Parliament, mostly from far-right political parties such as France's National Rally and the Alternative for Germany (AfD) but also from Christian Democrats like Czech MEP Tomas Zdechovsky, visited Kashmir. This happened at a time when foreign journalists and domestic politicians were barred from access to the region (Leidig 2020). Eviane Leidig reminds us that collaborations between Hindu nationalists and Fascist Italy as well as Nazi Germany existed in the 1930s. A leader of Hindu nationalism, V.D. Savarkar, once wrote that India should model its approach to its "Muslim problem" on that used by the Nazis to deal with their "Jewish problem" (Leidig 2020). He concludes that visions of these two nationalist movements as far away from each other

> are not necessarily contradictory, and they may continue to complement each other so long as the Muslim "other" remains their common enemy. If far-right nationalists have it their way, it is likely that Indo-European relations will be reshaped along Islamophobic lines.
>
> *(Leidig 2020)*

With political leaders like Donald Trump and Narendra Modi and growing far-right parties in Europe, an informal anti-Muslim network of statesmen and politicians is manifesting itself. Islamophobia today is a stark feature of many authoritarian political leaders. Their success has reinforced the acceptability of an Islamophobia that presents itself as an answer to an imagined "Muslim problem" that serves their respective nationalist and racist agendas.

Islamophobia in Austria and Germany Today

In Austria and Germany, the Islamophobic content is reminiscent of older forms of anti-Semitism. "Vienna shall not become Jerusalem" was a famous slogan of the Viennese mayor Karl Lueger of the governing Christian Social Party in 1910 (Hamann 2001, 404). Nearly 100 years later, the new leader of the FPÖ, Heinz Christian Strache, presented the slogan "Vienna shall not become Istanbul." It is as if the contemporary far-right has used a history book as a handbook for racist discourse. In a study comparing anti-Semitic discourse around the turn of the 20th century with Islamophobia around the turn of the 21st century, I showed the striking similarities in the two discourses: anti-Semitism and Islamophobia were and are used against more liberal political camps, specifically the Social Democrats, accused of facilitating the Judaification and Islamization of social life. While Judaification was understood as a process of transforming culture (through the Jewish spirit), politics (by assuming political power), economics, and the populace (through the "threat" of immigration), Islamization is framed as a cultural (implementing Islamic codes of conduct), social (creating counter-societies), political (taking over political power) transformation and as changing the populace (though a growing number of Muslims and the immigration of people from Muslim-majority countries). Islamization and Judaification paradoxically and inconsistently refer to the phenomena they frame as: a) an intentional plan by the two groups to undermine the dominant parts of society and b) a united endeavor of the political opposition to destroy the national (Christian) collective with the help of the alien Jewish and Muslim "other" (Hafez 2019a).

Today, anti-Muslim racism is especially implemented by the governing Austrian People's Party (ÖVP), a nominally centrist Christian Democratic party led by Sebastian Kurz, that implemented anti-Muslim legislation first with the FPÖ (Hafez, Heinisch, and Miklin 2019) (2017–2019) and later with the Green Party

(2020–) (Hafez 2020). This includes the ban on the Hijab in school for pupils, a law that regulates Islam differently than it does other churches and religious denominations (Hafez 2017), attempts to close down mosques, and the creation of a monitoring watchdog for "Political Islam."

In Germany, restrictive measures were implemented long before the AfD came into existence. Germany follows a restrictive Islam-related politics, looking at Muslims through the lenses of securitization (Hernández Aguilar 2018), as people who have to be disciplined (Hafez 2014a) and Europeanized (Hernández Aguilar 2015). Germany implemented discrimination against Muslim women via the Hijab ban in public administration as early as 2003 (Korteweg and Yurdakul 2014), although the German state is generally friendly toward Christian churches. But this discourse was often clothed in a less blatant and aggressive racist language, presenting itself as a civilizational mission that helps Muslims. It was the AfD that adopted many of the successful slogans and political claims from the FPÖ and other far-right parties in Europe. One election poster in Berlin says "Stop Islamization" (BBC News 2017). In 2016, the party adopted a policy platform that included anti-Muslim policies such as banning the burka, minarets, and the call to prayer (Bender 2016), all aimed at stopping the so-called "Islamization" (Connolly 2016) of Germany. The party adopted a manifesto stating that "Islam does not belong to Germany. Its expansion and the ever-increasing number of Muslims in the country are viewed by the AfD as a danger to our state, our society, and our values" (AfD 2017). The manifesto also described minarets as a "symbol of Islamic supremacy" (AfD 2017), called for hijab to be banned for civil servants and in public education, for the face-veil to be banned in public, and stated that "Islamic theology at state universities have to be abolished." It stated that Germany's Muslims are "a big danger to our state, our society, and our system of values" (AfD 2017). During the 2017 federal elections, the AfD ran a staunchly anti-Muslim campaign, using election posters that presented Islam as threatening German national identity. One poster depicted the belly of a pregnant white woman with the slogan, "New Germans? We'll make them ourselves" (Amann 2017). This poster is "reminiscent of Nazi-era propaganda encouraging German women to produce German children for the Fatherland." Another poster showed a piglet with the words: "Islam? It doesn't fit in with our cuisine." AfD released a poster during the elections that included the words "Burkas? We prefer bikinis" with a picture of two women wearing bikinis on a beach, thus clearly defining Muslims as the target of propaganda around which white German identity construction works.

But these discourses are not specific to the FPÖ or the AfD. Before the AfD emerged in 2013, a book by a social democrat under the title *Germany abolishes itself* (*Deutschland schafft sich ab*) became the bestselling book in Germany since World War II. The book, which proclaimed the racial inferiority of Muslims, gained much of its success from the widest-circulating yellow press, the famous *Bild Zeitung*, and the critically acclaimed quality press, the weekly *Der Spiegel*. The *Bild* portrayed Sarrazin as a martyr of the political class, daring to speak out against the threat posed to German society by its Muslim immigrants. He was widely described as a legitimate critic of Islam rather than as a racist, although the major thesis of his book was that genetics and cultural differences accounted for the deficits of minorities in Germany and that their strong numerical growth would destroy German society by making it "dumber." In fact, in his original manuscript, he used the word "race," dropping it after his publishing house recommended that he replace it with "ethnicity" (Hafez 2019c, 94–102). In a comparative analysis of the contemporary Berlin neutrality law and Muslim religiosity in the public sphere with central arguments of the late 18th- and early 19th-century German intellectuals' works on the status of Jewish law in the public sphere, Armin Langer found that religious othering exceeds a particular time and place. He argues that the cultivation of suspicion against religious minorities is central to constituting hegemonic national identities. Today, this is done by putting Muslims under suspicion by implementing programs ostensibly intended to target so-called Islamist extremism and using language and tactics similar to those used against Jewish communities at the turn of the 20th century (Langer 2020).

Conclusion

In this chapter, I have shown that while Austria and Germany differ vastly as to the historic role and success of far-right political parties in the post-World War II era, Islamophobia continues to play a major role in the racist imaginary of both countries. Islamophobia should be understood against the backdrop of a broader history of racism, including anti-Jewish racism that can be traced back not only to the Nazi era but also to both countries' widely neglected colonial eras. As several studies suggest, Islamophobia today follows a pattern of anti-Semitism found in both countries at the turn of the 20th century. The colonial attitude of having to civilize barbarians who are racialized as "the other" exists in today's discourse on threatening Muslims who are said to pose a danger to the security of the Austrian/German nation-state. Disciplining and controlling measures are put in place to contain and surveil Muslims who are seen as a threat to the national identity and national cohesion of the dominant society. The ruling elite in both countries is largely unwilling to open up space for the descendants of the poor working class *Gastarbeiter* (guest worker) who came 50 years ago and whose community today is seen through the lenses of the "Muslim threat."

While Austria today is institutionalizing this securitization of Muslims by setting up institutions such as the "Documentation Center for Political Islam," some authorities of the German state are rather alarmed by the rise of a blatant racist force such as the AfD and are trying to counter these developments by establishing institutions such as the Independent Expert Council on Islamophobia (*Unabhängig Expertenrat Muslimfeindlichkeit*). It seems the arrival of a blatant racist political party such as the AfD alongside the rise of a militant white supremacist (and Muslim) terror group like the NSU and the murder of centrist politicians by these organizations is creating a momentum within German society to counteract the rise of racist forces, even as the systemic racism embedded in the fields of education, security politics, goes unchallenged.

Still, the question raised by James Baldwin for Black Americans is open to an answer: Austrians and Germans have to find out why they have a problem with Muslims. This requires not only careful self-reflection but also a real political will to confront their history and relate it to today's realities.

Notes

1 Zimmerer (2013, 9). It was only in the late 1960s that Germans, inspired by the global process of decolonization, started to critically reflect on their colonial past. Germans were challenged to do this by historians of the German Democratic Republic (GDR), who had a more critical perspective on imperialism, by American historical scholarship and by studies done by scholars from the newly independent African states. Before this, official history-writing was dominated by former colonialists who attempted to present Germany as a benevolent empire. One example here is the former Governor of German East Africa Heinrich Schnee's *Deutsches Kolonial-Lexikon* (German Colonial Lexicon), which was designed to defend against the international claim that crime and violence ruled German colonies. For Schnee, this was a "colonial guilt lie" (*Kolonialschuldluege*) (Conrad 2012, 6–8). More recently, the claim for reparations launched by the Herero of Namibia against Germany brought the colonial past back onto the German agenda. During the global Black Lives Matter rallies sparked by the murder of George Floyd in May 2020, statues of German colonizers were torn down and debates about renaming names of institutions and streets referring to the colonial past were re-enlivened See Hasselbach (2020).

2 According to Max Blumenthal, Islamophobic rhetoric in political campaigning was first noticed on a local level in 2004, when politicians attempted to stop the construction of Islamic centers in various locations by linking them to extremism. See Blumenthal (2010).

References

AfD. 2017. "Manifesto for Germany, The Political Programme of the Alternative for Germany." https://cdn.afd.tools/wp-content/uploads/sites/111/2017/04/2017-04-12_afd-grundsatzprogramm-englisch_web.pdf

Amann, Melanie. 2017. "U.S. Ad Agency Boosts Right-Wing Populist AfD." *Der Spiegel*, August 30, 2017. www.spiegel.de/international/germany/u-s-ad-agency-boosts-right-wing-populist-afd-a-1164956.html.

Bangstad, Sindre, and Matti Bunzl. 2010. "Anthropologists Are Talking About Islamophobia and Anti-Semitism in the New Europe." *Ethnos: Journal of Anthropology* 75 (2): 213–28.

BBC News. 2017. "Germany's AfD: How Right-Wing Is Nationalist Alternative for Germany?" February 11, 2017. https://bbc.com/news/world-europe-37274201.

Bender, Ruth. 2016. "Germany's AfD Adopts Anti-Islam Stance at Party Conference." *WSJ*, May 1, 2016. www.wsj.com/articles/germanys-afd-adopts-anti-islam-stance-at-party-conference-1462120609.

Benz, W. 2011. *Antisemitismus und Islamkritik. Bilanz und Perspektive*. Berlin: Metropol.

Blumenthal, Max. 2010. *Republican Gomorrah: Inside the Movement That Shattered the Party*. New York: Nation Books.

Bridge Initiative Team. 2019. "Factsheet: Donald Trump as President of the United States." December 2, 2019. https://bridge.georgetown.edu/research/factsheet-donald-trump-as-president-of-the-united-states/.

Chinoy, Sahil. 2019. "What Happened to America's Political Center of Gravity?" *NYT*, June 26, 2019. www.nytimes.com/interactive/2019/06/26/opinion/sunday/republican-platform-far-right.html.

Connolly, Kate. 2016. "Frauke Petry: The Acceptable Face of Germany's New Right?" *The Guardian*, June 19, 2016. www.theguardian.com/world/2016/jun/19/frauke-petry-acceptable-face-of-germany-new-right-interview.

Conrad, Sebastian. 2012. *German Colonialism: A Short History*. Cambridge: Cambridge University Press.

Donia, Robert J. 1981. *Islam Under the Double Eagle: The Muslims of Bosnia and Hercegovina, 1878–1914*. New York: Columbia University Press.

———. 2007. "The Proximate Colony. Bosnia-Herzegovina under Austro- Hungarian Rule." www.kakanien.ac.at/beitr/fallstudie/RDonia1.pdf.

El-Tayeb, Fatima. 1999. " 'Blood Is a Very Special Juice': Racialized Bodies and Citizenship in Twentieth-Century Germany." *IRSH* 44: 149–69.

———. 2008. " 'The Birth of a European Public: Migration, Postnationality, and Race in the Uniting of Europe." *Am Q* 60 (3): 649–70.

Feichtinger, Johannes, Ursula Prutsch, and Moritz Csáky, eds. 2003. *Habsburg postcolonial. Machtstrukturen und kollektives Gedächtnis*. Innsbruck: Studien-Verlag.

Glenn, Evelyn Nakano. 2015. "Settler Colonialism as Structure: A Framework for Comparative Studies of US Race and Gender Formation." *Sociology of Race and Ethnicity* 1 (1): 52–72.

Grosse, Pascal. 2005. "What Does German Colonialism Have to Do With National Socialism? A Conceptual Framework." In *Germany's Colonial Pasts*, edited by Eric Ames, Marcia Klotz, and Lora Wildenthal, 115–34. Lincoln: University of Nebraska Press.

Hafez, Farid. 2014a. "Disciplining the 'Muslim Subject': The Role of Security Agencies in Establishing Islamic Theology Within the State's Academia." *Islamophobia Studies Journal* 2 (2): 43–57.

———. 2014b. "Shifting Borders: Islamophobia as Common Ground for Building Pan-European Right-Wing Unity." *Patterns of Prejudice* 48 (5): 479–99.

———. 2016. "Comparing anti-Semitism and Islamophobia: The State of the Field." *Islamophobia Studies Journal* 3 (2): 35–55.

———. 2017. "Muslim Protest Against Austria's Islam Law. An Analysis of Austrian Muslim's Protest against the 2015 Islam Law." *Journal of Muslim Minority Affairs* 37 (3): 267–83.

———. 2018a. "Schools of Thought in Islamophobia Studies: Prejudice, Racism, and Decoloniality." *Islamophobia Studies Journal* 4 (2): 210–25.

———. 2018b. "Islamophobia in Austria: National Report 2017." In *Enes Bayraklı & Farid Hafez, European Islamophobia Report 2017*, 27–66. Istanbul: SETA.

———. 2019a. "From Jewification to Islamization: Political anti-Semitism and Islamophobia in Austrian Politics Then and Now." *ReOrient* 4 (2): 197–220.

———. 2019b. *Reading Islamophobia Through the Lens of James Baldwin. The Leibniz Science Campus "Eastern Europe – Global Area": Understanding and Explaining Islamophobia in Eastern Europe, Connections* Special Issue No. 1, edited by Alexander Yendell, 21–26.

———. 2019c. *Feindbild Islam. Über die Salonfähigkeit von Rassismus*. Vienna: Böhlau Verlag.

Hafez, Farid, and Reinhard Heinisch. 2019. "The Political Influence of the Austrian Freedom Party in Austria." In *Do They Make a Difference? The Policy Influence of Radical Right Populist Parties in Western Europe*, edited by Benjamin Biard, Laurent Bernhard, and Hans-Georg Betz, 145–64. London and New York: ECPR Press Rowman & Littlefield.

Hafez, Farid, Reinhard Heinisch, and Eric Miklin. 2019. "The New Right: Austria's Freedom Party and Changing Perceptions of Islam." *Brookings*, July 24, 2019. www.brookings.edu/research/the-new-right-austrias-freedom-party-and-changing-perceptions-of-islam/.

Hamann, Brigitte. 2001. *Hitlers Wien. Lehrjahre eines Diktators*. München: Piper.

Hamann, Ulrike. 2015. *Prekäre koloniale Ordnung: Rassistische Konjunkturen im Widerspruch*. Bielefeld: Transcript Verlag.

Hasselbach, Christoph. 2020. "Germany's Colonial Era Brought to Light amid Global Protest." June 22, 2020. Accessed September 24, 2020. www.dw.com/en/germanys-colonial-era-brought-to-light-amid-global-protest/a-53898330.

Hegel, M. [1833–1836] 1987. *Lectures on the Philosophy of Religion*. Berkeley: University of California Press.

Hernández Aguilar, Luis Manuel. 2015. "Welcome to Integrationland: On Racism and the German Islam Conference." Diss. PhD thesis, Goethe-University Frankfurt am Main.

———. 2018. *Governing Muslims and Islam in Contemporary Germany: Race, Time, and the German Islam Conference*. Leiden: Brill.

Islam, Imrul. 2019. "NAMO." *The Bridge Initiative*, April 5, 2019. https://bridge.georgetown.edu/research/namo/

Jones, Robert P. 2020. *White Too Long: The Legacy of White Supremacy in American Christianity*. New York: Simon & Schuster.

Kalmar, Ivan. 2017. *Is Islamophobia the New Antisemitism?* Istanbul: SETA.

Kalmar, Ivan and Derek Penslar. 2005. "Orientalism and the Jews: An introduction." In *Orientalism and the Jews*, edited by Ivan Kalmar and Derek Penslar, xiii–xl. Waltham: Brandeis University Press.

Kim Sengupta Diplomatic. 2017. "Secretive American Conservatives Are Helping Bankroll Geert Wilders' Dutch Election Campaign." *Independent*, March 14, 2017. www.independent.co.uk/news/world/europe/dutch-elections-geert-wilders-us-backers-right-wing-conservative-think-tanks-a7629946.html

Klug, B. 2014. "The limits of analogy: Comparing Islamophobia and antisemitism." *Patterns of Prejudice* 48 (5): 442–59.

Korteweg, Anna C., and Gökçe Yurdakul. 2014. *The Headscarf Debates: Conflicts of National Belonging*. Stanford: Stanford University Press.

Ković, Miloš. 2017. "Austria-Hungary's 'Civilizing Mission' in the Balkans: A View from Belgrade (1903–1914)." *Balcanica* XLVIII: 107–22.

Kühne, Thomas. 2013. "Colonialism and the Holocaust: Continuities, Causations, and Complexities." *Journal of Genocide Research* 15 (3): 339–62.

Langer, Armin. 2020. "Judaism Is Not a Religion, But a Political Organization: German Jews Under Suspicion in the Age of Enlightenment and Parallels to Contemporary Islamophobic Discourses." *Islamophobia Studies Yearbook* 11, Special Issue: Muslims under general suspicion: Perspectives on the prevention of so-called Islamist extremism, edited by Farid Hafez and Sinyan Qasem, 91–110.

Lean, Nathan. 2012. *The Islamophobia Industry: How the Right Manufactures Fear of Muslims*. London: Pluto Press.

Lees, Charles. 2018. "The 'Alternative for Germany': The Rise of Right-Wing Populism at the Heart of Europe." *Politics* 38 (3): 295–310.

Leidig, Eviane. 2020. "The Far-Right Is Going Global, Foreign Policy." January 21, 2020. https://foreignpolicy.com/2020/01/21/india-kashmir-modi-eu-hindu-nationalists-rss-the-far-right-is-going-global/.

Madley, Benjamin. 2005. "From Africa to Auschwitz: How German South West Africa Incubated Ideas and Methods Adopted and Developed by the Nazis in Eastern Europe." *European History Quarterly* 35 (3): 429–64.

Messerschmidt, Astrid. 2017. "Rassismusthematisierungen in den Nachwirkungen des Nationalsozialismus und seiner Aufarbeitung." In *Rassismuskritik und Widerstandsformen*, edited by Karim Fereidooni and Meral El, 855–67, Wiesbaden: Springer.

Michaels, Jennifer E. 1996. "Breaking the Silence: Elisabeth Reichart's Protest Against the Denial of the Nazi Past in Austria." *German Studies Review* 19 (1): 9–27.

Okey, Robin. 2007. *Taming Balkan Nationalism: The Habsburg 'Civilizing Mission' in Bosnia, 1878–1914*. Oxford: Oxford University Press.
Peck, Raoul Peck, and James Baldwin. 2017. *I Am Not Your Negro*. New York: Vintage International.
Pickel, Gert, and Alexander Yendell. 2016. "Islam als Bedrohung? Beschreibung und Erklärung von Einstellungen zum Islam im Ländervergleich." *Zeitschrift fur Vergleichende Politikwissenschaft* 10: 273–309.
Prutsch, Ursula. 2003. "Habsburg Postcolonial." In *Habsburg postcolonial. Machtstrukturen und kollektives Gedächtnis*, edited by Ursula Prutsch, Moritz Csáky, and Johannes Feichtinger, 33–43. Innsbruck: Studien-Verlag.
Raphael-Hernandez, Heike, and Pia Wiegmink. 2017. "German Entanglements in Transatlantic Slavery: An Introduction." *Atlantic Studies* 14 (4): 419–35.
Said, Edward. 1978. *Orientalism*. London: Penguin Books.
Sartre, Jean Paul. 1948. *Anti-Semite and Jew*. New York: Schocken Verlag.
Sauer, Walter. 2012. "Habsburg Colonial: Austria-Hungary's Role in European Overseas Expansion Reconsidered." *Austrian Studies* 20: 5–23.
Schilling, Britta. 2015. "German Postcolonialism in Four Dimensions: A Historical Perspective." *Postcolonial Studies* 18 (4): 427–39.
Shooman. Yasemin. 2014. " . . . *weil ihre Kultur so ist": Narrative des antimuslimischen Rassismus*. Bielefeld: Transcript Verlag.
Todorova, Maria. 2009. *Imagining the Balkans*. Oxford: Oxford University Press.
Wodak, Ruth. 1990. "The Waldheim Affair and Antisemitic Prejudice in Austrian Public Discourse." *Patterns of Prejudice* 24 (2–4): 18–33.
Wodak, Ruth, and Anton Pelinka, eds. 2002. *The Haider Phenomenon in Austria*. New Brunswick, New Jersey: Transaction Publishers.
Zimmerer, Jürgen. 2005. "The Birth of the Ostland Out of the Spirit of Colonialism: A Postcolonial Perspective on the Nazi Policy of Conquest and Extermination." *Patterns of Prejudice* 39 (2): 197–219.
———. 2013. "Kolonialismus und kollektive Identität: Erinnerungsorte der deutschen Kolonialgeschichte." In *Kein Platz an der Sonne: Erinnerungsorte der deutschen Kolonialgeschichte*, edited by Jürgen Zimmerer, 9–38. Bonn: Bundeszentrale für politische Bildung.
Zuckermann, Moshe. 2012. "Judensolidarität und Islamophobie in Deutschland. Anmerkungen zu einer ideologischen Verschwisterung: Ein Essay." In *Jahrbuch fünf Islamophobieforschung*, 11–16. Wien: New Academic Press.

6

"THEY ARE FROM MARS"

The Othering of Jews and Muslims in European Legal Debates

Mareike Riedel

The regulation of minority religious practices constitutes an important site for observing the dynamics of religious othering in Europe. Attempts to place restrictions on minority religious practices have become increasingly widespread across Europe. Much legislative and judicial attention has thereby focused on Muslim practices, which are seen to test the boundaries of liberal tolerance in the secular state. Liberal law, with its appeal to universality and objectivity, offers dominant groups in society a powerful and authoritative language and framework to draw the boundaries between "us" and "them." Whether it is the permissibility of wearing the veil in public contexts, the accommodation of Muslim personal status law, or issues of forced marriage, public debates demanding legal intervention have frequently slipped into a discourse that paints Muslims in orientalizing and racializing terms as backward, fundamentalist, illiberal, premodern, and uncivilized. In contrast, European societies emerge as the primary locus of civilizational progress, secular modernity, and the liberal rule of law (Mancini 2012; Razack 2004).

Religious slaughter, that is the slaughter of animals without prior stunning according to religious laws, has been another subject of emotive public controversy and legal action, in which the law has served as a site for the othering of religious minorities, particularly Jews and Muslims. European law requires animals to be stunned prior to slaughter, either with a bolt shot into the head for larger animals, such as cattle, or via electric shock for poultry. The relevant EU Directive allows for an exemption to this requirement for religious reasons in order to account for the right to religious freedom.[1] This exemption is particularly relevant for Muslims and Orthodox Jews. Both Jewish and Islamic religious rules require animals to be in perfect health when slaughtered, meaning that they must be unharmed from any form of prior stunning. In Judaism, the Talmud requires the prevention of unnecessary pain. In the process of *shechita*, which fulfills this requirement according to Jewish oral law, the animal is killed by cutting its trachea and esophagus with

DOI: 10.4324/b22926-7

a sharp knife and letting its blood drain completely as the dietary laws of kashrut also require Jews to not ingest blood. Similarly, in the Muslim tradition, where the prescribed method is called *dhabihah*, the meat must be made fit for consumption by humans through exsanguination and the animal must be killed in the least painful way. Other than in Orthodox Judaism, however, there is disagreement among different religious schools in Islam about whether certain forms of pre-stunning are permissible for the production of halal meat. Therefore, a ban on slaughter without prior stunning does not necessarily prevent the production of halal meat for some Muslim communities, while it does for all those observant Orthodox Jews who eat a kosher diet, with no exception.

A number of countries do not allow for an exception to the pre-stunning requirement, including Sweden, Norway, Iceland, and Belgium (Bergeaud-Blackler 2007, 966). In Switzerland, too, no such exemption exists. In other European countries, such as Germany, Spain, Italy, the Netherlands, the UK, Poland, and Ireland, religious slaughter is permitted to various degrees, yet these exemptions have not been uncontroversial, and new legal bans have been put in place where an exemption existed previously, such as temporarily in Poland in 2013[2] and in Belgium in 2017, a ban that the Court of Justice of the European Union upheld.[3] While many Jewish and Muslim groups have opposed such bans as an infringement on the right to practice their religion, advocates of a ban on religious slaughter cite animal welfare as their main concern. They argue that the cut through the throat of a conscious animal inflicts unnecessary pain and suffering (Joseph 2016). Animal welfare organizations have been at the forefront of seeking a ban on religious slaughter, yet they have often been joined by anti-minority and anti-immigrant movements and parties that mobilize the issue as a site to foster an anti-Islam agenda (Klug 1989).

The strange coalition of animal welfare and anti-minority sentiment is not new. During the 19th and early 20th centuries, animal welfare organizations and antisemites campaigned against *shechita*, the Jewish method of butchering, to end what they perceived as a cruel, barbaric, and premodern rite. Indeed, there is an uncanny historical echo to the contemporary othering of Muslims in Europe that is reminiscent of historical European discourses on Jews, whereby Jews were depicted as either eternal outsiders or premodern foreigners in need of regeneration and reform before being granted equal rights as citizens. For a long time, Jews constituted a paradigmatic religious Other for Christian Europe. Despised as killers of Christ, greedy moneylenders, a nation within a nation, much of Europe's shifting cultural, social, and political anxieties over difference were projected on its Jews (Nirenberg 2013). Today, similar anxieties over the religious Other reverberate through debates about the integration of Islam in Europe.

In analyzing these echoes and similarities, it has been suggested that Muslims are the new Jews and that Europe's Jewish question has turned into a Muslim question. From this point of view, Muslims have replaced Jews as Europe's primary Other (e.g. Bunzl 2007). However, while Islamophobia is certainly more prominent in public discourse today than antisemitism, the othering of Jews and Muslims has been historically intertwined. A growing body of scholarship seeks to illuminate this "shared story" of Jews and Muslims as Christian Europe's constitutive Others (Jansen & Meer 2020; Kalmar & Penslar 2005b; Katz 2018a; Renton & Gidley 2017). Gil Anidjar (2003), for example, has explored the intertwined histories of Jews as the internal theological enemy and Muslims as the external political enemy and their role in the constitution of Europe as Christian. This shared story, however, is not just a thing of the past but continues to play out in contemporary politics of religious difference in secular societies. In the context of France, for example, Ethan Katz observes that "the presence of Jews in conversations of Muslims – France's current, undisputed ethnic and religious Other – constantly reiterates that Jews remain different too" (Katz 2018b, 100). One of the issues that casts doubt on Jewish inclusion, Katz argues, is the Jewish insistence on embodied religious practices, such as dietary laws or dress, that mark them as distinct often in similar ways to Muslims. Katz's observation points to a strange tension between the public affirmation of successful Jewish integration on the one hand and a persistent uneasiness around Jewish difference as an irritant for secular law alongside Muslim difference in Europe on the other hand.

In this chapter, I consider European debates about the legal status of religious slaughter as another such moment when the othering of Jews and Muslims converges. Considering these debates allows us to explore law as a potent site for the othering of religious minority groups and the creation of hierarchies between the "civilized" and the "uncivilized" through the language of animal welfare and belonging in the secular state. Moreover, by shedding light on how the exclusion of one Other exposes the ambivalent inclusion of another Other, the religious slaughter debates also offer a glimpse of some of the ways in which the Jewish and the Muslim question remain intertwined in contemporary Europe. The chapter begins with a discussion of studies on historical debates about *shechita* as a site for the othering of Jews before turning to contemporary controversies about religious slaughter in Europe that have focused on Muslims yet inevitably included Jews too. It should be noted that my focus in this chapter is neither on the question of whether religious slaughter is indeed better or worse than other forms of slaughter, a question that remains a topic of debate in the scientific literature on pain and suffering of animals, nor do I aim to discuss the normative legal question of whether a ban would unduly infringe upon the right to religious freedom. Moreover, my analysis focuses on particular themes and does not represent the entire debate. Consequently, I do not wish to suggest that opposition to religious slaughter is always antisemitic or Islamophobic per se. The suffering of animals is a genuine concern. However, as I aim to show in this chapter, it is important to acknowledge how some animal welfare arguments for restricting the religious rights of Jews and Muslims have mobilized a civilizational discourse that marginalizes minority groups while elevating majority groups.

Between Antisemitism and Animal Welfare: *Shechita* in 19th- and Early 20th-Century Europe

Polemics over religious slaughter have a long history in Europe. The rise of the animal welfare campaigns that began to gain momentum in the mid-19th century put the treatment of animals under greater scrutiny. Animal welfare campaigns targeted a range of practices that they deemed inhumane, including vivisection, certain forms of hunting, and the conditions in European slaughterhouses. At the time, the slaughter of animals without prior stunning was not exclusively practiced by Jews, and methods of stunning were only slowly becoming more widespread. Animal welfare societies started agitating against what they perceived as inhumane and cruel slaughter methods, thereby drawing attention to the Jewish practice of *shechita*. Antisemites soon seized on the opportunity to capitalize on the animal welfare discourse to target Jews through attacks on religious slaughter. The laws of *kashrut*, including the slaughter of animals without prior stunning for the production of kosher meat, continued to mark Jews as distinct even after they had been emancipated and granted equal rights as citizens.

The practice involves the letting of blood, allowing to appeal to deep-seated prejudice toward Jews as cunning, brutal, and bloodthirsty. Blood has held a prominent place in the way that Christian societies have imagined and perceived Jews, the outsider within (Biale 2007). One of the most significant tropes was the blood libel that accused Jews of stealing Christian blood, suggesting that "Jews needed to imbibe the blood of Christians because of their congenital blood loss and their religious rituals" (Heng 2019, 11). The term "ritual slaughter," which is often used to refer to *shechita* (and nowadays also to Muslim butchering practices), evokes a semantic association with the blood libel charge of ritual murder (see Julius 2010, 341). Alongside circumcision, another practice involving blood that had long pre-occupied Christian societies, *shechita* provided a fertile ground for antisemitic campaigns to capitalize on both growing societal concerns about the treatment of vulnerable animals and deep-seated cultural tropes about Jewish Otherness and suspicion toward the ability of Jews to assimilate.

As studies of historical slaughter debates have shown (Judd 2007; Metcalf 1989; Kushner 1989; Smith 2007; see also Deckha 2013), animal welfare societies did not simply become unwitting victims to antisemitic campaigns but have either tolerated their interventions as necessary for the cause or appealed to such prejudice themselves. Certainly, not all animal welfare activists of the time played with this prejudice, and many indeed distanced themselves strongly from such discourse. Nonetheless, these two issues often blurred into one another. Moreover, even if not all of these campaigns succeeded in introducing bans, they nonetheless constituted *shechita* as an important site for the struggle over the legal and social status of Jews in European societies at a time of significant social, cultural, and political change.

One of the first successful campaigns against *shechita* took place in late 19th-century Switzerland, where the Swiss Animal Protection society pushed for a referendum on the matter. Slowly, the campaign moved from concerns about animal cruelty to questions of Swiss national identity and the conditions of Jewish belonging in Swiss society. One of the most prolific opponents of *shechita*, the president of the animal welfare society of the canton of Aargau, suggested, for example, that Jews could only be granted an exemption if they continued to be second-class citizens. Having been emancipated into Swiss law and society, however, meant there was an equal duty for all Swiss citizens, no matter if Jewish or Christian, to respect Swiss morals (Akiyama 2011). Abolishing *shechita* was a way to forcefully assimilate Jews into Swiss culture and its Christian roots, as one participant in the debate made clear: "As far as we are concerned, if the Jews cannot be satisfied with the meat we Christians have to eat, then they can leave" (in Metcalf 1989, 35). Moreover, for campaigners, the ban was necessary in order to prevent Switzerland from falling back into heathendom (Metcalf 1989, 34). The same activists stressed that their advocacy was not meant to attack Jews or to deny them their religious freedom but only sought to ensure the humane treatment of animals. Nonetheless, some linked *shechita* to the blood libel and expressed the hope that a ban on *shechita* would discourage immigration from Eastern European Jews as well as encourage the emigration of Swiss Jews (Metcalf 1989, 34–35). While the referendum was ultimately successful in installing a ban on *shechita* in 1893, the Swiss government itself, which had been opposed to the ban, continued to allow for the import of kosher meat.

Calls for a ban on religious slaughter in England date back even earlier to the mid-19th century. The RSPCA, founded as the Society for the Prevention of Cruelty to Animals in 1824, became an important player in the campaign against *shechita*. Initially, the issue gained little traction, but soon anxieties over a growing number of Jews migrating from Eastern Europe and Russia to England became enmeshed with the animal welfare campaign against *shechita*, turning the practice into a focal issue for those suspicious of Jews and their relationship with British values and society (Lever 2019, 891–892). The depictions of Jews as cruel and backward began to find their way into early anti-*shechita* debates. For example, in 1904 the Humanitarian League distributed a pamphlet arguing that "any religion whose observance cannot be reconciled with the modern standard of humanity stands self-condemned as a barbarous survival of a barbarous time" (in Julius 2010, 342). Largely due to government reluctance and successful Jewish lobbying, these interventions never led to legal change in England.

The developments in England and Switzerland also resonated in Germany. Much like their counterparts in Switzerland, some *shechita* opponents contended that the slaughter of animals without prior stunning posed a risk to Germany's reputation as a civilized state since the alleged brutality through the practice of non-stunned slaughter would render the country's people more brutal themselves (Judd 2003, 122). While initially these campaigns were not concerned with Jews given that slaughter without prior stunning was still widespread also among the Christian population, at the turn of the 20th century, the debate began to center on the Jewish practice at a time when German society experienced a rise in nationalism coupled with a growing suspicion of minorities, in particular the recently emancipated Jews. Soon, parts of the animal protection discourse began to play on these suspicions, reinforcing images of Jews as deviant and cruel, thus drawing a link between *shechita* and the blood libel (Judd 2003, 124). In the German parliament, the Reichstag, proposals to ban the practice were introduced, with its advocates pointing to an alleged Jewish contempt for German culture and Christianity (Judd 2003, 124).

While supporters of *shechita* invoked religious freedom, opponents of the practice claimed that *shechita* had no religious basis since it was an ancient tradition of a "foreign Oriental race" (Venerito 2018, 296). Campaigns to end *shechita* presented Jews as bloodthirsty and dangerous (Judd 2003, 125–126), and *antisemites* depicted Christians as victims who were forced to eat meat from animals slaughtered through *shechita* (Venerito 2018, 196). Yet these campaigns had little success. Due to competing agendas and power struggles at various levels of government across Germany, a nationwide ban was never implemented. Only Saxony implemented a ban on the practice from 1892 until 1910, later followed by Bavaria in 1930. It was only with the rise of Nazism that Germany banned the practice in the whole country as one of the first legal changes in 1933, soon leading to the complete loss of right for Jews in Germany. Although the legislation did not single out Jews, by requiring the stunning of animals prior to slaughter with no exception, *shechita* was effectively banned. Italy followed suit in 1938, and similar bans were installed in countries occupied by Nazi Germany.

Shechita also became a contested issue in the Scandinavian countries. Norway adopted a ban on the slaughter of non-stunned animals in 1929 after a long campaign. One of the Board members of the Norwegian Animal Protection Society called *shechita* "meaningless" and "gruesome" and concluded that if Jewish merchants and businessmen would decide to leave Norway as a result of the ban, there would be plenty of Norwegians ready to do their jobs (Metcalf 1989, 38). The Norwegian animal welfare movement had not shied away from demonizing Jews in order to further its aims, alluding to fears of the primitive and the ritual (Snildal 2014, 129). The campaign painted Jews as different from Norwegians, whose feelings would be offended by Jewish practices. A member of the Agrarian Party insisted during the debate on the draft law that Norway had not invited Jews into the country and that the Norwegian people were "under no obligation to supply the Jews with animals for their religious orgies" (in Metcalf 1989, 39). Nonetheless, Jews were allowed to continue importing kosher meat from Sweden, where a similar debate had been brewing since the early 20th century.

Beginning in 1902, a number of parliamentarians repeatedly urged the Swedish parliament to adopt a ban on *shechita* but remained unsuccessful initially. The legal problem was that a ban on slaughter without prior stunning would have also affected the so-called Danish-American method of slaughtering pigs and thereby Sweden's bacon and pork exports (Metcalf 1989, 41). Nonetheless, campaigns to ban *shechita* continued and contributed to prejudice toward Jews. While some advocates made an effort not to single out the Jewish community, others adopted a language of "brutality" and contrasted the "religion of the 'white race'" to the

Jewish religion, claiming that the Torah was full of cruelty toward animals (Metcalf 1989, 43). While not everyone agreed with this view and some voiced their objection to such prejudice, a bill banning the slaughter of animals without prior stunning was ultimately adopted in 1937. The ban is still in place today. Similar debates took place in Denmark, where proponents of a ban described *shechita* in Orientalist terms as an "oriental practice" that is "alien to our Nordic individuality" (in Metcalf 1989, 45). The argument echoes a common European perception of Jews at the time that explained their difference as a matter of their "oriental origins" (Kalmar & Penslar 2005a). Much like initially in Sweden, however, economic concerns about the effects of such a bill on Danish meat exports meant that the campaign proved ultimately unsuccessful. In addition, Copenhagen's more sizeable Jewish community was able to yield much more political influence than the small communities in Sweden and Norway (Metcalf 1989, 46).

Targeting Muslims, Striking Jews? *Shechita* and *Dhabihah* in Europe Today

After World War II, overt antisemitism became increasingly unacceptable in public discourse, and European governments began to embrace Jews and Judaism as part of a shared European tradition, encapsulated in the dubious references to the Judeo-Christian tradition of Europe.[4] The contention over religious slaughter, however, has not disappeared. Some of the pre-war laws banning the practice are still in place, such as in Sweden, Norway, and Switzerland, while religious slaughter has remained a controversial issue in other countries. Since the end of World War II, there has been an ebb and flow of campaigns to ban the practice, even though the focus of these campaigns has now increasingly shifted to the practice of *dhabihah* as the problem to be tackled by law. Debates about religious slaughter remain enmeshed with questions about minority rights, religious freedom, and belonging, questions that have now turned to Islam and Muslims. In large parts of Europe, Muslim migration from the former European colonies as well as various national guest worker programs attracting laborers from Islamic countries changed the demographic composition of European societies, which began to turn their attention to this new Other within.[5] Yet this does not mean that prejudice toward Jews has been completely replaced. Instead, this prejudice still surfaces in debates about the permissibility of religious slaughter as a civilizational discourse that continues to establish an implicit divide between "us" – the secular, enlightened, and humane society – and "them" – the premodern, inhumane, and savage groups. Contemporary debates about religious slaughter thereby link two Others – Jews and Muslims – in complex ways.

For example, during the 1980s in Britain, the Bradford controversy put Muslim slaughter practices into the political spotlight after the local town council had decided to provide halal meat in high school canteens for Muslim students. Although the policy was largely aimed at accommodating the religious needs of Muslim students, often its critics hardly made a distinction between Jews and

Muslims. Instead, as Brian Klug (1989) has shown, opponents of religious slaughter presented both groups as needing to abandon their "alien practices" (Klug 1989, 23). Analyzing letters sent to newspapers on the matter, Klug describes how the rhetoric of those allegedly concerned with animal welfare easily slipped into "clichés about Britain and Christian civilization" (Klug 1989, 21) and ultimately tied the question of slaughter methods to broader debates about immigration and belonging in British society with its standards of "humanity" and "progress" to which minorities have to assimilate. The British National Front, a far-right fascist party, too joined the debate and distributed a leaflet calling to "Stop this Evil!" (in Klug 1989, 18).

Post-war debates about banning religious slaughter have not been limited to Britain. In Germany too, the increased presence of Muslims drew attention again to religious slaughter. After the end of World War II, the country abolished its ban on *shechita* that had been installed by the Nazis and restored the religious rights of Jews in an attempt to heal relations with its small remaining Jewish community. The legal toleration of religious slaughter only came under greater public scrutiny when Muslims demanded the same right. Following a large-scale post-war guest worker program, the number of Muslims had grown significantly between the 1960s and the late 1980s. During the 1980s, resentment toward the presence of "foreigners" grew, and these groups were increasingly seen as endangering the cultural and ethical values of Germans, including the proper treatment of animals. As David Smith (2007) has documented, although framed in terms of animal welfare, organizations pushing for an end to religious slaughter frequently relied on implicit distinctions between a German "us" (the civilized and humane) and "them" (the uncivilized and backward). The Animal Welfare Society *Tierschutzbund*, for example, claimed that there was no reason to continue "the dreadful practice that meets with horror and disappointment among the German population" (in Smith 2007, 96).

While many critics of religious slaughter focused on Muslims, others addressed both Jews and Muslims. The Society Against the Abuse of Animals argued that neither "Semitic" nor "Islamic" law would prohibit the pre-stunning of animals. In 1985, the then-president of the *Tierschutzbund*, who opposed both Jewish and Muslim slaughter practices, proclaimed that the goal of

> Christian-oriented countries of the west is not only to deliver high-technology industrial goods to the people of the Third World, but rather also to instruct them in dealing with sentient, suffering animals, and to convince them that the use of slaughter without stunning, while stemming from a deep-rooted tradition, is not demanded by religion.
>
> (Smith 2007, 96)

The fight against religious slaughter was thus branded as a broader civilizing mission to help the alien Other both within and outside to arrive in modernity and to remake their religion to suit the values of predominantly Christian societies. During the 1980s, Smith observes, many West German animal welfare activists often hailed from a Christian conservative background and embraced cultural homogeneity and assimilation as a societal ideal, which required the abolishment of "foreign practices" such as religious slaughter (Smith 2007, 99). Eventually, the subject came before the German Constitutional Court, which decided in 2002 in favor of the Muslim claimant who had brought the case after he had been denied the right to practice religious slaughter.[6] However, until today, civilizational discourse remains a rhetorical tool in the tool box of German animal welfare activists. In 2019, one of the state-level branches of *Tierschutzbund* released a statement arguing that an end to religious slaughter would be a sign of a progressive and successful integration of Muslims into European culture, an open and humane culture where there is no justification for such practices.[7]

The campaign against religious slaughter often dwells on a clash between secularism and religious tradition, in which minority religious practices are branded as dangerous challengers to the secular rule of law. In 2014, Denmark removed the religious exemption from its slaughter provisions, effectively banning both kosher and halal meat production. Dan Jørgensen, Danish Minister for Agriculture and Food, stated that "animal rights come before religion."[8] The fight against religious slaughter was thereby presented as a broader pushback against religious overreach into the secular liberal society. Animal welfare activists were eager to stress that the ban did not single out minority religious slaughter practices: "We don't call it a ban on kosher (practices) but a ban on slaughter without stunning because for us, and I think for the government as well, it is a matter of animal welfare,"[9] said a campaign manager for the World Society for the Protection of Animals in Copenhagen. While the language of the law may not single out Jews or Muslims, in effect it remains a law that only targets religious minorities, who are the only religious communities practicing this form of slaughter.

Supporters of the ban, however, argued that the move had nothing to do with religious intolerance toward minorities. In defense of the ban, Minister Jørgensen referred to the existing bans in Sweden and Norway that are "known as remarkably tolerant countries."[10] Yet, as discussed earlier, the bans on slaughtering animals without prior stunning were to a significant extent motivated by intolerance for Sweden's and Norway's Jewish communities. In practice, the law changed little for the Jewish community, which had already relied on the import of kosher meat. Moreover, the leaders of Denmark's Muslim community had issued a religious decree that pre-stunned animals would be considered halal.[11] Nonetheless, the symbolic message was not lost for Jewish and Muslim communities, many of whom interpreted the ban as antisemitic and Islamophobic (Miele 2016, 49). There was also concern that the ban would set the stage for further restrictions on the rights of religious minorities, such as the practice of infant male circumcision. In 2017, Denmark, alongside Iceland, indeed debated banning the circumcision of underaged boys for religious reasons.[12]

In 2017, the Belgian regions of Flanders and Wallonia joined Sweden, Switzerland, Denmark, and other European countries by introducing a ban on the slaughter of animals without prior stunning. The Flemish law had been introduced by the far-right nationalist party Vlaams Belang (Flemish Importance), which opposes multiculturalism and has espoused anti-Muslim views.[13] Despite the capture of the issue by right-wing populists, supporters of the ban emphasized that the law was about animal welfare and consumer rights and not about anti-minority sentiment. While a growing concern for consumer rights and awareness of animal welfare may have been important drivers in the Belgian campaigns against religious slaughter, anti-minority discourse reared its head too. Opponents of religious slaughter explicitly chastised observant Jews alongside Muslims for their unwillingness to change their practices. The director of the Belgian group Global Action in the Interest of Animals blamed Jews and Muslims for failing to modernize:

> They want to keep living in the Middle Ages and continue to slaughter without stunning – as the technique didn't yet exist back then – without having to answer to the law. Well, I'm sorry, in Belgium the law is above religion and that will stay like that.[14]

Muslims and Jews are represented as premodern who fail to understand the secular rule of law. Commenting on the refusal of Jewish communities to adopt non-lethal stunning in order to satisfy the law, one Belgian activist similarly presented the Orthodox Jewish insistence on *shechita* as a tradition that places Jews outside progressive secular society and renders them as stubborn religious fundamentalists, alien to Belgian society:

> With Kashrut [the laws governing food in Judaism], you have scholars who are fundamentalists, a total unwillingness to evolve. That's a problem in a secular society. . . . It is like we are from two different planets, we are from Earth and they are from Mars or Jupiter.[15]

Jewish and Muslim groups soon lodged a legal challenge against the Flemish ban, which the Belgian Constitutional Court referred to the Court of Justice of the European Union. Against the legal opinion of the Advocate General Gerard Hogan, who had found the ban to violate the right to religious freedom in his non-binding opinion,[16] the Court backed the Flemish ban in December 2020. The Court argued that the ban did not completely outlaw religious slaughter but only regulated that animals had to be stunned, thereby striking a fair balance between animal welfare and religious freedom.[17] The minister for animal welfare, Ben Weyts from the right-wing party Vlaams Belang, celebrated the decision by stating that Flanders was "writing history."[18] For Jewish organizations, however, the decision was a blow given that Jewish law does not allow for stunning, casting doubt on the sincerity of European institutions to cherish and protect Jewish life.[19]

While contemporary attacks on religious slaughter cannot be understood apart from a growing Islamophobia in Europe and a broader backlash against multiculturalism, the religious slaughter debates also point us to an ambivalent inclusion of Jews in European countries. Although historically campaigns served at least to some extent an antisemitic agenda, currently some campaigns against religious slaughter have been ceased by those seeking to limit the presence of Islam in Europe. However, the fact that a ban affects Europe's Jews alongside Muslims can create a "political dilemma," especially for right-wing populist parties, which have often been strong advocates for a legal ban on religious slaughter as part of an anti-Muslim agenda. Many of these parties seek to present themselves as allies for European Jews and are staunch supporters of the state of Israel as a "Western bulwark" against the alleged threat of Islam. For example, the Flemish party Vlaams Belang, which oversaw the introduction of the ban on religious slaughter, has positioned itself as an ally of Jews through the support of Israel and by appealing to the fears among local Belgian Jews of antisemitism among the Muslim population.[20] Nonetheless, the ability to further an anti-Muslim agenda appears to quickly trump concerns for Jewish needs as the ban on religious slaughter shows. Similarly, despite frequent antisemitic comments of its members, the German populist party Alternative für Deutschland (AfD, Alternative for Germany) has also been eager to express its support for Israel and counts a number of Jewish members, organized as Jews in the AfD (Juden in der AfD).[21] Yet the party's 2017 election program that claims that "Islam does not belong to Germany" also calls for the abolishment of religious slaughter as a form of "animal abuse/torture" – a ban that would affect both Muslims and Jews in Germany.[22]

This tension also became visible in the Netherlands in 2011, when the Lower House of the Dutch Parliament debated a ban on the slaughter of unstunned animals, which had been proposed by the Partij voor de Dieren (Party for the Animals) (Kurth & Glasbergen 2017, 416–417). During the 1970s and 1980s, a number of Dutch parties had already begun pushing for an end to religious slaughter, including the right-wing Party of the Farmers (Boeren Partij) as well as the anti-immigrant Centrum Party (Centrum Partij), attacking the practice as barbaric and primitive – yet without success (Vallenga 2015, 216–217). The 2011 proposal received significant support from the populist nationalist Partij voor de Vrijheid (Party for Freedom, PVV), led at the time by Geert Wilders and espousing strong anti-Muslim views, including a ban on religious slaughter, which the party considers to be "barbaric" and hence incompatible with the values of European civilization (Vallenga 2015, 222). However, as Sipco Vallenga (2015) has noted, while the party is Islamophobic, it is not (openly) antisemitic and refrains from presenting Jewish culture and religion as a similar threat. Instead, similarly to the Flemish populist parties, it seeks to build friendly relationships with both Dutch Jews and Israel. Even though supporting a ban on religious slaughter puts a strain on these relationships, the majority of PVV members supported the proposal in order to end what it perceived to be the "disgusting" practice of halal slaughter.[23] The Dutch Upper House ultimately rejected the bill. Yet some of the participants in the debate wondered if religious slaughter would have been banned if it only concerned Muslim meat production (Kurth & Glasbergen 2017, 428).

Banning religious slaughter as part of an attempt to exclude Muslims challenges a broader European project to affirm the Jewish past and present as part of its collective identity – not only for right-wing politicians. Unsurprisingly, this tension is particularly evident in Germany, a country that is still wrestling with its relationship with the Jewish community. The German Constitutional Court's decision in 2002 has not prevented further attempts to target Muslim slaughter practices. In 2019, the Christian Democratic Party in the state of Lower Saxony picked up an earlier proposal by the right-wing populist party Alternative für Deutschland and pushed for an end to granting Muslims the right to slaughter sheep without prior stunning for the Muslim festival of Eid al-Adha. Although the political move was aimed at the state's Muslim community, the Jewish community immediately protested, rejecting the plans of the Christian Democrats as an "affront" that they would not accept.[24] The German Federal Commissioner for the Fight Against Antisemitism at the time, Felix Klein, called the proposal an attack on Jewish and Muslim religious life. A ban, he argued, would thwart efforts to protect Jewish life in Germany. While the focus on Jewish life in his statement is understandable given that Klein's mandate is focused on antisemitism, his intervention singled out Jews as in need of protection from the proposed legal ban, even though the proposal had Muslims as its obvious targets.[25]

We can observe a similar tension around efforts to include Jews while restricting minority rights in Denmark. Even though the country proceeded with its ban on religious slaughter, the subsequent proposal to outlaw religious infant male circumcision, a practice that cannot be alternatively maintained in a similar way to the provision of kosher meat through import, was ultimately rejected. The Danish prime minister Mette Fredriksen explained the decision by affirming Jewish – yet not Muslim – belonging:

> Many Jews don't find it compatible to live in a country where circumcision is banned, and I simply don't think we can make a decision with which we don't live up to our promise – that the Jews will remain part of Denmark.[26]

Conclusion

In this chapter, I have pointed out some similarities in the dynamics of historical debates on *shechita* and present-day controversies over the permissibility of religious slaughter in European countries. In considering the debates about the legal status of religious slaughter as a site for the othering of Jews and Muslims, the aim is neither to suggest that all opponents of religious slaughter are prejudiced toward Jews and Muslims nor to downplay the sincerity of animal welfare concerns. Moreover, the secularization of Western societies certainly contributes to a decrease in sympathy for religious concerns. However, there is reason to be suspicious when minority religious practices are singled out for legal intervention under the banner of animal welfare, particularly in light of the enduring ubiquity of practices such as factory farming and long-distance animal transport across Europe (see also Porat 2021). The focus on banning religious slaughter in order to end the inhumane treatment of animals creates, as Joe Wills points out, a "false consciousness" that locates the mistreatment of animals solely among minority groups while rendering majority practices as either humane or at least necessary.[27] Animal welfare campaigns indeed also draw attention to majority practices around the treatment of animals, yet these campaigns have often engendered neither the same amount of public outrage nor legislative action. This is partly because the issue of Jewish and Muslim religious slaughter practices lends itself more easily to appeals to anti-minority sentiment that linger in the majority population, helping to shore up support. As Brian Klug observes:

> For they are not merely methods, they are icons, symbols of a moral or metaphysical opposition: the "ritual" versus the "humane." The connotations of these two words reverberate through the popular rhetoric on the subject. . . . The semantics of the controversy do not end here. The antithesis between "humane" and "ritual" is continued in a variety of synonyms. "Humane slaughter" is also known as the "Western," "Christian," "British" or "English" method. "Ritual slaughter" is called "Jewish," "Muslims" and "Semitic." Thus the very labels lend themselves to a polemic which opposes Us to Them. Our methods to Theirs.
>
> (Klug 1989, 22)

Even if contemporary debates do not exhibit the same othering vitriol in public and parliamentary discourse as the earlier debates during the 19th and early 20th centuries (although openly antisemitic and Islamophobic language still populates the online world), history shows that restrictions on the rights of religious minorities cannot be understood as disconnected to broader projects of collective identity formation in European societies along an increasingly racialized line of religious difference. Through the legal debate on religious slaughter, Jews alongside Muslims are racialized as cruel and in need of legal intervention. As Will Kymlicka and Sue Donaldson note, there is a long history of mobilizing animal issues to construct and legitimize racial hierarchies in Western societies by making the treatment of animals a "measuring stick that operates to signify white/Western cultures as uniquely humane and civilized while stigmatizing minorities/non-Western cultures as backward or barbaric" (Kymlicka & Donaldson 2014, 121; see also Deckha 2013). While animal welfare is an important concern and the suffering of animals warrants significantly more legal and political attention, it is important to not lose sight of how legal bans on religious minority practices remain enmeshed with a broader civilizational mission that seeks to construct and maintain Western identity as the primary locus of progress and modernity. Moreover, even if appeals to Christianity have become more muted in contemporary religious slaughter debates, there remain vestiges of an older Christian–Jewish/Muslim divide that enables the majority predominantly Christian culture to mobilize secularism and secular law against the intrusion of "their" archaic religion.

Moreover, through repeated attacks on religious practices, even if those attacks are primarily aimed at Muslims, European societies signal that they are willing to alienate Jews by casting them as in need of reform and regeneration in order to live up to the standards of a "civilized and humane society," despite frequent public affirmations of Jewish belonging in European societies. By attacking Muslim practices, Jews are made "collateral damage," as UKIP's spokesman for agriculture admitted freely when the party expressed its support of a ban on non-stunned slaughter in 2015. As he explained to the *Jewish Chronicle*: "This isn't aimed at you – it's aimed elsewhere – it's aimed at others. . . . You've been caught in the crossfire; collateral damage."[28]

Even if campaigns to ban religious slaughter do not succeed, their success lies elsewhere: They exert pressure to conform and signal the necessity to abolish difference in order to belong (Kushner 1989, 20). The symbolic function of such appeals to the power of law in order to restrict the rights of religious minority groups forms an important dimension of the ongoing debates about religious slaughter in Europe. Menachem Margolin, a Belgian rabbi, indeed worried:

> To have the government interfere in this way is damaging to the reputation of the Jewish people as a community. It implies that we as a group are irresponsible with the welfare of animals and need government supervision which is, of course, a very negative view of us.[29]

At the same time, while some Muslims may not be affected by a ban due to the permissibility of stunning in some Islamic schools of thought, the focus on religious slaughter constitutes yet another important site for the othering of Muslims in the name of liberal law and values alongside the headscarf and the forced marriage debates.

Although the repeated attacks on the religious rights of Jewish and Muslim communities further alienate already marginalized populations, these developments might in turn provide the ground for greater Muslim–Jewish unity. Already in 1968, the British newspaper *The Times* pondered whether by "defending their rights in the abattoirs . . . Muslims and Jews will find the makings of a devoutly-to-be-wished détente?" (in Carlton & Kaye 1985, 501). The discussions about the Belgian ban on religious slaughter seem to have served to some extent as such a catalyst. In 2016, Muslim and Jewish leaders launched the Muslim Jewish Leadership Council in Vienna, an initiative that aims to protect the rights of religious minorities in Europe.[30] With the rights of religious minorities under pressure, this shared experience of legal marginalization might help European Muslims and Jews to overcome some of the rifts that have kept them divided in order to join forces in counteracting some of Europe's exclusionary tendencies that play out in the field of law.

Notes

1 Council Regulation (EC) No. 1099/2009 on the Protection of Animals at the Time of Killing.

2 Poland outlawed religious slaughter without prior stunning in 2013, but the Polish Constitutional Court overturned the law in 2014. In 2020, a new law was drafted that would

have banned religious slaughter for export meat, which would have had a significant impact on the country's sizeable export industry of halal and kosher meat production. The law was ultimately not signed but was followed by a new proposal: https://www.dw.com/en/whats-in-kaczynskis-kosher-beef/a-55702908

3 *Liga van Moskeeën en Islamitische Organisaties Provincie Antwerpen VZW and Others v Vlaams Gewest* (29 May 2018), C-426/16, ECLI:EU:C:2018:335 (CJEU).

4 On the European embrace of Jewish culture and history even in the absence of a significant Jewish population, see Gruber (2002). On the term "Judeo-Christian," see, e.g., Topolski (2020).

5 Of course, Muslims had been living in Europe for much longer, but their numbers increased significantly during this period. Moreover, there is a much longer tradition of the Muslim as Other in Europe, and the present-day controversies have to be understood in light of this history.

6 *Bundesverfassungsgericht* (BVerfG, German Federal Constitutional Court), 15 January 2002 – 1 BvR 1783/99.

7 https://landestierschutzverband-bw.de/nachrichtenleser/traditionelle-schächtung-ist-tierquälerei.html

8 https://www.independent.co.uk/news/world/europe/denmark-bans-halal-and-kosher-slaughter-minister-says-animal-rights-come-religion-9135580.html

9 https://www.washingtonpost.com/national/religion/danish-jews-muslims-fight-for-exemption-to-ritual-slaughter-ban/2014/02/25/6672ecde-9e5a-11e3-878c-65222df220eb_story.html

10 https://www.economist.com/erasmus/2014/02/18/much-ado-about-not-much

11 https://www.aljazeera.com/news/2014/2/18/danish-halal-law-changes-nothing-says-imam

12 https://www.nytimes.com/2018/06/02/world/europe/denmark-circumcision.html

13 https://www.politico.eu/article/belgium-becomes-eu-test-case-on-halal-and-kosher-slaughter-religious-freedoms-animal-welfare/

14 https://www.nytimes.com/2019/01/05/world/europe/belgium-ban-jewish-muslim-animal-slaughter.html

15 https://www.politico.eu/article/belgium-becomes-eu-test-case-on-halal-and-kosher-slaughter-religious-freedoms-animal-welfare/

16 Advocate General's Opinion in Case C-336/19 *Centraal Israëlitisch Consistorie van België and others* (10 September 2020).

17 Court of Justice of the European Union (Grand Chamber), Case C-336 *Centraal Israëlitisch Consistorie van België and others* (17 December 2020).

18 https://www.bbc.com/news/world-europe-55344971

19 See note above.

20 https://www.nytimes.com/2005/02/12/world/europe/fear-of-islamists-drives-growth-of-far-right-in-belgium.html

21 https://www.faz.net/aktuell/politik/inland/die-afd-und-der-antisemitismus-israels-falsche-freunde-16605456.html

22 Wahlprogramm der Alternative für Deutschland für die Wahl zum Deutschen Bundestag am 24. September 2017 (April 2017), https://www.afd.de/wpcontent/uploads/sites/111/2017/06/2017-06-01_AfD-Bundestagswahlprogramm_Onlinefassung.pdf, at 37 and 73.

23 Vallenga (2015, 222) notes that all but one of PVV's MPs voted in support of the proposal. This one MP eventually left the PVV, partly because of this particular issue.

24 https://www.welt.de/politik/deutschland/article198563321/CDU-will-Muslimen-betaeubungsloses-Schaechten-verbieten.html

25 https://de.qantara.de/content/debatte-ueber-das-schaechten-nach-cdu-vorstoss-in-niedersachsen

26 https://cphpost.dk/?p=118305

27 https://www.alaw.org.uk/2020/09/the-troubling-case-of-non-stun-slaughter-a-comment-on-the-opinion-of-advocate-general-hogan-in-centraal-israelitisch-consistorie-van-belgie-and-others/

28 https://www.thejc.com/news/uk/ukip-s-agriculture-spokesman-says-he-did-not-want-shechita-ban-policy-1.64957
29 https://www.thejc.com/news/world/flanders-belgium-ban-on-kosher-slaughter-begins-1.477865
30 https://mjlc-europe.org/Mission

References

Anidjar, Gil. 2003. *The Jew, the Arab: A History of the Enemy*. Stanford: Stanford University Press.

Akiyama, Yoko. 2011. "Die Hegemonie der Mehrheit in einer Multikulturelle Gesellschaft. Unter Besonderer Berücksichtigung des Schächtverbots im Jahr 1893 in der Schweiz." *Eurostudia* 7 (1–2): 59–71.

Bergeaud-Blackler, Florence. 2007. "New Challenges for Islamic Ritual Slaughter: A European Perspective." *Journal of Ethnic and Migration Studies* 33 (6): 965–80.

Biale, David. 2007. *Blood and Belief. The Circulation of a Symbol between Jews and Christians*. Berkeley; Los Angeles; London: University of California Press.

Bunzl, Matti. 2007. *Anti-Semitism and Islamophobia: Hatreds Old and New in Europe*. Chicago: Prickly Paradigm Press.

Carlton, Roger, and Ronald Kaye. 1985. "The Politics of Religious Slaughter." *New Community*, (Winter): 490–503.

Deckha, Maneesha. 2013. "Welfarist and Imperial: The Contributions of Anticruelty Laws to Civilizational Discourse." *American Quarterly* 65 (3): 515–548.

Gruber, Ruth Ellen. 2002. *Virtually Jewish. Reinventing Jewish Culture in Europe*. Berkeley; Los Angeles; London: University of California Press.

Heng, Geraldine. 2019. *England and the Jews*. Cambridge: Cambridge University Press.

Jansen, Yolande, and Nasar Meer. 2020. "Genealogies of 'Jews' and 'Muslims': Social Imaginaries in the Race-Religion Nexus." *Patterns of Prejudice* 54 (1–2): 1–14.

Joseph, Anna. 2016. "Going Dutch: A Model for Reconciling Animal Slaughter Reform with the Religious Freedom Restoration Act." *Journal of Animal Ethics* 6 (2): 135–52.

Judd, Robin. 2003. "The Politics of Beef: Animal Advocacy and the Kosher Butchering Debates in Germany." *Jewish Social Studies* 10 (1): 117–50.

———. 2007. *Contested Rituals: Circumcision, Kosher Butchering, and Jewish Political Life in Germany, 1843–1933*. Ithaca: Cornell University Press.

Julius, Anthony. 2010. *Trials of the Diaspora. A History of Anti-Semitism in England*. Oxford: Oxford University Press.

Kalmar, Ivan Davidson, and Derek Jonathan Penslar. 2005a. "An Introduction." In *Orientalism and the Jews*, edited by Ivan Davidson Kalmar and Derek Jonathan Penslar. Hanover and London: Brandeis University Press.

———, eds. 2005b. *Orientalism and the Jews*. Hanover and London: Brandeis University Press.

Katz, Ethan B. 2018a. "An Imperial Entanglement: Anti-Semitism, Islamophobia, and Colonialism." *American Historical Review* 123 (4): 1190–209.

———. 2018b. "Where Do the Hijab and the Kippah Belong? On Being Publicy Jewish or Muslim in Post-Hebdo France." *Jewish History* 32 (1): 99–114.

Klug, Brian. 1989. "Ritual Murmur: The Undercurrent of Protest against Religious Slaughter of Animals in Britain in the 1980s." *Patterns of Prejudice* 23 (2): 16–28.

Kurth, Laura, and Pieter Glasbergen. 2017. "Dealing with Tensions of Multiculturalism: The Politics of Ritual Slaughter in the Netherlands." *European Journal of Cultural Studies* 20 (4): 413–32.

Kushner, Tony. 1989. "Stunning Intolerance. A Century of Opposition to Religious Slaughter." *Jewish Quarterly* 36 (1): 16–20.

Kymlicka, Will, and Sue Donaldson. 2014. "Animal Rights, Multiculturalism, and the Left." *Journal of Social Philosophy* 45 (1): 116–35.

Lever, John. 2019. "Halal Meat and Religious Slaughter: From Spatial Concealment to Social Controversy - Breaching the Boundaries of the Permissible?" *Environment and Planning C: Politics and Space* 37 (5): 889–907.

Mancini, Susanna. 2012. "Patriarchy as the Exclusive Domain of the Other: The Veil Controversy, False Projection and Cultural Racism." *International Journal of Constitutional Law* 10 (2): 411–28.

Metcalf, Michael F. 1989. "Regulating Slaughter: Animal Protection and Antisemitism in Scandinavia, 1880–1941." *Patterns of Prejudice* 23 (3): 32–48.

Miele, Mara. 2016. "Killing Animals for Food: How Science, Religion and Technologies Affect the Public Debate About Religious Slaughter." *Food Ethics* 1: 47–60.

Nirenberg, David. 2013. *Anti-Judaism: The Western Tradition*. New York; London: WW Norton.

Porat, Iddo. 2021. "The Starting at Home Principle: On Ritual Animal Slaughter, Male Circumcision and Proportionality." *Oxford Journal of Legal Studies* 41 (1): 30–58.

Razack, Sherene H. 2004. "Imperilled Muslim Women, Dangerous Muslim Men and Civilised Europeans: Legal and Social Responses to Forced Marriages." *Feminist Legal Studies* 12 (2): 129–74.

Renton, James, and Ben Gidley, eds. 2017. *Antisemitism and Islamophobia in Europe. A Shared History?* London: Palgrave Macmillan.

Smith, David. 2007. "'Cruelty of the Worst Kind': Religious Slaughter, Xenophobia, and the German Greens." *Central European History* 40: 89–115.

Snildal, Andreas. 2014. "An Anti-Semitic Slaughter Law? The Origins of the Norwegian Prohibition of Jewish Religious Slaughter c. 1890–1930." PhD Thesis, University of Oslo. https://www.duo.uio.no/bitstream/handle/10852/82684/PhD-Snildal-2014.pdf?sequence=1.

Topolski, Anya. 2020. "The Dangerous Discourse of the 'Judeo-Christian' Myth: Masking the Race-Religion Constellation in Europe." *Patterns of Prejudice* 54 (1–2).

Vallenga, Sipco. 2015. "Ritual Slaughter, Animal Welfare and the Freedom of Religion: A Critical Discourse Analysis of a Fierce Debate in the Dutch Lower House." *Journal of Religion in Europe* 8: 210–34.

Venerito, Barbara. 2018. "Antischächtbewegung und Antisemitismus in Deutschland von 1867 bis 1914." PhD Thesis, Free University Berlin. https://refubium.fu-berlin.de/handle/fub188/23680.

7

ALBANIAN MUSLIMS

Religious Othering and Notions of European Islam

Flora Ferati-Sachsenmaier

Introduction

At the turn of the 21st century, Albanian Muslims[1] constituted the largest Muslim community in Southeast Europe. However, they also represent a unique national context, one in which, although Muslims were a relative majority, Islam never played a central role in shaping Albanian political life and national identity. As many scholars have noted, it could not, because historically speaking, Albanians have belonged to one of the four main recognized religions: Islam, Christian Orthodoxy, Roman Catholicism, and Bektashism (an Islamic Sufi movement). Religious diversity has been present among Albanians for centuries and has left a deep legacy in Albanian literature, culture, and history.[2] However, the insistence of the Albanian elites on building a nation-state identity based on a non-religious identity primarily dates back to the 19th century. Closely tied to the intellectual and political movements to establish a modern nation-state of Albania, a national identity without a religious basis was propagated by the activists of the Albanian Renaissance Movement (in Albanian, Rilindja Kombëtare), who saw religion as a potentially divisive force that could impede efforts to establish an independent Albania.

Proponents of the modern nation-state of Albania, Rilindasit as they were called, worked to create a new way of understanding modern Albanian nationalism that would supersede existing religious differences, advancing the notion of Albanianism, so-called. As prominent Rilindas poet Pashko Vasa succinctly summarized it, Albanianism meant that "[Albanians] should swear an oath not to mind church or mosque, for the faith of Albanians is Albanianism." Thus, modern Albanian nationalism, with its emphasis on the language, ethnicity, and shared culture, begins to develop very differently from the modern nationalist movements of Albania's neighbors and Greece. Unlike the Serbian and Greek nationalist projects in which religion formed the cornerstone of their national identities, Albanian nationalism

DOI: 10.4324/b22926-8

makes no reference whatsoever to religion. It has neither religious symbolism nor religious myths. As scholarship has shown, "Albanian nationalism forms an exception to this common Balkan pattern of overlapping ethnic and religious identities and religiously inspired nationalisms." (Dujzings 2002, 60). Within the territories where Albanians constitute either an absolute majority or minority – the first modern Albanian state, created in 1912; Serbian-ruled Kosovo between 1912 and 1999; North Macedonia; southern Serbia; or parts of Montenegro – at no point were "religious identities and religious institutions utilized by [Albanian] political leaders to achieve political and national cohesion" (Cesari 2015, 502).

In this chapter, I ask why, despite this enduring absence of any reference to religion as a repertoire of national identity, there has been a continuing tendency in some political and intellectual discourses to depict the Albanians as religious other, and specifically as an essentialized Muslim other. As I will argue, Serbian nationalist discourses, Serbian Orthodox Church clerics, as well as some influential Serbian intellectuals have a long history of depicting Albanians as Muslims and other. The same pattern can be observed in the case of Macedonian (Slav) nationalist discourse with regard to Albanians in North Macedonia and in Greek nationalist discourses vis-à-vis Albanian Çams, an Albanian minority from Çamëria, a region located in northwestern Greece today.

The main argument this chapter makes is that the religious othering of the Albanians as Muslim other has to be understood in the context of the territorial claims and political struggles over the territories where Albanians live. One distinctive feature of the discourse is that the depiction of Albanians as Muslim other has always gone hand in hand with an anti-Ottoman, anti-Turkish, and therefore an anti-Islam discourse. In fact, the two have been used interchangeably. The main purpose of accentuating Islam instead of the Albanian national identity and embedding this into anti-Ottomanism is to claim that no such people as Albanians actually exist.

The religious othering of Albanians as Muslim other not only runs contrary to how Albanians have understood the relationship between national identity and religious belonging since the late 19th century, but it has also resulted in a set of state-led discriminatory policies against Albanians in the 20th century. These include the large-scale Albanian population transfers from Kosovo and today's North Macedonia to Turkey during the interwar period, the repression of the ethnic identity of Albanian Muslim Çams, and their subsequent expulsion from Greece in 1944. Moreover, Serbian government made religious claims to Kosovo, at all stages of the conflict, and this went hand in hand with othering Kosovar Albanians as Muslim others. Finally, the chapter will argue that, from the 19th until the 21st century, Albanian secular-political elites have responded to these dimensions of religious othering with two key terms: *Albanian exceptionalism*, used to discuss religious tolerance, which stresses that the Albanian Islamic tradition is shaped by a unique Albanian national tradition that promotes religious coexistence and tolerance, and *European Islam*, used to emphasize Albanian indigenousness in Europe.

The Historical and Political Dimensions of Religious Othering: The Case of the Albanians in the Balkans

By the middle of the 19th century, as it became clear that the Ottoman Empire was losing its hold on power in the European part of its Empire, and as several Christian Balkan states were gaining their independence, a central question emerged: who were the region's "non-Turkish speaking Muslims?" (Clayer and Bougarel 2017, 38). The way the question was framed and – often – answered revolved around notions of the compatibility of Islam with European modernity, the pre-Ottoman existence of local Balkan peoples, and their Islamization processes. As the political context of the period was characterized by the nation-state formation processes, one important question that emerged was about the right of Balkan Muslims to have their own nation-states.

Two specific population groups were seen as belonging to indigenous Muslim Balkan populations: the Albanians and the Slavic-speaking Bosnian Muslims. They pre-dated the Ottoman arrival in the 14th century, the argument went, and had only gradually converted to Islam – although not all did so, as shown by the presence of multi-religious traditions among the Albanians. It was mainly the Albanians who lived largely in four vilayets[3] across the Balkans who were seen as comprising this distinctive local Muslim population. Not only was their language different from Turkish, "as regards the Albanian Muslims more specifically, but the idea also arose that they were different from the Turkish Muslims because they had opted for a different Islam, supposedly less orthodox and more free thinking, that of the Bektashi brotherhood" (Clayer and Bougarel 2017, 38). Prominent Albanian intellectuals of all religious backgrounds advanced these ideas locally in the late 19th century, but the most influential advocates laying the foundations for this way of thinking were the leaders of the Albanian Bektashi order.

For Albania's famous national poet Naim Frashëri, himself from the Bektashi order, the decoupling of Albanians from the Ottoman Empire religiously, linguistically, and culturally was crucial for building the national modern Albanian identity. Naim Frashëri saw Sunni Islam as an instrument of foreign rule and an impediment to national unity, and his literary work features traces of national romantic sentiments and adamant distancing from Orthodox Sunni Islam.[4] After all, the Ottomans had employed coercive policies and measures to prohibit the teaching of the Albanian language and forced Albanian Muslims to attend Turkish schools. As late as the 19th century, for instance, "in the whole of Albania only two Albanian schools existed, while there were some 5,000 Turkish or Greek schools" (Misha 2001, 38). As an alternative to Ottoman Orthodox Sunni doctrine, Naim Frashëri and other Bektashi leaders created new religious visions and institutions. They built hundreds of Bektashi lodges (tekkes) in which Albanian Muslims and Christians could pray together,[5] places where new forms of religious understanding and tolerance were cultivated. Moreover, they opened up clandestine schools in the Albanian language, advocated for purging Turkish words from the Albanian language, and when they could, even supported armed groups with nationalist agendas. In 1878, before the convening of the League of Prizren in

Kosovo, it was located in the Bektashi tekke in Frashër, a town in southern Albania, where Abdyl Frashëri summoned Albanian intellectuals, religious leaders, and local officials to discuss and advance demands for national unity and liberation from the direct Ottoman rule.

Thus, the assertion that Albanian Muslims were practicing a non-orthodox form of Islam was to some extent true. While there were conservative Albanian (Sunni) Muslims who remained loyal to the Ottoman Empire, Bektashism became the new vehicle for articulating Albanian national political aspirations and cultural revival. Famously, it transmitted these ideals through literature, by introducing an entirely new genre that was imbued with national epic elements and depicted Sunni Islam as a tool of Ottoman domination over Albanian territories (Shuteriqi et al. 1983, 186). Although a minority religion, the significance of Albanian Bektashism lay in its forging of a new way of understanding religion and promoting religious tolerance among Albanians, emphasizing close cooperation with Albanian Christians, Muslims, and Catholics over the allegiance to Sunni Islam Ottoman Turks.

In the decades that followed, other prominent Albanian intellectuals and religious figures such as poet and Franciscan priest Gjergj Fishta and Fan S. Noli (the founder of the Orthodox Autocephalous Church of Albania) continued propagating the idea of a civic understanding of religion in the Albanian-populated territories across the Balkans. Their literary work and political legacy reveal the shaping of the national ideal of Albanianism: before one is Muslim, Christian, Catholic, or Bektashi one is first and foremost Albanian. Gjergj Fishta's famous line "it is true that we indeed have both Eid and Easter, but Albanianism is what unites us all" is taught and repeated among Albanians up to the present, especially during religious holidays. Fan S. Noli who held the first Orthodox liturgy in Albanian in 1908, and subsequently translated it into Albanian Orthodox rituals and liturgies, remains one of the most influential figures in modern Albanian history. Noli was convinced that the founding of the Albanian Orthodox Church was essential to the survival of the Albanian state, a position that was frowned upon by the Greek Orthodox Church and Greece in general because they held territorial ambitions in Albania.

As will be discussed in the next section of the chapter, despite Albanian ecumenism and the divide between Albanian Bektashism and Sunni orthodoxy, Serbian nationalist and Christian Orthodox religious discourses have insisted on casting Albanians as "Muslim other." In other words, the anti-Ottoman and anti-Orthodox Sunni Islam, and anti-Greek Orthodox legacy which is deeply ingrained in the Albanian collective modern understanding of themselves are completely missing.[6] Accordingly, some Balkan Christians have repeatedly downplayed the religious diversity of Albanians, and they have emphasized Albanian Islam, portraying it predominantly in the essentialist view.

Beginning in the middle of the 19th century, Serbian nationalists, the Serbian Orthodox Church, and prominent Serbian intellectual figures began propagating a counter discourse about the Albanians. Inspired by the Kosovo myth, this narrative revolves around the 1389 Battle of Kosovo. In essence, the Kosovo myth is a religious othering myth that portrays a struggle of Christians Serbs against Muslims

(Ottoman Turks). In the Serbian popular historical discourse, the myth's central figure is Serbian Prince Lazar, who led the battle against Sultan Murad I at the battle of Kosovo. The Serbs explain the death of Prince Lazar as his decision to sacrifice the Serbian Kingdom on Earth for the Kingdom of Heaven. Prince Lazar thus attains Christ-like features; he is a religious martyr, and his martyrdom is the martyrdom of Serbian nationhood itself. He sacrifices himself for the "defense of Christian Europe" against "Islam." As a result, the Serbian nation is imagined as a chosen people with a special covenant with God.

Historians know little about the battle except that Sultan Murad and Prince Lazar were both killed and a broad coalition of Balkan troops fought against the Ottomans. Hence, the battle was not solely Serbian or Serbian Orthodox Christian. And in the medieval period, the Serbs fighting under Prince Lazar certainly didn't think of themselves as part of a Serbian nation. It was the Serbian Orthodox Church that first turned Prince Lazar into a religious martyr, declaring him a saint shortly after his death, emphasizing his "martyrdom for the faith," and depicting Serbs as a chosen, "heavenly people." Why did the Kosovo myth become such an integral element of anti-Albanian political discourse during the 20th century?

As Albanian religious and intellectual figures were propagating the idea that the faith of Albanians is Albanianism in an effort to shape their movement for an independent nation-state, Serbian poets and political figures were cementing the idea of a collective Serbian identity in which ethnic and Orthodox religious identity were inseparable. In the Serbian national movement of the 19th century, the revival of the Kosovo Myth became a central theme in the discourse of the national struggle for independence from the Ottoman Turks. From being merely a legend, a part of folk-epic oral traditions, the Kosovo myth becomes fully incorporated into the modern Serbian national movement. Two of the main figures responsible for this revival were Serbian literary figure Vuk Karadžić and national poet Petar Petrović Njegoš, a bishop and writer from Montenegro. In his famous poetic drama *The Mountain Wreath*, Njegoš revitalized the Kosovo Myth and gave it a nationalistic mission for the future. Njegoš expressed not only open hatred toward Islam in the form of Ottoman Turkish rule but also referred to local Muslim populations that had converted to Islam as "Turks" or "Turkifiers."

The Mountain Wreath celebrates the 18th-century ethnic cleansing of these infidel convert "Turks" by Montenegrin Serbs and combines nationalism and religious credo to justify the violence. For instance, one of the verses from the *Mountain Wreath* reads:

> The blasphemers of Christ's name
> We will baptize with water or with blood!
> We will drive the plague out of the pen!
> Let the song of horror ring forth,
> A true altar on a bloodstained rock.

(Goldhagen 2012)

Thus, by the late 19th century, Kosovo had assumed a new significance in the Serbian collective national imagination. For Serbian national and religious elites, the loss at Kosovo had to be avenged, and "Turkish" and "Muslim" infidels, which included Albanian Muslims, would have to pay. This mythological self-understanding erased the six centuries of historical intermezzo between a Serbian medieval kingdom and the modern state of Serbia and made Kosovo a religious pledge and a national duty. On the other hand, for the Albanian national and intellectual elites, the province had to be protected from both Ottoman-Turkish yoke and Serbian ethno-clerical territorial claims. Albanians began to respond to this religious othering discourse with an Albanian Islam that was native to Europe; their "Europeaness" came from the fact that Albanians were not Muslims from the East but rather native people of the Balkans whose Islamic tradition was influenced by its national context of religious diversity and tolerance.

These national struggles over shaping and re-shaping the perceptions of ethno-national and religious identities in the Balkans were not limited to the region. A number of famous European intellectuals and public figures took positions on these matters as well. Their positions on the Muslim identity and national identity of Albanians were often discussed in the framework of the right to have their own state. German historian Leopold von Ranke maintained that "it was a mistake to regard the [Muslims] of Bosnia and Albania as intruders, and that to wish to return them to Asia would be a historical absurdity" (Clayer and Bougarel 2017, 37; von Ranke 1829, 523–558). Dora d'Istria, a Romanian princess of Albanian origin, wrote extensively on what set Albanian Muslims apart from the Ottoman-Turkish Muslims. But these ideas were based on ethnicized and even racialized conceptions. For example, Dora d'Istria, emphasized the "Aryan race" of the Albanians and referred to the Ottoman Turks as the "Asiatic race" (Clayer and Bougarel 2017, 37).

The process of religiously differentiating "Albanian Muslims" from the Ottoman Muslims thus took a rather an essentialist-national view, stressing their pre-Ottoman Christian roots and the superficiality of the conversion to Islam under the Ottoman rule. Albanian ideologists and foreign observers asserted that many Albanian Muslims had converted to Islam primarily to escape taxation and some still secretly practiced their Christian beliefs. Moreover, the evident religious diversity, the prevalence of interreligious marriages, and multi-confessional places of worship among Albanians – were all used as arguments to prove that Albanian Islam was compatible with a European identity and Western modernity. Therefore, not only Christian Orthodox Serbs in the Balkans would be entitled to have their own national state but also Albanians as well.

Between the second 19th and early 20th centuries, a discourse had been established that differentiated between "Ottoman Muslims" and "local Muslims" in the Balkans. This was foreboding a post-Ottoman reality, as there was a gradual process that would take decades to fully complete in the Balkans. It also marks the era in which we see the notions of "Albanian Islam" and "European Islam" begin being juxtaposed to the idea of "Turkish" or "Asiatic Islam." The quest of the Albanians to establish their independent state from the Ottoman Empire seems to have particularly fueled the debate about "European Islam." The Serbian nationalistic narrative, however, preferred not to disentangle the two. The reasons for this were the Serbian territorial ambitions over Kosovo.

Religious Othering and State Policy Measures Against Albanian Muslims in the 20th Century

In the early 20th-century Balkan Peninsula, the Albanian-inhabited regions were at the center of what, in the terms of the Great Power rivalry and interference, was called the Eastern Question. "These regions were claimed either wholly or in part by Serbs, Montenegrins, Greeks and Bulgarians as part of their historical territories, with the hope of dividing [these territories] between them" (Vickers 1995). As the Ottoman rule officially came to an end in the Balkans,[7] the Albanians declared their national independence in 1912, the last of the Balkan peoples to do so. The internationally recognized state of Albania declared in 1913 at the London Peace Conference, however, left more than one-third of the Albanians outside the confines of the new state. The outcome was that Serbia and Greece became the largest winners of the carved-up Albanian territories in the Balkans, with Serbia given the entire vilayet of Kosovo and Macedonia, while Greece received regions of Çamëria and Ioaninna that border the southern part of today's Albania.

Kosovo was a predominantly Albanian populated province that had been under the Ottoman rule for 500 years when the Serbs invaded it in 1912. As explained, the Kosovo Myth was used to rally public support for the Serbian military conquest of Kosovo, which was accompanied by the systematic destruction of villages and atrocities against Albanian civilians (Carnegie Endowment for International Peace 1914; Freundlich 1913). Serbs saw the conquest as revenge for Kosovo, claiming that they were not only avenging the loss of Kosovo from the Ottoman Turks after almost 500 years but also liberating it from the local converted Muslim infidels. As all objective historical accounts have shown, one distinctive feature of the Serbian–Montenegrin violent conquest of Kosovo was the practice of forced conversion of Albanian Muslims and Catholics to Christian Orthodoxy. For instance, "by May 1913 the Austrian consul in Prizren [a city in southern Kosovo] reported that 2,000 Muslim families in the town of Peja [alone] had been converted, and that those who refused were tortured and shot" (Malcolm 1998). We know of these atrocities and forced conversions from accounts of foreigners, Albanian Catholics from Kosovo, and the Albanian Catholic Archbishop of Skopje, Lazër Mjeda, who sent a detailed account of the events to Rome.

Despite the destruction during 1912–1913, Albanians still remained a majority in Kosovo, parts of Macedonia, parts of Montenegro, and what is today called southern Serbia. To explain the enduring linguistic, ethnic, and distinctive Albanian character of these regions, some Serbian academics revitalized the so-called Arnautaši thesis. Initially circulated in the late 19th century,[8] the thesis claimed that the majority of Albanians in Kosovo were Albanianized Muslim Serbs.[9] Espoused most prominently by the Serbian historian Jovan Tomitsch in 1913, the Arnautaši thesis argued that Serbian historians had over-estimated the Great Exodus of Serbs from Kosovo in 1690 – an exodus for which the Albanians were typically blamed. This exodus had been a dominant narrative in Serbian history, used to explain the fact that there were more Albanians (Muslims) in Kosovo than Serbians (Christian Orthodox). In Tomitsch's re-evaluation, the main reason for these numbers was not the exodus, but the processes of "Islamicization" and "Albanianization" of Orthodox Serbs in Kosovo. Supposedly, this conversion was caused by waves of migration from the northern plains of Albania into the Kosovo valley. No evidence was given about precisely *when* this alleged massive migration of Albanian Muslims into Kosovo occurred; Serbian academics like geographer Jovan Cvijić, however, took great pains to describe *how* the Albanian-speaking Muslim community allegedly converted "native Serb Christians." He emphasized the role of Albanian Muslim clans and their supposedly coercive measures, deceit, and intermarriage, all of which eventually led to the Albanized Islamization of the "native Serb Christians" (e.g., Cvijić 1918). The point of the argument was to undermine any Albanian origin story for the ethnic or national category of the majority population living in Kosovo by making them originally Serbs and, of course, to endorse Serbia's conquest and rule in its newly conquered territories of Kosovo and Macedonia (Müller 2005, 182–85).

In the national struggles of the Balkan Christian nations and territorial expansions in the Balkans, religious othering served as an essential component of attempts to assert political rule over Albanians outside the Albanian state. Whether in historical discourses, religious discourses, or policy measures, religious othering of Albanians was used to legitimize territorial claims and, once lands were acquired, as a raison d'être to govern Albanian subjects. After 1913, for instance, the Greek authorities categorized Albanians in the acquired territories of Çamëria and Ioannina as either Muslim Chams or Christian Chams. Since the region of southern Albania had historically been largely Christian Orthodox, and the Greek language was used by many as the main language of commerce and education, the Greek authorities registered the Orthodox Cham Albanians as Greeks. But they registered Albanian Chams as either Muslim Chams or Muslim Turks. The hope was to turn the Albanian Orthodox communities into "loyal nationals" in these newly annexed territories by Greece after 1912.

In 1918, large parts of Albanian territories in the Balkans were incorporated into the newly established Serb-dominated Kingdom of the Serbs, Croats, and Slovenes[10] which encompassed the territory of current-day Kosovo, Macedonia, as well as parts of Montenegro. As subjects of the kingdom, Albanians were given the status of a non-sovereign linguistic minority. Although the Kingdom of the Serbs, Croats, and Slovenes had signed international treaties pertaining to minorities' right to education, Albanians were not allowed to receive education in their mother tongue nor to run their own schools. As it has been noted by many scholars, significantly smaller minority groups than Albanians, such as Hungarians and Germans, were allowed to use their native languages and organize their schools (Sevic 2000). This was because the state authorities didn't recognize Albanians as a national minority in either a national or an ethnic sense. The majority Albanian population in Kosovo were recognized as non-Slav nationals of the Kingdom but were not granted the same status as Serbs, Croats, and Slovenes or other minorities for that matter. They were portrayed in discourses as either "Albanianized Muslim Serbs," according to *Arnautasi thesis* propaganda, or simply as Muslims. In line with this legal and citizenship categorization, the Albanians of Kosovo and Macedonia were allowed to have a specific political party to represent their interest in the Yugoslav Kingdom – Xhemijet or the Islamic Association for the Defense of Justice.

Reduced to a linguistic and religious category, during the interwar period, Albanians in the Yugoslav Kingdom could receive their education in either Serbian secular schools or Muslim religious schools. The study of Islamic scriptures in Albanian was forbidden, and it could be conducted only in Arabic or Turkish. Albanians received their secular education in Serbian in the so-called People's Schools, ethnically mixed state-run schools that followed a standardized, government-approved curriculum (Wachter 1998; Redzepagic 1968). However, Serb and Albanian pupils were separated for religious instruction that was taught by Orthodox priests and Slav-speaking Muslim teachers, respectively. "By 1930 there were no Albanian-language schools, except for a few utterly clandestine ones, in the whole of Kosovo; nor was there a single Albanian-language publication on sale there" (Malcolm 1998, 267). The banning of the Albanian as a language of religious instruction was related to the process of religious othering, as the authorities hoped that suppressing the national identity of Albanians would eventually lead to the creation of a less problematic religious identity – "Albanians as Serbian-speaking Muslims," similar to that of Bosnian Muslims. The Albanian language is distinctively different from Slavic languages, whereas Bosnian is a Slavic language and was seen therefore as helpful in strengthening both Muslim identity (in form of a Turkish or Slav Muslim identity) and serbianization of the Albanians in Kosovo and Macedonia.

Why was the Kingdom of Yugoslavia so suspicious of Albanian Muslim clergy? The Serbian authorities initially allowed private religious Muslim schools in the Albanian-inhabited territories. As scholarship has demonstrated, however, they soon became suspicious of the Albanian Muslim clergy in Kosovo and Macedonia because they used the limited opportunity – in the domain of religious education – to disseminate non-religious and nationalist ideals such as "faith of Albanian is Albanianism." There were reasonable grounds for this suspicion. In interwar Yugoslavia, Albanian Muslim clergy not only supported national and cultural activities, but they also began to secretly teach in Albanian in Muslim primary schools and seminaries and, in some cases, even completely abandoned the use of Turkish and Arabic in studying religious scripture. As in the late 19th century, when Albanian books were being clandestinely disseminated in Bektashi lodges in response to repressive Turkish measures against education in Albanian; it was Albanian Muslim hodjas and imams who spread Albanian-language books in interwar Yugoslavia. This lets them provide Albanian pupils with religious and secular education at the same time (Vokrri 1990, 303–14). But the Serbian authorities did not remain idle in face of these developments and developed a response policy to prevent Albanian nationalism from taking roots in Muslim schools: they either closed them down altogether or replaced Albanian imams with Bosnian Muslims. "This policy was driven by the same rationale as that of prohibiting secular schooling in Albanian – to undermine the feeling of Albanian national identity by stimulating the supremacy of collective identification based on religion" (Kostovicova 2002).

There are several new studies documenting the Muslim clergy's importation of illegal Albanian books from Albania. For instance, in what is today Western Macedonia, in the Polog Valley, influential local religious community leaders such as Mulla Ferik Maliki and Osman Efendi Abdullahu were at the forefront of the struggle for national Albanian ideals. A devoted teacher, Osman Abdullahu, was known for saying "Pa vatan nuk ka Iman," or "there is no faith or belief without homeland."[11] For Abdullahu, the Albanian language and nation were of primary importance, and religion was secondary. As historian Ismet Jonuzi-Krosi has shown, several of these influential religious figures were members of political organizations with pan-Albanian orientations such as "Besa" (Jonuzi-Krosi 2020). All in all, in the Albanian-speaking world in interwar Yugoslavia, the efforts to religiously other Albanians through the education system to create "Serbian-speaking Muslim" citizens backfired. Religious Albanian figures (both Muslim and Christian) served as an important guardrail against the de-Albanization processes. Hoping that Albanians could be changed into Muslim Slavs or Serbs, Serbian policymakers tried to dominate Islamic religious institutions by employing Slav mullahs and imams. They were vigorously shunned by Albanians. And when the efforts to end the "Albanization" of Kosovo through assimilationism failed, the massive expulsion of Albanian Muslims to their Turkey state became the next form of religious othering.

In 1937, Serbian historian Vasa Cubrilovic, a professor at the University of Belgrade, gave a lecture addressing the presence of Albanians in the Yugoslav territory, a geographic area he declared had been Serbian since the middle ages. The title of the lecture – the Expulsion of the Albanians – was radical enough, but the content, a call for a final solution to the Albanian problem, was even more chilling. A leading member of the Serbian Academy of Arts and Sciences, Cubrilovic, was obsessed with the ethnic composition of Kosovo and the fact that Albanians constituted an ethnic majority not just there but also in South Serbia and in parts of Macedonia – which he considered "the Albanian triangle." He enumerated failures in assimilating the Albanians (both Muslims and non-Muslims) and the failure of colonization measures, after the Serbian conquest of Kosovo in 1912. In his speech, he maintained:

> There is no possibility for us to assimilate the Albanians. [They] cannot be dispelled by means of colonization alone. They are the only people who, over the last millennium, managed to resist the nucleus of our state. If we proceed on the assumption that the gradual displacement of the Albanians by means of gradual colonization is ineffective, we are left with only one course – that of mass resettlement. In this connection, we must consider two countries: Albania and Turkey. [And] we will not stop at nothing to achieve this final solution.[12]

Cubrilovic used an old Turkish term for Albanians, calling them "Arnauts," and suggested referring to the Albanians simply as Turks. The term Turks had a specific function to play, of course, in the entire discourse of religiously othering Albanians as Muslims. As he went on to say:

> It is well known that the Moslem masses are generally readily influenced by religion and are prone to superstition and fanaticism. Therefore, we must first of all win over the clergy and men of influence through money and threats in order for them to give their support to the evacuation of the Albanians. Agitators, especially from Turkey, must be found as quickly as possible to promote the evacuation, if Turkey will provide them for us. Another means would be coercion by the state apparatus. The law must be enforced to the letter so as to make staying intolerable for the Albanians.

About a year after Cubrliovic's speech, some of his recommendations began to be implemented. Turkey signed an agreement with the Yugoslav Kingdom agreeing to take up 200,000 Albanian Muslims from Kosovo and 40,000 from Macedonia. Although there had been several waves of emigration of Albanians to Turkey before, this was forced migration. As de Rapper has documented, "Yugoslavia strove to organize the departure of Albanians on the basis of international agreements, and managed to provoke a wave of departures to Albania and Turkey" (De Rapper 2000). These efforts only partially materialized, because the Turkish government didn't ratify the agreement and World War II put the plans on hold. What is important to recall, however, is that in Serbian nationalistic thinking, the departure of Albanians was seen as part of "de-Islamization" and "de-Albanization" of these territories. Turkey was to serve as their receiving alien state, and in the agreement between Yugoslavia and Turkey, Albanian Muslims were already called Turks. In fact, the Albanian Muslims who were sent to Turkey were received under the category of national refugees.

In neighboring Greece, religious othering of Albanians as a discursive and policy measure was also in full swing. Following the annexation of the region of Ionnina and Çamëria,[13] that is between 1913 and 1914, Albanian Çams as they are known, were reduced to a linguistic minority. They could not receive education or liturgy in the Albanian language or have a separate Albanian Orthodox Church. Historically, Greece has denied any existence of an Albanian minority in Greece, but in the immediate aftermath of World War II, it is estimated that between 40,000 and 70,000 Albanians (largely Muslim Çams) were forcibly expelled from Çamëria to Albania. Their lands and property were confiscated, and their citizenship was revoked. The official Greek position was that Albanian Çam (Muslims) left on their own homelands to "avoid legal retribution after having collaborated with Nazis" during World War II. However, historical accounts have persuasively argued that the expulsion of Albanian Çams took place against the backdrop of the efforts to homogenize Greece ethnically and religiously.

In sum, from 1913 on, religious othering of Albanians was employed as a central mechanism of the rule over Albanian subjects outside the Albanian state. In Greece and Kingdom of Yugoslavia, although Islam was just one of the recognized religions practiced by Albanians, it became central to the discourse of religious othering of Albanians. Subsequently, this influenced not only the position of Albanians as citizens of the Serb Kingdom and eventually Yugoslavia but also in Greece. The purpose of depicting Albanians as Muslim others and constantly referring to them as Turks was, first, to negate their national or ethnic Albanian origin and, second, to either assimilate or force them to migrate to Turkey or Albania. Thus, the politicization of Islam didn't begin with Albanian Muslims but with their neighboring Orthodox states whose nationalism blurred religion and ethnicity.

Religious Othering of Albanians During the Godless Communist Era

The communist era found Albanians divided into two communist countries in the Balkans. In Tito's federal Yugoslavia, Albanians lived in Kosovo, Macedonia, South Serbia, and Montenegro, comprising the third-largest ethno-national group. Their position as a minority influenced their struggles for political and cultural rights. Yugoslavia was more tolerant of religious freedoms for the Albanians than of their political and cultural rights. The Yugoslav communists controlled religious institutions, including Islamic ones, by collectivizing religious property and turning it into state property. Clerics were paid state salaries, and liberal Muslim figures were incorporated into the Communist state apparatus. The slogan of Communist Yugoslavia was "brotherhood and unity" which was an effort to forge a supranational identity in the federation.

In Albania itself, Albanians of different religions lived harmoniously during the first half of the 20th century. Under King Zogu, the Albanian government reformed its religious institutions, including the Islamic ones. It abolished sharia courts as early as 1929 and banned the veil in 1937. At the time that the Yugoslav Kingdom was trying to Slavicize Islamic institutions as part of its de-Albanization policies in Kosovo and Macedonia, in Albania itself, political struggles were never tainted with a religious flavor. One can argue that secularization processes developed more quickly in Albania than in Yugoslavia – even before the Godless communist era of the Balkan Peninsula arrived. Albanian intellectuals of different religious backgrounds played an essential role in the secularization of Albanian society. They utilized the notion of "European Islam" and the Albanian Bektashi legacy to galvanize support for these reforms and for the modernization of Islam (Clayer and Bougarel 2017, 117). It was not that religion didn't matter at all to Albanians. It mattered, but in the form of a guardrail of the Albanian nation's existence and as an exceptional case of religious tolerance and as an indication of a progressive European society.

Enver Hoxha, the infamous dictator who ruled Albania for 41 years, was a son of a Muslim imam. In fact, in Albanian, Hoxha means Muslim teacher. But this personal history did not prevent him from banning religion altogether. Between 1967 and 1990, Albania was officially the first atheist state in the world. Hoxha's declaration of war on *religion as such* led to severe persecutions and the destruction of important cultural sites and heritage. He banned the use of religious names, fasting during Ramadan, and religious dietary rules such as not eating pork. He turned mosques and monasteries into Marxist cultural centers. Because of Albania's entrenched religious diversity, the war on religion could be waged against all religions, and although evidence suggests that he was little harsher with Islam, Hoxha's regime did precisely that; there are accounts of murdered Muslim clerics and Catholics priests buried together in the same grave.

Interestingly, though Albanians in Kosovo and Macedonia enjoyed much more religious freedoms than Albanians in Albania in the communist period, during their political struggles for access to university and equal political rights in the Yugoslav federation, they never used religion to make their political claims. They remained loyal to the idea that the "faith of Albanians is Albanianism," even though religiously speaking, Albanian Muslims had a relative majority.

The end of the communist era in Yugoslavia was followed by the bloody disintegration of the federation. Before the Yugoslav wars began, however, political and religious figures had already brought religion back to the center of political life. After five decades of communist intermezzo, it was a communist turned overnight nationalist, Serbia's infamous President Slobodan Milosević, who discovered the relevance of religion in the new nationalistic epoch. It was in Kosovo, on 28 June 1989, on the occasion of the 600th anniversary of the Kosovo Battle, that Milosević rose to power. It is estimated that on that day, a million Serbs from Serbia traveled to Kosovo to stand at the site of the Battle and hear Milosević say:

> Six centuries ago, Serbia heroically defended itself in the field of Kosovo, but it also defended Europe. Serbia was at that time the bastion that defended the European culture, religion, and European society. Six centuries later, now, we are gain engaged in battles and are facing battles. They are not armed battles, although such things cannot be excluded yet. However, regardless of what kind of battles they are, they cannot be won without resolve, bravery, and sacrifice, without the noble qualities that were present here in the field of Kosovo in the days past.

When Milosević spoke about Serbia's role as a bastion of defense of Christian Europe against the Ottomans and of unfinished battles, he implicitly referred to the Kosovar Albanians. His speech suggested there were still Ottoman remnants in Kosovo in 1989, the Albanian Muslims. After 1989, religious othering of Albanians as Muslims returned to political life and was again fully incorporated into the Serbian-dominated Yugoslav state ideology. The Serbian Orthodox Church played an active role in highlighting the religious importance of the event. It played the nationalistic drums for Milosević; months prior to the Milosević's speech in Kosovo, the relics of Prince Lazar (Serbian prince who died at the Battle of Kosovo in 1389) were carried throughout the most important Serb-inhabited territories in Yugoslavia. Moreover, the place where Milosević held the speech was full of symbols related to Serbia's Kosovo myth. Just above his head stood the gigantic numbers 1389–1989 commemorating the 600th anniversary of the Kosovo Battle. There were images of the flower that were used as a symbol for Prince Lazar's blood and the Serbian Orthodox cross with a "C" on the four corners that means "Only Unity Saves the Serbs."

Similar to the interwar period under the Kingdom of Yugoslavia, Albanian schools and newspapers were closed down, and Albanian intellectuals were interrogated and prosecuted in Kosovo and elsewhere in Yugoslavia. Kosovar Albanians responded to these repressive measures by creating parallel institutions in education and healthcare and established a Kosovar Albanian government in exile which had its main seat in Germany. Their resistance to oppressive Serbian rule was initially peaceful. They called for an independent state of Kosovo and mobilized international support for it. However, the political struggle of Albanians in Kosovo and Macedonia was not framed in religious terms; it was entirely secular in nature. When the peaceful resistance movement of the Kosovar Albanians failed to create desired political outcomes, the Kosovo Liberation Army (UÇK) appeared on the scene, a guerrilla army fighting for the liberation and independence of Kosovo from Serbia. But neither the peaceful resistance movement nor UÇK used religion or religious symbolism to achieve their goals. It was for this reason that, unlike in Bosnia and Herzegovina, the Kosovar Albanian political struggle for liberation against Serbia did not attract support from the Muslim world. Moreover, an MIT report on the destruction of cultural heritage in Kosovo has shown that the Kosovar Albanians did not burn a single church until open war broke out in 1998–1999 (Herscher and Riedlmayer 2000).

At that time of open war and the NATO-humanitarian intervention in Kosovo, Serbia's military and paramilitary forces burned down some of the oldest mosques and Islamic libraries, destroying 218 mosques and other cultural institutions related to Albanian history and heritage. In 1999, Serbia's ethnic cleansing campaign forced more than 90% of Kosovar Albanians to flee to neighboring Macedonia and Albania. Neither the nationalistic political elites nor the Serbia Orthodox Church distanced itself from these events; in fact, Bishop Atanasije infamously stated: "We blame Milosevic not for trying to defend the nation, but for failing" (Harden and Gall 1999).

Conclusion

Religious othering was an essential dimension of politically othering and discriminating against Albanians in the 20th century. It was prominently espoused by Serbian nationalistic circles, whether literary figures, distinguished academics, state officials, and Serbian Orthodox clerics. Moreover, similar patterns can be found in Greek and Slav Macedonian discourses vis-à-vis Albanians. These discourses served de-Albanization processes linked to the minority status of Albanian subjects in the Serb and Greek conquered Albanian-inhabited territories after 1912. Albanians were religiously othered as "Muslims" even though in their self-and-collective imaginations, Albanians didn't identify themselves as Muslims per se.

This was because, unlike Serbian and Greek nationalisms, Albanian nationalism was secular and propagated a more linguistic, culture, and shared history-based notion of national belonging.

In these discourses, Balkan Christian neighbors have portrayed Albanian Islam in essentialist Muslim images as "Asiatic," "violent," and "barbaric." These terms helped to make the case that Islam never had a place in Europe and those who converted to Islam had no place either. With the demise of the Ottoman Empire, Balkan indigenous peoples such as Albanians and Bosnians (some of whom had converted to Islam) came under pressure to make a case for having their own nation-states. Christian Balkan states like Serbia and Montenegro, which attained their national independence early due to Russia's support, became particularly keen to dispute the ethno-national origin of Albanians. In this chapter, I show that they referred to them as either "Muslims" or "Turks," but not as Albanians. They were motivated by territorial expansionist ideas which for conventional reasons they clothed them in religious symbolism and religious nationalism. As citizens of the Serb-dominated Kingdom of Yugoslavia and Communist Yugoslavia, Albanians in Kosovo, Macedonia, southern Serbia, and parts of Montenegro became the minority with the fewest rights, though they were one of the largest minority groups in terms of numbers. In the long course of the 20th century, Albanians responded to this religious othering discourse and policy by putting emphasis on the "civil religion" of Albanianism, which lacks any religious elements, religious myths, and symbolism. Albanian Islam and its surrounding discourses and identities have been shaped by a unique context in the Balkans.

Notes

1 When using the term *Muslim*, I follow those scholars who use it in the "sociological meaning of the word Muslim." That is to say, while some of their social realities, self or collective understandings might be influenced by the historical legacies related to certain interpretations of Islam, the term Muslim doesn't indicate as such the level of religiosity.
2 Some of the most influential Albanian intellectual and political figures belonged to different faiths. For instance, Naim Frasheri was a Bektashi, Gjergj Fishta was a Franciscan priest, and Fan Noli was an Orthodox Christian.
3 Vilayet is a Turkish word that refers to a major administrative district or province within the Ottoman Empire.
4 Sami Frashëri was also an editor of an influential Turkish daily newspaper in Istanbul at that time.
5 The Bektashi lodges were mainly concentrated in southern Albania.
6 As Noel Malcom has persuasively argued, one important reason the Albanian elites insisted on building this anti-Ottoman discourse was the fact that there was a real danger that newly independent Christians states of the Balkans would be seen as the sole heirs of national struggles against the Ottomans and thus the only legitimate successors to the former Ottoman territories in the Balkans. See Malcolm (2020, 82).
7 The Ottoman rules came to an end with Balkan Wars (1912–1913), also known as the First and Second Balkan wars.
8 This is credited to Milojevic and Gopcevic. They were the first to circulate the idea.
9 See, for example, Jovan Hadzi-Vasilijevic.

10 The Kingdom of Serbs, Croats, and Slovenes, as it was officially called came into being in 1918.
11 Author's translation.
12 Cubrilovic's memorandum, original and English translation.
13 Çamëria is located in today's northwestern region of Greece.

References

Carnegie Endowment for International Peace. 1914. *Report of the International Commission to Inquire Into the Causes and Conduct of the Balkan Wars*. Washington, DC: Published by the Endowment.

Cesari, Jocelyne, ed. 2015. *The Oxford Handbook of European Islam*. Oxford: Oxford University Press.

Clayer, Nathalie, and Xavier Bougarel. 2017. *Europe's Balkan Muslims: A New History*. Translated by Andrew Kirby. London: Hurst.

Cvijić, Jovan. 1918. *La péninsule balkanique. Géographie humaine*. Paris: A. Colin.

De Rapper, G. 2000. Les Albanais à Istanbul [Albanians in Istanbul]. Dossiers de l'IFEA 3. Istanbul: Institut Français d'Etudes Anatoliennes, Georges Dumézil (IFEA). www.ifea-istanbul.net/dossiers_ifea/Bulten_03.pdf.

Duijzings, Ger. 2002. "Religion and the Politics of 'Albanianism: Naime Frashëri Bektashi Writings." In *Albanian Identities: Myth, Narratives and Politics*, edited by Stephanie Schwander-Sievers and Bernd J. Fischer. London: Hurst.

Freundlich, Leo. 1913. *Albania's Golgotha: Indictment of the Exterminators of the Albanian People*. Translated by R. Elsie. Peja: Dukagjini Balkan Books.

Goldhagen, Daniel Jonah. 2012. *Worse Than War: Genocide, Eliminationism, and the Ongoing Assault on Humanity*. London: Abacus.

Harden, B., and C. Gall. 1999. "Church of Milosevic's Rise Now Sends Mixed Messages." *New York Times*. www.nytimes.com/1999/07/04/world/crisis-balkans-serbian-orthodox-church-milosevic-s-rise-now-sends-mixed-message.html

Herscher, A., and A. Riedlmayer. 2000. "Monument and Crime: The Destruction of Historic Architecture." *Kosovo. Grey Room* 1: 109–122. Accessed August 18, 2020. www.jstor.org/stable/1262553.

Jonuzi-Krosi, Ismet. 2020. *E verteta per Organizaten "Besa": Dega e Tetoves me Rrethinë (1935–1944)*. Tetovë: Tringa Design Tetovë.

Kostovicova, Denisa. 2002. "Shkolla Shqipe and Nationhood." In *Albanian Identities: Myth, Narratives and Politics*, edited by Stephanie Schwander-Sievers and Bernd J. Fischer. London: Hurst.

Malcolm, Noel. 1998. *Kosovo: A Short History*. London: Palgrave Macmillan.

———. 2020. "Myths of Albanian National Identity: Some Key Elements, as Expressed in the Works of Albanian Writers in America in the Early Twentieth Century." In *Rebels, Believers, Survivors: Studies in the History of the Albanians*. Oxford: Oxford University Press. doi:10.1093/oso/9780198857297.003.0012.

Misha, Piro. 2001. "Invention of a Nationalism: Myth and Amnesia." In *Albanian Identities: Myth, Narratives and Politics*, edited by Stephanie Schwander-Sievers and Bernd J. Fischer. London: Hurst.

Müller, Dietmar. 2005. "Das Kosovo und die Albaner im Serbischen Nationscode, 1880–1914." In *Staatsbürger auf Widerruf: Juden und Muslime als Alteritätspartner im rumänischen und serbischen Nationscode ; ethnonationale Staatsbürgerschaftskonzepte 1878–1941*. Wiesbaden: Harrassowitz.

Redzepagic, Jasar. 1968. *Razvoj Prosvete i Skolstva Albanske Narodnosti na Teritoriji Danasnje Jugoslavije*. Pristina: Zajednica Naucnih Ustanova Kosova I Metohije.

Sevic, Zeljko. 2000. "The Unfortunate Minority Group-Yugoslavia's Banat Germans." In *German Minorities in Europe: Ethnic Identity and Cultural Belonging*, edited by Stefan Wold, 143–65. New York: Berghahn Books.

Shuteriqi, Dhimitër S., et al., eds. 1983. *Historia e letërsisë shqiptare që nga fillimet deri te lufta antifashiste nacional-çlirimtare*. Tiranë: Akademia e Shkencace e RPS të Shqipërisë, Instituti I Gjuhësisë dhe i Letërsisë.

Vickers, Miranda. 1995. *The Albanians: A Modern History*. London: Tauris.

Vokrri, Abdulla R. 1990. *Shkollat dhe arsimi në Kosovë ndërmjet dy luftërave botërore: (1918–1941)*. Prishtinë: Enti i Teksteve dhe i Mjeteve Mësimore i Kosovës.

von Ranke, Leopold. 1829. *Die Serbische Revolution: Aus Serbischen Papieren und Mitteilungen*. Hamburg: F. Perthes.

Wachter, B. Adrew. 1998. *Making a Nation, Breaking a Nation: Literature and Cultural Politics in Yugoslavia*. Standord: Stanford University Press.

8

OTHERING IN ISIS

Mark Juergensmeyer

"The Shi'a are devils," a former fighter for the Islamic State told me. He was one of the hundreds of jihadi warriors who had been rounded up, tried, and convicted after the fall of Mosul and the termination of the Islamic State's territorial control in Syria and Iraq. He was now beginning a long-term sentence in a maximum-security prison in Kurdistan in Northern Iraq. It was there that I was able to talk with several former fighters, including this tall 30-something bearded Sunni Arab, whom I will call Muhammad.

"But the Shi'a are humans, like you and me," I said in response. I said this not only because I had no animosity against Shi'a Muslims but also because Muhammad had earlier told me that when he was younger he had Shi'a playmates when they were children growing up in Mosul. "They were your friends," I reminded him.

"Yes, but that was before I learned the truth," he said. The truth to which Muhammad was referring was the ISIS apocalyptic ideology that cast Shi'a as heretics and worse – as incarnates of evil. This characterization made it possible to hate them, but more strikingly, to kill them with impunity. It is one thing to disagree with someone on religious grounds; it is quite another to see them as your mortal foe. It was the Shi'a, Muhammad explained to me, in league with Zionists and American Crusaders, who were conspiring against the Sunni Arabs and their ability to live full Muslim lives in a restored Caliphate. They could and should be stopped. He drew his finger across his throat to make the point.

At this moment, I began to feel somewhat uncomfortable. His reference to Americans included me, after all, and we were alone in the empty conference room, just the two of us and my interpreter. I realized at that moment that the ballpoint pen with which I was keeping notes could be used as a weapon. I quietly slipped it into my pocket.

DOI: 10.4324/b22926-9

Seeing me hide my pen, Muhammad grinned and said, "oh not you, professor. I just mean Americans in general." Though I didn't quite understand the distinction he was making at the time, I felt a bit relieved.

Imagining the Other

I knew why he disliked the Shi'a. It was not the Shi'a boys with whom he had played as a child whom he hated but the Shi'a in power after the fall of Saddam Hussein and the imposition of American rule. Muhammad's own father had been in Saddam's army, where he was well treated and well rewarded. The family was able to maintain a comfortable middle-class existence in the suburbs of Mosul. Muhammad's childhood memories were those of a pleasant, secure, and well-funded family reverie.[1]

All of that came crashing down when the American troops arrived and dismantled Saddam's army. Worse, the U.S. occupation government would not allow any former members of the military to serve in the new army. Legions of militia emerged, both Shi'a and Sunni, to fill the security gap. Mosul, it seemed to Muhammad, was on the battlefield of gang warfare. His father lost his job, and the family was suddenly plunged into poverty. Muhammad was 13 at the time, and the memories of the family tragedy were etched into his mind.

Two years later when al Qaeda in Iraq came recruiting, Muhammad was ready to join. When I asked him why, he looked puzzled as if his family's situation was a sufficient explanation. But then he gave other answers. He said he was curious, and besides, all of his friends were doing it. He met with some of the leaders and found them to be inspirational. At age 15 with no other prospects for his future, he joined the movement.

At first, he saw the al Qaeda movement primarily as a way of restoring power and dignity to Sunni Arabs. Unlike the global mission of al Qaeda led by Osama bin Laden, the Iraqi version was stridently anti-Shi'a. Its ideology portrayed the Shi'a as satanic agents and gave justification for any kind of assault against them and those that supported them. In Iraq after 2003, that meant the American military. Guerilla attacks against Americans along with Shi'a religious and government establishments were part of the movement's mission. Though when he first joined, Muhammad said that he didn't accept all of the ideas, but he knew that the Shi's were evil. He had experienced it indirectly in his own home.

After joining the jihadi movement, Muhammad served a variety of roles. It was very egalitarian, he said, in that they would rotate the duties of those who were involved with the organization. His job would be to help in transporting weapons, providing communications, and participating in fighting teams. In the early days, he said, there was a great sense of camaraderie among the militants and the sense that all were equal within it.

Within two years, however, Muhammad was arrested. He was part of a team that was cornered and captured. Although they did not have specific evidence of his committing crimes, he was culpable of being part of what was regarded as a terrorist organization. He was sent to a prison camp, Camp Bucca, in the extreme southern tip of Iraq near the city of Umm Qasr. The American military had taken over this detention facility when they occupied Iraq in 2003 and named it after Ronald Bucca, a New York City fire marshal who died in the collapse of the World Trade Center Towers in the 9/11 attacks.

Muhammad loved being in prison. "The Americans were so stupid," Muhammad told me, "thinking that they would punish us by putting us all together into this facility with nothing else to do but to learn from one another." The camp was nicknamed "Jihadi University" by the militants of al Qaeda in Iraq who were detained there. The inmates organized themselves into classes that were taught by the more experienced fighters. The subjects taught were Islamic theology, militant organization, and strategy.

It was in Camp Bucca, Muhammad told me, that his commitment to the movement changed. He became less concerned with anti-Shi'a support for Sunni Arab empowerment and focused more on religion and the promised Caliphate. He increasingly saw his participation in the movement as one that was a requirement of his religious duty to live a strict and righteous life and to punish those who were impediments to this rigid Islamic lifestyle. The prime impediments were the heretics, namely, Shi'a, and the invaders, primarily their American enablers. Hence, the goals of the movement were not changed, but his motives were transformed into one of a spiritual quest. His view of the enemy had hardened as well. He saw them now as demonic foes, agents of the devil and worthy to be annihilated.

After two years, Muhammad was released from prison. He was 19 years old at the time and ready for new adventures, though then the al Qaeda movement was largely moribund. Abu Musab al Zarqawi, the leader of al Qaeda in Iraq, had been killed, and the Awakening Movement designed by U.S. General Petraeus had armed traditional Sunni tribal leaders and their militia to turn against the jihadi movement.

Muhammad rejoined what remained of the movement but found that it was rife with infighting. The old spirit of egalitarian camaraderie had vanished. He got into fights with some of the other militants, one of whom stabbed him in the stomach. Muhammad lifted up his shirt to show me the scars that he still bore from that experience. After that, he retreated from active militancy. For a time, Muhammad lived a relatively normal life. He got married and fathered a daughter and worked at odd jobs. But he was waiting, he said, for the opportunity to return to the struggle.

He soon had his chance. In 2011, when movements of democratic protest associated with Arab Spring swept throughout the Middle East and new opportunities for Sunni Arab militancy emerged in neighboring Syria, Muhammad was thrilled. In 2012, he crossed over the border to join the jihadi activists. At first, he was associated with al Nusra. Then in 2013, when an Iraqi activist who had been in al Qaeda in Iraq started a new movement in Syria, Muhammad joined it. Muhammad admired the new leader, Abu Bakr al Baghdadi. He cheered when his home city of Mosul was conquered by ISIS in 2014, and when Abu Bakr al Baghdadi mounted the pulpit of the central mosque in the city to proclaim himself as the Caliph of the Islamic State.

Muhammad returned to Iraq to work with the movement. He was still with the military wing of ISIS, but increasingly, he became unhappy with the local leaders with whom he had to deal on a regular basis. He said that he was loyal to al Baghdadi as the Caliph, and admired the spokesperson for the movement, Abu Muhammad al-Adnani. But he found the local organization to be corrupt, self-serving, and ineffective. Though not formally resigning from the movement, he would just wander off from time to time and distance himself from it.

Paradoxically, it was during one of those times that he was again captured. He was in a gray area between ISIS and government territory when Iraqi soldiers identified him. His face was familiar, he said, since he had been associated with the movement for years. The trial and conviction came relatively quickly, and ever since he has been in the prison where I met with him.

What about now, I asked Muhammad. If he had the opportunity, would he join the movement again? It depended, he said, on the leadership. He did not like violence, he said, and thought that at times the militants in the movement went too far. But the movement had no choice other than to fight back militantly, he said, since the Shi'a oppressors were violent. So they had to respond in kind. If the Islamic State was actually established anyone within it had to live by its pure and rigid standards. They would have to convert or die. Christians were people of the book, they could buy their way out. But others, including Shi'a and Yazidi, would have to leave or die.

Muhammad had been attracted to al Qaeda and the Islamic State in part because it presented him with an exciting and radically new view of the world. It was one in which great cosmic forces were at work. This confrontation was a clash between good and evil that would usher in the last days of the planet and signal the arrival of the Islamic savior, the Mahdi. Though only the hard core of the fighters was propelled by this belief, at least Muhammad and some of the other Sunni Arabs in ISIS-controlled territory shared it. It was the dominant motif for the true believers of the movement.

This "ISIS apocalypse," as William McCants described it in a perceptive book with that title, is a kind of extreme variant of Wahhabi Muslim apocalyptic thinking (McCants 2015). Soon after the fiery leader of al Qaeda in Iraq, Abu Musab al-Zarqawi, was killed in 2006, his successor, Abu Ayyad al-Masri, turned to apocalyptic thinking to characterize the movement as the Caliphate that would emerge at the end times. He thought that the Mahdi would be coming soon and that the faithful had to act quickly to establish a Caliphate to receive him. His successor and self-proclaimed Caliph of the Islamic State, Abu Bakr al Baghdadi, shared that view. The name of the ISIS online magazine, *Dabiq*, referred to a town in northern Syria that was the location of the battle of Marj Dabiq between the Ottoman Empire and the Mamluk Sultanate in 1516. It was an ISIS belief that this town would be the location of the final battle between true believers and infidels that would usher in the apocalypse. For that reason, the ISIS leadership battled hard to retain control over the town, and when it fell to Syrian government forces in 2016, they renamed their magazine. The new name was *Rumiyah*, which also has apocalyptic significance, since the forces from Rumiyah (Rome, and by extension all of Europe and the West) would attack the Muslim forces and be defeated in the final apocalyptic battle.

The strict code of behavior and extreme brutality in dealing with perceived enemies are aspects of the ISIS movement that are grounded in some accounts of medieval Islamic history and practice. The relation between this kind of reign of terror and religion is problematic, however. One can claim that the ISIS policies are vicious because their religious understanding requires the faithful to act this way. More likely, however, their yearning for an intimidating form of extreme violence needed justification, which they found in ancient tradition. Either way, it is an eerie relationship between religion and extreme violence.

Many Muslims assert that the ISIS ideology is not true to Islam either in spirit or in history. Yet the leaders of ISIS claimed Muslim authority for their actions, strict shari'a law as the basis of their jurisprudence, and the promise of salvation for those recruited into its ranks. The religious credentials of al Baghdadi gave some credibility to this religious appeal. He was a cleric whose family claimed ancestry from the family of the Prophet. He received a PhD degree in Islamic Studies from the Islamic University of Baghdad (not Baghdad University, as is sometimes misreported, which is a secular state institution). His thesis was on how to perform proper recitations of the Qur'an (not Quranic studies, as sometimes reported).

Still, al Baghdadi knew the scriptures and the tradition of Islam better than most jihadists. Osama bin Laden had no religious credentials, for example; though he pretended to be an engineer, his college training was in business management. Ayman al Zawahiri was a medical doctor, and al Baghdadi's predecessor in leading al Qaeda in Iraq, Abu Musab al Zarqawi, was a street thug from Jordan. By contrast, al Baghdadi looked fairly legitimate. His credentials alone did not make the movement Islamic, however. Nor did the Islamic whitewashing of the regime's terrorist actions and cruel restrictions make them Muslim. The judgment is in the eye of the beholder. And to most Muslims, ISIS represented the antipathy of the faith. For the few, the true believers in ISIS' cosmic war, the movement constituted their whole world.

When Muhammad became a convert to this ISIS apocalyptic worldview, he was able to see his old Shi'a enemies in a new light. Not just as political foes but as subhuman transcendent beings. The language of the ISIS movement provided him with a virtual lexicon of othering hatred.

The Rhetoric of Othering

In surveying the language of othering in the Islamic State movement, I have largely relied on the articles in *Dabiq* and *Rumiyah*, the glossy online publications of the movement. Though these articles are in English in order to reach a global network of jihadi activists, the articles are peppered with Arabic terms, especially when referencing those who are considered as enemies or as those who are not true believers in the ISIS version of the faith. I have also considered many terms that were used in online postings on Twitter and Telegram, some in English and others in Arabic, that have been monitored by my own research assistants and others who have followed the communications among the far-flung jihadi network on digital social media. I am particularly grateful to my former student, Mafid Taha, for his help in identifying and translating these terms.

Perhaps the most common word for an ISIS "other" is *kafir*, anyone who deviates from the movement's apocalyptic interpretation of Islam. The term can also be transliterated as *kafr*, *kaffar*, or *karif*. Etymologically, the term comes from the root K-F-R that refers to farmers planting seeds in the ground and covering them with soil. By analogy, a *kafir* hides the truth or hides from the truth, either by an act of deviousness or indifference. It has come to mean any unbeliever or someone who rejects Islam. It is often associated with the word *shirk*, which means a believer in a false God or gods. In Islamic history, there has been wide variation in the use of these terms. They have not always been applied to people of the book, for example – Jews and Christians. In the ISIS lexicon, however, the term *kafir* applies to virtually anyone who is not a follower of the narrow apocalyptic Islamic theology that the movement propounds, including the people of the book.

Interestingly, this term also applies to other Muslims. ISIS was quite liberal in its application of the term *kafir* to anyone who did not abide by the narrow theology of the movement. This is the practice known as *takfir*, accusing others of being heretics. This process of othering was central not only to its theology but also to its organization. It created a sharp we–they distinction that was intended to heighten the sense of belonging within the ISIS community. Even more important, it gave license to hate – even kill – those who were in the category of "other."

The fellow Muslims that the ideologues of the Islamic State hated most were Shi'a Arabs. This is understandable given the political realities of Syria and post-Saddam Iraq. In Syria, even though the Sunni Arabs of Eastern Syria were the majority of the population, the Damascus government of Bashar al Assad privileged his own religious community, the Alawites, a Shi'a Muslim sect. The Sunnis in Syria felt that they were treated like second-class citizens and deprived of leadership in public life. In Iraq, the Sunni Arabs of Western Iraq had been a privileged class under Saddam Hussein, who was himself a Sunni, but after the U.S. invasion and occupation of the country, democracy was imposed, and this meant majority rule. Since the majority of Iraqis are Shi'a Arabs, their political parties have dominated post-Saddam Iraqi politics, and the Sunni Arabs in western Iraq, like their Syrian Sunni neighbors, felt like second-class citizens as well.

So it is understandable that the Shi'a were despised. They were considered the oppressors. But this attitude entered into ISIS theology in specifically religious terms. The Shi'a were regarded as *rafisdah*, "rejectors" of the true Islam. They were also called *murtadin*, apostates, or *mutajawiz*, transgressors. Perhaps the harshest term for Shi'a was *dajjal*, a word that means a deceiver, a false prophet who lures people to Satan. This view of the otherness of Shi'a Islam is expressed in the title of a special issue of the ISIS online magazine, *Dabiq*, that was headed "The Rafidah: From Ibn Saba to the Dajjal." This chapter was a purported history of the Shi'a tradition, though it never used the term "Shi'a," calling them *rafidah*, rejecters and *dajjal*, false prophets. It is this attitude toward Shi'a that greatly distinguishes ISIS from al Qaeda. Early on in their relationship when the movement that became ISIS was still related to al Qaeda, Osama bin Ladin and Ahman al Zawahiri attempted to dissuade ISIS from adopting such harsh rhetoric toward the Shi'a. But al Baghdadi and his colleagues were not deterred. They saw the Shi'a as their political foes, and worse – false prophets that could be killed with impunity.

Perhaps even more striking is that the ISIS ideology not only regarded Arab Shi'a as "others" but also viewed some Arab Sunnis as "others" as well. The Saudi imams are singled out as devious religious tricksters. The term that ISIS uses is *murtad*, apostates, a word applied to people who pretend to be Muslim but are not true believers. Because of their deception, they are even more despised than some of the more obvious enemies of ISIS. An article in the ISIS online journal, *Dabiq* (issue 13, page 7), is hardly subtle. It is titled, "Kill the Imams of Kafr." In the article, it says that the Saudi Imams are "undoubtably *murtaddin*." And it goes on to say that their "apostasy is even grosser than any other, having studied the clear texts proving their collapse into *kafr*." The diatribe against the Saudi Imams ends with saying that "they are truly nothing more than the slaves of *taghut*." In this context, *taghut* means "false gods," though the word originates with the term for stepping over one's boundaries. Over time, however, it has come to mean an apostate.

This othering of Saudi imams is all the more remarkable considering how similar the ISIS ideology is to Wahhabi Muslim beliefs. The Wahhabi reform movement of the 18th-century Arabian peninsula joined forces with the tribal leadership of the Saud family to create an imposing and powerful coalition of political and religious forces that dominate the country of Saudi Arabia even in the present day. The theology of Wahhabi Islam is very conservative, advocating a return to primal Muslim society and adopting the strict punishment and harsh restrictions of an earlier era of Islam. The sanctions for beheading as a punishment for some crimes such as adultery, for example, or cutting off a hand as a punishment for stealing, are practices that ISIS have in common with its similarly conservative Wahhabi kin. What ISIS finds revolting, however, is the easy familiarity that Saudi Imams and members of the Saud ruling family have with Western oil executives and political leaders, including the former U.S. President, Donald Trump. The article excoriating the Saudi imams in *Dabiq* was accompanied by pictures of the clergy in relaxed accompaniment with Trump and his entourage.

The sin of the Saudi imams – the thing that made them into "others" – was their familiarity with Crusaders and Zionists, the terms that most jihadis, including ISIS, have for Christian and Jews. The inclusion of Jewish and Christian people as "others" may seem a bit surprising, since the Qur'an and by extension Muslims throughout Islamic history have given special respect to Jews and Christians as "people of the book." All three of the Abrahamic faiths – Judaism, Christianity, and Islam – accept the Hebrew Bible as a shared scripture. For this reason, there has been some discussion within Muslim circles about whether they can be considered *kafir*. But this has not deterred the ISIS ideologues, who consider all Jews as Zionists and all Christians as Crusaders.

By calling Jews "Zionists," and Christians "Crusaders," jihadis are evoking the images not only of two non-Muslim traditions but also of particular facets of them that imply a hostility to Islam. The Zionist desire for a Jewish homeland on the turf of ancient Israel is, from the point of view of many Muslims, an imposition of non-Muslim culture and political control in the center of Arab Islam. The attempt of Crusaders in the 11th through the 13th centuries to assert Christian domination over the holy places in Jerusalem is seen as a similar attempt to remove Muslim control over what is one of its most sacred locations and humiliate Islam in the heart of the Muslim Arab world. These terms are effective, therefore, in transforming Jews and Christians from the people of the book who are part of the same Abrahamic family, to others – Zionists and Crusaders who are hostile to Islam. The fourth issue of the ISIS online magazine, *Dabiq*, is titled "The Failed Crusade"; it focuses on what ISIS regards as the unsuccessful attempt to eradicate the territorial control of the Islamic State in Syria and Iraq.

ISIS ideologues are aware, however, that many if not most Westerners are not all that religious. Though nominally Jewish and Christian, they are largely secular in beliefs and lifestyle. Hence, ISIS often speaks of Western culture as *dahri*, atheist – literally those who are limited by time – or as the attitudes of *mulhid*, or *mulhad*, or *al-mulhadin*, atheists or nonbelievers. These are terms that earlier in Muslim history referred to apostates or heretics but which have come to be applied to those who do not believe in any religion – secularists or atheists. Another term for secularists is *eilmani*, which can also mean "worldly."

More harsh terms for Westerners are *jahil*, which simply means "ignorant," in the sense of a child who is unaware of what is really going on, or *aljahil*, something like a clumsy oaf. The ISIS online magazine, *Dabiq*, also refers to Western leaders as *iblis*, devils or satans. In one article, Dabiq said that such Western leaders were truly nothing more than the slaves of *taghut*, idols or false gods. On more than one occasion, the magazine and online Twitter chatter talked about the U.S. military and its leaders as *khanazeer*, "pigs."

The prime hatred of ISIS rhetoric is toward Jewish and Christian political leaders and military, though clearly anyone associated with these faiths is tarred with their ascription to communities deemed Zionists and Crusaders. This even applies to Jews and Christians who are Iraqi by ethnic heritage and part of Jewish and Christian communities that have lived in the region for centuries. Though Arabic-speaking and Iraqi citizens, they are considered "others" not only because their religious traditions are not Muslim but also because they are associated even in a second-hand way with the dominant Zionist and Crusader politicized forms of Judaism and Christianity. Even though Jews have lived in the region since the first diaspora in the 6th century BCE, they still are branded as other by ISIS. Among the Iraqi Christian communities are Assyrians, one of the remaining pockets of a thriving culture that reaches back to biblical times. Assyrian Christians in Iraq speak an Eastern Aramaic language and are proud of their distinctive Middle Eastern heritage as one of the oldest continuous Christian communities in the world. But from the point of view of ISIS if they are Christian, they are tainted with the Crusader devils. A number of churches have been bombed in Iraq and within ISIS-held territories, Christians were treated as second-class citizens. An enormous number of both Jews and Christians have fled the country to Israel, Europe, or the United States.

Though Jews and Christians are the primary recipients of ISIS' othering, other religious traditions are also considered as outsiders, unworthy of respect. They are usually not mentioned in ISIS literature, largely because the movement does not interact with members of their faiths in any meaningful way. The general term, *mushrik*, "polytheists," is used for adherents of other religious traditions such as Hinduism, Buddhism, and Sikhism. Though this term clearly brands them as an "other," it is not as pejorative as the terms used for Jews and Muslims.

There is one non-Jewish and non-Christian religious group, however, for which ISIS has a special hatred. These are the Yazidis, a small religious community centered at Sinjar on the Western edge of Iraq's Kurdistan region near the border of Syria. Their homeland was a part of the territory that was overtaken and controlled by ISIS when the movement marched to Mosul in 2014 and proclaimed its Islamic State. To ISIS, the Yazidis were more than *mushrik*, idol worshippers and polytheists. They were *eibad alshaytan*, worshippers of the devil, and for that reason considered not just to be "other," but subhuman.

The ISIS treatment of the Yazidis is one of the great tragedies of the establishment of the Islamic State. The Yazidi faith is ancient, reaching back thousands of years before Islam and Christianity to ancient Babylonian religion. Some scholars suggest that it has Persian influences linked with Zoroastrianism and Mithraism; some have even suggested influences from ancient Vedic religion from India. Part of the Yazidi mythology is the divine reverence for the sun. They are branded as devil worshippers, however, because of another aspect of their mythology.

Yazidi cosmology asserts that at the beginning of creation, there were seven angels. One of them was Melek Taus, the Peacock Angel. In Yazidi mythology, the Peacock Angel is involved with the creation of humanity and comes down to earth for this purpose but refuses to bow to Adam, and returns to God. Many Muslims, however, including the ideologues of ISIS, identify the Melek Taus figure with Idris, the devil or fallen angel, who disobeyed Allah and was eternally damned. For this reason, the Yazidis long before ISIS have been incorrectly regarded as devil-worshippers. ISIS took up that epithet and raised it to a whole new level.

When the Yazidi homeland was conquered by the Islamic State, the ISIS warriors immediately branded the Yazidis not just as "others" but also as extreme others – devil worshippers and agents of satan. This meant that the ISIS fighters had moral permission to treat them in the most harsh terms. The Yazidi men would often be taken out and killed on the spot. The younger women would be taken into sex slavery, where they would be sold in auction houses to ISIS cadres who would bid small amounts of money for them. The older women would sometimes be impressed into household slavery chores. Younger girls and boys would also be impressed into slavery.

I met with one of these young Yazidi boys who had been captured and put into slavery. Our meeting was in a village near the northern Iraqi city of Dohuk during the fighting over the last vestiges of ISIS control in Baghouz in 2019. When I talked with him, Ayman had just escaped from ISIS control three days earlier. He seemed remarkably relaxed for a teenager who had been through such harrowing experiences, but he seemed glad to tell his story.

Ayman was born and raised in the main Yazidi town of Sinjar that was overrun by ISIS forces in 2014 when Ayman was only 11. First, his father and older brothers were separated from his mother, sisters, and himself, and he has never heard from the men in the family since then. ISIS cadres usually killed the Yazidi men almost as soon as they were captured. Later Ayman was separated from his mother and sister as they were taken away to be sold into slavery by ISIS, and they too have disappeared. The mother was most likely impressed into housework and the sister into sex slavery, though both may no longer be alive. ISIS was in the habit of killing its Yazidi slaves as they retreated from the territory that they had once held.

Ayman was also put up for sale as a slave, but only after he went through a forced transformation. ISIS tried to make a Muslim out of him. First, they changed his name. Then he was sent to Raqqa, the ISIS capital in Syria, and placed in a camp with boys from various backgrounds, though he was kept from interacting with any Yazidis. He was given lessons in the Qur'an and in the ISIS version of radical Islam. He was forced to speak only Arabic, and in time, he lost his fluency in Kurdish, his mother tongue.

When he was deemed sufficiently Muslim and his Arabic was up to par, Ayman was ready to be sold as a slave. He was put up for auction, and he was purchased first by a Moroccan ISIS volunteer in Syria who put him to work as a household servant, cleaning his rooms and helping in the kitchen. Things got worse when he was sold again, probably after the Moroccan fighter was killed, this time to a Saudi ISIS fighter with two wives who forced him to do housework and chores. He was subjected to regular beatings and various other kinds of abuse. I didn't pressure him for details, but he said it was the worst part of his captivity.

His captivity under the Saudi man came to end, probably because his master was killed during the last intense year of ISIS fighting. Ayman was still under ISIS control, however, and was commanded to become a soldier. He was now 16 and sufficiently able to fight. He was given a gun and a few weeks of training on how to use it, and he became one of the last ISIS fighters holding on to a sliver of territory between Syria and Iraq in Boubadran and Baghouz.

In the last week before I talked with him, when he was fighting for ISIS in Baghouz, he was struck by a mortar round and his right leg was shattered. He was carried off to a field hospital where a splint was attached to his leg and he was provided makeshift crutches. When he was able to walk, Ayman realized that the leadership structure of the ISIS fighting forces was falling apart in the intense battle for survival. Someone in the hospital whispered that he should simply flee. He did just that, hobbling out of the war zone at night to a checkpoint commanded by the forces he had been shooting at just hours earlier.

He surrendered to the Kurdish forces that were battling ISIS, explaining that he was in fact a captured Yazidi who had been forced to fight. He was brought back to a hospital near his old town of Sinjar, which had been destroyed during the ISIS control and in the subsequent battle to liberate it from ISIS. He was interviewed on Iraqi television, and by luck, people who knew his family saw the interview and informed his grandfather, the only known surviving member of the family.

His grandfather traveled to the hospital for a tearful reunion and brought the boy back to the village where I met them the next day after they arrived. Both Ayman and his grandfather seemed eager to tell the story of what had happened to the family. Ayman was remarkably composed despite the trauma of five years of slavery and a dramatic escape. At times he laughed when he recounted some of the odd things that happened to him. But his face darkened when discussing the worst of his experiences, the beatings, the violence, and the abuse.

Everyone Is Other

As Ayman's story tragically reveals, there are dark consequences to being dubbed an "other" by ISIS. It is not just a matter of social ostracism or being treated as a second-class citizen. In the case of Yazidis such as Ayman, it could justify persecution, slavery, and death.

As the months of ISIS control moved into years, the movement gradually began to turn in on itself. The othering that was initially reserved for non-Sunni Muslims (with the exception of Saudi imams), Christians, Jews, and other religious communities, began to be applied to those Sunni Arabs whom leaders within the movement did not respect or trust.

Several of the men who had escaped from ISIS control and were encamped in refugee camps in Kurdistan told me that though they initially had supported ISIS control in Mosul, over time ISIS turned against their own people, including them. One of the men said that he was discovered to be smoking cigarettes and listening to Western music on his radio, music that was coming from a station in nearby Kurdistan. He was imprisoned for a month and lost his government-supported job. Another man listening to our conversation added a more gruesome story of his own. Though initially he supported the ISIS leadership and had a decent job as a result, when it was discovered that he had formerly been a policeman working for the Iraqi government, he was detained. For days, he did not know what his fate would be until one night he was taken out with a group of other men in the jail to a dark soccer field. When he heard the sound of gunfire, he realized that they were all marked for extermination. He dropped down to the ground and pretended to be dead. Later when the ISIS shooters had left the scene he crawled to a fence and escaped, eventually arriving in the refugee camp, alive to tell the story.

Muhammad, the ISIS warrior with whom I had a conversation in a Kurdistan prison, never abandoned his belief in the ISIS caliphate ideology. But he did reject the movement's organization, and for that reason he found himself to be an "other." He was harshly critical of the in-fighting and power-plays within the leadership of the movement, he said. He left the organization before he was caught and convicted. Now in prison, he is regarded by many of the other former ISIS fighters as a turncoat, and he has become a marked man. The warden, concerned about his safety, moved him to a more remote cell in the prison, where he isolated him from the rest of the prisoners. The warden thinks that Muhammad has rejected ISIS. But when I talked with Muhammad, it was clear that he was ideologically still a true believer. He had not abandoned the apocalyptic ISIS ideology. It was only the political organization of the movement that he criticized. Nonetheless, that was sufficient reason for many of his old colleagues to regard him as an "other," a concept that was increasingly growing in size. The paranoia of ISIS leadership seemed to regard almost everyone as other outside their inner circle. And even within it, many were suspect. The process of othering, it seems, is unending, and can expand at an almost exponential rate. As othering in ISIS has shown, it can even devour its own.

Note

1 This account of Muhammad's life is drawn from his narrative that is included in my book, Mark Juergensmeyer, *When God Stops Fighting: How Religious Violence Ends* (Oakland: University of California Press, 2022).

References

Juergensmeyer, Mark. 2022. *When God Stops Fighting: How Religious Violence Ends*. Oakland: University of California Press.

McCants, William. 2015. *The ISIS Apocalypse: The History, Strategy, and Doomsday Vision of the Islamic State*. New York: St Martin's Press.

9

THE RELIGIOUS AND THE SECULAR

Othering in Legal and Political Debates in Palestine in 2013

Irene Schneider

Yassir Arafat, founder of Fatah, the main branch of the Palestinian Liberation Organization (PLO) and, after the Oslo treaties in 1993–1995, the first president of Palestine, is generally considered a secular politician. His party was founded in 1959 as part of the anti-colonial struggle, and the leftist orientation of this liberation movement was, as Frode Løvlie argues, long taken for granted (Løvlie 2014, 100). Arafat himself, however, was not as staunch a secularist as one might have expected from his political career, especially with regard to family law: he is quoted as calling family law – and therefore the definition and regulation of gender roles and rights as well as definitions of masculinity and femininity – a "wasps' nest" (*ʿushsh al-dabābīr*).[1] While this might seem only to mean that he regarded it as a sensitive topic, further consideration reveals that there is more to it. Family law is administered in Palestine by Sharia Courts and those courts apply in the West Bank an old version of the Jordanian family law, the Jordanian Law of Personal Status (JLPS) of 1976, and in Gaza the Egyptian Family Rights Law (EFRL) of 1954, both of which draw heavily – as does most family law in Muslim states – on classical Islamic law, albeit codified and slightly modernized. After Oslo, and in preparation for what was hoped would soon be an independent Palestine, Arafat issued Decree 1/1994, which ensured that legislation and laws that were effective before 5 June 1967 in the West Bank and Gaza Strip would remain in effect. At the same time, he created the Sharia Court High Council (SCHC, *al-Majlis al-Aʿlā li-l-Qaḍāʾ al-Sharʿī*), nominating in 1994 Muḥammad Abū Sardāna as Supreme Judge (*Qāḍī al-Quḍāt*), equal to the rank of a minister (Welchman 2000, 89, 92). Representatives of the so-called Sharia establishment[2] thus gained great political and legal influence in Palestine.

In general, family law and gender relations are of particular importance for national identities and cultural authenticity. This is also true for Palestine, which in 2020 is still struggling, and hopefully not failing, to become an independent

DOI: 10.4324/b22926-10

state with its own national identity. Secular or religious? Rooted in traditional gender hierarchies or oriented toward gender equality? Family law debates, gender relations, gender roles, social and legal duties, rights and obligations of men and women toward each other and in the family, the construction of the family as the core of society, and culturally developed concepts of femininity and masculinity can be described as powerful markers of national identities and an important expression of cultural authenticities, in short as "pillars and weak points in the construction of identity" (Hélie-Lucas 1994, 393; see also Buskens 2003; Hammami 2004). By leaving not only the legal framework of the pre-Oslo time intact and waiting for a Palestinian family law to enter the picture but also giving such a religious institution as the Supreme Judge a prominent position as a quasi-minister, Arafat might well have implemented or at least deepened a secular – religious cleavage. The strong Palestinian civil society has fought since the 1990s (Moors 2003, 6; Hammami 2004) for a secular law, or at least a civil family law, to be developed parallel to the religious laws, while the powerful Sharia establishment, especially its conservative representatives, has been prepared to outlaw the secular part of Palestinian society as the other – and to establish itself as the "real" national identity of Palestine in what I call a hegemonic and powerful discourse.

In this chapter, I will analyze only one aspect of this highly fascinating debate and focus on one sequence of otherings in the discourse about a draft for a new Palestinian family law drawn up by a national committee created and commissioned by President Mahmud Abbas around 2010. My analysis is based on the Sharia establishment's refutation of that draft law, issued in the form of an influential Communiqué on 2 November 2013. This Communiqué rejected the 2010 Draft that had dared to challenge what the Sharia establishment considered its monopoly: interpreting Islamic law and creating or, better, controlling gender roles and a traditional gender hierarchy.

Othering is considered in this context as a process of not only creating one's own identity but also setting it against an identity that is defined as other, with the aim of disparaging that other and driving him/her out of the discourse by establishing one's own dominant position in this discourse. This chapter will focus not only on the linguistic way of doing this but also on the political process that it sets in motion. The structure of this chapter is as follows: after (1) an introduction to the theoretical tool of othering, (2) I lay out the Palestinian political-legal background to enhance understanding of the secular–religious tension in a modern Muslim state before I analyze (3) the Sharia establishment's text in detail. Finally, (4) I summarize with concluding remarks.

What Is Othering?

Othering is a process that uses discursive practices to form both hegemonic and subaltern subjects (Thomas-Olalde and Velho 2012, 27). It includes the creation of a collective self-image that is positive (Thomas-Olalde and Velho 2012, 29) and that allows the perception that "we are the good ones" and "they are the bad ones" to prevail. Historically based on several philosophical and theoretical traditions that cannot be outlined here (but see, for example, Jensen 2011, 64; Thomas-Olalde and Velho 2012, 28–40), it includes processes of essentializing and collectivizing the other, thus establishing it as a homogeneous group (Thomas-Olalde and Velho 2012, 30) that can easily be attacked. The concept of othering was and still is one of the key concepts of post-colonial theory. It was implicitly included in Edward Said's *Orientalism* (1994). Said, analyzing scientific texts about "the Orient" as well as political texts, journalistic pieces, literature, and travel books, pointed to the constructive character of "the Orient" created by Westerners. It was, he argued, a pure representation and not a "natural" depiction of the Orient to which without exclusion every scholar and writer adhered (Said 1994, 21). He concluded "that European culture gained in strength and identity by setting itself off against the Orient as a sort of surrogate and even underground self" (Said 1994, 3).

The term "other" was coined by Gayatri Spivak in her article "The Rani of Simur," which dealt with British rule in India. Spivak pointed out three dimensions to it. The first is about power: making the subordinates aware of who holds the power and thus making them see "[w]ho they are subject to" (Spivak 1985, 254), or, as Sune Qvotrup Jensen puts it, the "powerful producing of the other as subordinate" (Jensen 2011, 64). The second dimension concerns the sociological construction of the other as pathologically and morally inferior (Spivak 1985, 254–55; Jensen 2011, 65), and the third includes what can be labeled "knowledge is power," that "the master is the subject of science or knowledge" (Spivak 1985, 256), or, as Jensen puts it, that "technology is the property of the powerful empirical self, not the colonial other" (Jensen 2011, 65). Jensen describes Spivak's understanding of othering as a multidimensional process that can easily be combined with intersectionality and other approaches (Jensen 2011, 65). Ashcroft et al. point to the dialectical character of this process in which the colonizing other is created at the same moment as the colonized others (Ashcroft, Griffith, and Tiffin 2000, 156).

In this chapter, I add two further aspects to this post-colonial approach – Sadiq Jalal Al-ʿAzm's and Simone de Beauvoir's approaches. Al-ʿAzm (1981) has, in his reply to Edward Said, pointed to the fact that there exists also an "Orientalism in reverse" which leads to Occidentalism, the construction of the Westerners as others. He states: "Accordingly, in trying to deal (via its Orientalism) with the raw reality of the Orient, the Occident does what all cultures do" (Al-ʿAzm 1981, 355).

Perceiving and constructing the other happens not only between societies but also within every society. Individuals and social groups aim to create an own identity by differentiating themselves from the other. While the aspect of othering the "Orient" or the "Orientals" has – despite Al-ʿAzm's reprimand – been researched most often only for colonial, post-colonial, and neo-colonial dependencies of Asian and African states from (former) colonial powers, research on othering within societies has so far concentrated on the West and consisted mostly of studies on immigrants from Asia and Africa (see, for example, Scharff 2011; Thomas-Olalde and Velho 2012). Again the "Oriental," or person with Asian or African background, was the focus of European perception and constructed as the other.

The topic of this chapter has therefore been chosen deliberately to fill a research lacuna on othering among different parts of society in a non-European country, Palestine. It will focus on the opposites of the secular and the religious, a binary often ignored, as Muslim countries are considered to be molded by religion, monolithic, and lacking an open public debate.[3] This cannot be right, certainly not for Palestine with its vibrant civil society, strong women's organizations, and a secular past coming, as outlined earlier, from the context in which it arose as a liberation organization fighting an anti-colonial battle for independence and political equality.

The second addition, taking the concept of othering one step further, is the inclusion of the gender aspect. I am analyzing the question of family, which inevitably includes the construction of gender roles, gendered rights, masculinity and femininity, and equality versus hierarchy. Gender equal approaches are the aim of the civil society in Palestine and elsewhere in the Muslim world, whereas – generally, but there are of course exceptions[4] – the Sharia establishment defends a traditional patriarchal model of gender relations connected to a hierarchy which they root in the Quran. According to the often-discussed verse 4:34, for example, men are described as standing above women.[5]

On a very general level, societies – and Muslim society is no exception to this – divide into male and female and regard, as de Beauvoir (d. 1986) has outlined so succinctly in her book, the man as the norm, the starting point, and the woman as the other, the exception: "A man never begins by positing himself as an individual of a certain sex: that he is a man is obvious" (de Beauvoir 2011, 25).

With otherness being a fundamental category of human thinking: "And she is nothing other than what man decides; she is thus called 'the sex,' meaning that the male sees her essentially as a sexed being, for him she is sex, so she is it in the absolute" (de Beauvoir 2011, 26). She continues: "He is the Subject; he is the Absolute. She is the Other" (de Beauvoir 2011, 26). De Beauvoir points out that often in the past, women accepted this situation. "The tie that binds her to her oppressors is unlike any others" (de Beauvoir 2011, 28). Women have, she argues, only recently – referring to her living time – started to challenge their position as the other, especially as the subordinate (de Beauvoir 2011, 28–30). This is true for Europe as well as the Middle East, as both societies can be considered patriarchal societies in the past and still today.

The approach of this chapter is to combine these two perspectives with the approach of othering and to ask, as Oskar Thomas-Olalde and Astride Velho do, to what extent the term othering can help us to better grasp and understand hegemonic practices and processes of subject formation (Thomas-Olalde and Velho 2012, 27) not only in the Palestinian context but also generally.

Mapping Out the Secular and the Religious in Palestine

The emergence of modern Muslim nation-states after World War I and World War II turned the former early modern multi-ethnical, multi-lingual, multi-religious Muslim Empires like the Ottoman Empire that controlled the Middle East from the 13th century until 1922 and to which Palestine belonged, into new political and social entities. As James Gelvin argues, these pre-modern empires shared three characteristics: they did not interfere much in the day-to-day lives of their citizens, but expected the populations not to rebel and to pay taxes; they were governed by imperial elites who frequently were of a different religion and descent and spoke a different language than the majority of those they ruled; and, third, they rarely attempted to impose any sort of uniformity on their population with regard to language or culture or identity (Gelvin 2014, 15–16). The emergence of what Gelvin calls a "culture of nationalism" (Gelvin 2014, 17) not only transformed these empires into what is now known as modern nation-states – among them Israel and Palestine[6] – but also imposed a necessity to define an own identity. It thus launched processes of othering considered necessary to build up an own identity and nationalism.

Palestinian nationalism developed during the period between World War I and World War II, particularly during the British Mandate (1922–1948). Since 1922, the immigration of Jews to Palestine had been part of the policy of the British Mandate based on the Balfour Declaration. In this declaration, the British government "view[ed] with favour the establishment in Palestine of a national home for the Jewish people" (see Gelvin 2014, 81). When they arrived in Palestine, the Jewish people brought with them their form of nationalism, Zionism, molded in response to the violent antisemitic pogroms they were exposed to, especially in Eastern Europe (Gelvin 2014, 93). The Palestinians, as former subjects of the multi-ethnic and multi-religious Ottomans, were confronted with this strong Jewish nationalism and started to shape their own national identity. Helga Baumgarten identifies three more or less chronological phases: the Movement of Arab Nationalists, Fatah, and Hamas (Baumgarten 2005, 26). Whereas the Movement of Arab Nationalists represented the nationalist phase influenced by pan-Arabism, during which there was no separate Palestinian identity, Fatah was and is an "expression of a more Palestinian nationalism" in the context of the anti-colonial leftist struggle against the West, while Hamas embodies "Palestinian nationalism's religious variant" emerging in the 1980s after secular political models had failed according to the perception of the people of Palestine and the Arab countries (Baumgarten 2005, 26). Fatah was, according to Baumgarten, a "tru[e] mass-movement" until Hamas came along (Baumgarten 2005, 26). This development did not take place without tensions and, according to Mkhaimar Abusada (2010, 1–2), clashes between secular and religious groups intensified after PLO secularism failed to bring a solution to the conflict with Israel which had occupied East Jerusalem, the West Bank, and Gaza in 1967. The strengthening of political Islam was also triggered by the rise of the Israeli right, especially the Likud party, which came to power in 1977, Abusada argues, and the growth of Jewish extremists and their attacks on the Muslim holy shrines, the Israeli policy of land confiscation, and the spread of Jewish settlements in an area that was expected to become the State of Palestine (Abusada 2010, 2). Islam for many Palestinians became a source of hope and salvation from the Israeli occupation.

The tensions between secularism and Islam intensified, according to Abusada, after the PLO and Israel signed the Oslo agreement in September 1993 and the Palestinian Authority (PA) was established in 1994. Whereas Fatah supported the Oslo agreements and Arafat became the first president of Palestine residing in Ramallah, Hamas rejected them. Its opposition to the agreements stems from the fact that it saw the kind of autonomy agreed upon as more dangerous than the occupation and, in fact, as a reorganization of the occupation in a way more beneficial to Israel (Abusada 2010, 3). The tension between these two political Palestinian parties escalated in 2006 after Hamas won the parliamentary election. The struggle that followed led to a regional split with Fatah controlling the West Bank with the government and the parliament in Ramallah and Hamas controlling Gaza, establishing a second government in Gaza City. The parliament in Ramallah was shut down, whereas the parliament in Gaza City is still governing (summer 2020) under Hamas's supervision but is not recognized by Fatah or internationally (Brown 2012, 10).

The development of political Islam, the emergence of the PA as a quasi-state after Oslo, and the implementation of structures and institutions including a parliament and ministries in Ramallah and, after 2007, parallel structures in Gaza City are, however, only one side of the coin. The Islamic legal legacy has always been strong, especially in family law, as in all Arab and Muslim modern nation-states (Schneider 2014, 58–75). Arafat's decision not to repeal the existing laws, including the family law, and even to support the Sharia court system with the creation of the position of a Supreme Judge have had at least two substantial consequences.

First, the applicable laws, i.e., the JLPS of 1976 in the West Bank and the EFRL of 1954 in Gaza (see Schneider 2018), remained in force unchanged, whereas the neighboring countries, Jordan and Egypt, undertook substantial reforms – Jordan with the new JLPS of 2010 (Engelcke 2017) and Egypt with an important reform of the divorce law in 2000 (Sonneveld 2012). In Palestine, in contrast, while different drafts were discussed, no new law was passed and the political split between Hamas and Fatah made negotiations about a new Palestinian family law even more difficult.

There is, however, a Basic Law[7] that was issued in 2003, before the split. Several articles of the Basic Law are important in understanding the political situation and the struggle between the secular and religious camps for the development of a future new family law. According to Article 5 of the Basic Law, Palestine shall be a democratic parliamentary system, which is, according to Article 6, governed by the rule of law. According to Article 9, all Palestinians shall be equal before the law and the judiciary without distinction based upon race, sex, color, religion, political views, or disability.[8] According to Article 4 (1) of the Basic Law, Islam is the official religion in Palestine, and, according to Article 4 (2), the principles of Islamic Sharia are "a" principal source of legislation (Basic Law Article 4 (2)). But what does this mean? Asem Khalil, professor of law at Birzeit University, explained that the secular character of the Palestinian state was never intended to be anti-religious (Khalil 2009, 31). Article 4 is seen to be in a certain tension with 10 (2), according to which the Palestinian National Authority shall "work without delay to become a party to regional and international declarations and covenants." International law and human rights are often seen – especially by the traditional representatives of the Sharia establishment – as opposed to Islamic law. The Sharia establishment points to Article 4 (2) and the important role of Islam and Islamic law, whereas more secular jurists and women's organizations refer to Articles 9 and 10. There was a decisive step taken toward the implementation of human rights when, in 2014, and after vehement debates, Palestine signed the CEDAW (Convention on the Elimination of all Forms of Discrimination against Women)[9] and other international treaties without any reservations.

Second, Article 47 of the Basic Law states that the Parliament is the elected legislative authority. The President has, according to Article 43, the right to issue decrees amending the existing law in certain situations and he has done this in different legal areas,[10] but not in family law. There is, however, no right to legislate in the Basic Law given to the Sharia courts and its administrative system, the SCHC.[11] But this is exactly what the SCHC did de facto, and this is the second consequence of Arafat's lenient position toward the Sharia-based part of the legal system. The Supreme Judge Department of the SCHC has issued rulings (*taʿmīmāt*) in what can be called an extraordinary legislation process that de facto amends the existing family law. Yūsuf Idʿīs, Supreme Judge, for example, issued a ruling with regard to divorce based on redemption (*khulʿ*) which amended the applicable law (JLPS of 1976 in the West Bank).[12] *Khulʿ* is defined in Article 102 of the JLPS of 1976 as a divorce[13] according to which a woman may gain her freedom after paying back the dower to the husband – but only if he consents. Men, on the other hand, had and still have the unrestricted right to repudiate their wives whenever they wish in a divorce called *ṭalāq*, which can be translated as "repudiation" (JLPS Articles 83–101; EFRL Articles 67–77). In the new ruling of 2012, the Supreme Judge gave women the right to file a petition and ask for divorce only before the consummation of the marriage, in what was called judicial *khulʿ*, even *against* the husband's wish. Being a high religious authority, the Supreme Judge called the Palestinian society patriarchal (*mujtamaʿ dhukūrī*) and expressed his wish to protect women from men's oppression (Schneider 2016a). Applied in the Sharia courts since 2012, this ruling has, strictly speaking, amended the applicable law, despite not having been issued through one of the legal channels, the parliament, or as a presidential decree (Schneider 2018, 177–79). Rulings like these reflect the powerful position of the Sharia establishment, especially the SCHC and its head, the Supreme Judge (*Qāḍī al-Quḍāt*), who acted as a quasi-legislator in the realm of family law. More than 20 years after Oslo, in the second decade of the 21st century, the Supreme Judge, first appointed by Arafat in 1994, has become not only a powerful person atop the Sharia court system and the SCHC, both centers of institutionalized Islamic law and legal thinking, but he is also a prominent political player in Palestine (Schneider 2016a).[14]

The majority of women's organizations and civil society organizations fighting for (more) gender equal rights may be seen to have a more secular approach, voting for international law as laid down in CEDAW and being in favor of a new Palestinian family law as a civil and not a religiously influenced law. If this is not possible, they argue, there could be two parallel family laws: one civil and one religious (Schneider 2021, 200, 264), leaving it to the citizens to choose which one they want to refer to. In addition, scholars such as Hebron University professor of law Mutaz Qafisheh have advocated for reform of the family law that would adapt it to international standards. He discusses how the discrepancies between the two legal systems could be harmonized and international law could be translated[15] into the Palestinian context in legally sensitive issues such as divorce or marriage with or without a guardian (Qafisheh 2018). There are also representatives of the Sharia establishment such as the female judge Ṣumūd al-Ḍamīrī who argues in favor of a modernized Islamic law that gives women more rights (Damiri 2018). The women's organizations including WCLAC (Women's Centre for Legal Aid and Counseling),[16] WATC (Women's Affairs Technical Committee),[17] and the GUPW (General Union of Palestinian Women)[18] support such approaches. Different actors are invited to debates on these issues that take place in the Palestinian public and media and in which the traditional power of the Sharia establishment is contested.[19]

Muhammad Khalid Masud discusses the idea of "public" with reference to Pakistan and defines the public sphere "as a space that the modern media and mass education have helped to create and where public debates on issues of common concern are taking place" (Masud 2005, 155). For him, this space has at least two characteristics of publicness: a plurality of voices and a fragmentation of traditional authority. The public sphere for Masud is the site the traditional scholars have to share with lay members of society who publicly discuss Sharia (Masud 2005, 155–56). While the framing of this debate is religious, he states, and "it is not a secular critique, it is certainly not led or dominated by the religious 'orthodoxy' either" (Masud 2005, 155–56). What Masud describes for Pakistan is true for Palestine, too (see Schneider 2021, 14), where discussions about law but also other topics normally include representatives of the Sharia establishment and civil society, and to a lesser extent, the state. Debates are controversial and fierce and reflect an ongoing power struggle over the (future) identity of the Palestinian state.

The ICNL (International Center for Not-for-Profit Law), an independent global supervisor of civil society activities, states that Palestine, both the West Bank and Gaza, has an active civil society[20] and describes Palestine as "an exceptional case," explaining that "Palestine's unique history has in many ways proved conducive to the development of a vibrant and active civil society, by both regional and global standards" (ICNL, 12 July 2017; see also Shaʿbān 2016). By 1994, when the PA was created, nongovernmental organizations (NGOs) active in the region already had a long history of providing many essential social services. After coming to power, the PA attempted to assert heavy-handed control over these NGOs (ICNL, 12 July 2017) and when the PA produced a draft NGO law modeled on the highly restrictive Egyptian law, the reaction of Palestinian NGOs was swift and well organized. After a protracted struggle between the PA and the Palestinian civil society sector, the NGOs won what has been termed "a near total victory."

The aforementioned NGO law, finally passed in 2000, was for many years the most liberal and least restrictive NGO law in the Middle East (ICNL, 12 July 2017).

Othering the Secular: Communiqué (Arab. Bayān) of the Sharia Establishment of 2 November 2013

Since there is as yet no Palestinian family law, the difficult legal situation in Palestine is sensitive and hotly contested. Across Palestinian society, from state representatives to civil society organizations and representatives of the Sharia establishment in both Gaza and the West Bank, there is broad agreement that a new unified Palestinian family law is required. However, different actors disagree on what the law should entail. Should it be compatible with international law and thus support gender equal rights? Should it be more secular or religious, and, if based on Islamic law, which interpretation of Islamic law should prevail? Should it be a more moderate and modern version oriented toward gender equality and therefore more in accordance with international law, or a more conservative version in keeping with what is still a traditional society, preserving male privilege and curtailing women's rights, for example, in questions of divorce?

Several draft laws have been drawn up since the creation of the Palestinian Authority, as mentioned in the literature, for example, for the years 2001, 2003, 2005/06, 2007, and 2008; the early ones were, according to Welchman, provided by the Sharia establishment (Welchman 2004, 108–9; Goudarzi-Gereke 2018, 51–53). The parliamentary deadlock and the 2007 political split further diminished the chances of a unified law and the question of whether a unified family law should be introduced by presidential decree was raised. According to Ashraf Abū Ḥayyeh, a member of the civil society organization WCLAC, in 2007, the Minister for Women's Affairs, in cooperation with the Head of SCHC, forwarded a draft prepared by a presidential committee to President Abbas. Civil society, however, intervened and prevented the draft from being passed, pointing to a lack of consensus on family law among civil society groups and state institutions and demanding that civil society groups were to be given the chance to comment on the draft (Abu Hayyeh 2011). In 2008, the GUPW, the Ministry of Women's Affairs, and civil society groups issued the Charter of the Rights of the Palestinian Woman (*Wathīqat Ḥuqūq al-Mar'a al-Filasṭīniyya*) with basic rights for women, but this did not have the status of a draft law.[21] In 2010, a group of women activists met with Prime Minister Salām Fayyāḍ to discuss the issue but nothing came out of this (Abu Hayyeh 2011).

Around this time President Abbas took a fresh approach toward a Palestinian family law and created the National Committee of the Family Law (NCFL, *al-Lajna al-Waṭaniyya li-Qānūn al-Usra*),[22] overseen by Ḥasan al-ʿŪrī, his legal advisor. The idea was, as al-ʿŪrī outlined in an interview with me, to bring together different parts of society, such as representatives of the Sharia establishment, representatives of civil society, and, especially, women from the women's organizations, representatives of the universities, as well as specialists of the Ministries of Justice and Women's Affairs. It was not an easy task for him, he explained to me, and he knew he had to make a selection from among many experts in all areas.[23] However, this initiative shows that instead of issuing a presidential decree, Abbas wanted to initiate a wide-ranging discursive process among experts in different fields – law, society, and politics – and to bring about a draft law through intensive debates between representatives of the religious and the secular parts of society. The aim was to extinguish the "wasps' net" and replace it with a sound concept of how family law in Palestine in the 21st century should look. The result was the Draft Law of 2010 (DCAF 2012, 156–16), circulated as a Draft Law under the heading of the NCFL. Since the Sharia establishment used this text as the target for its critique, we must consider it in detail.

Draft Law of 2010

Before dealing with the draft law, a short introduction to Islamic law seems appropriate. Generally, to describe it in the frame of a Weberian ideal type, Islamic classical marriage and inheritance laws belong to the patriarchal type and are based on different rights and duties of men and women (Schneider 2019, 335). The husband is head of the family; as head of the family, he represents his family in public, is financially responsible for its well-being, and at the same time controls his wife's body and sexuality while having prerogatives such as polygyny, repudiation rights, and guardianship for the children. Women inherit less than men.

The lack of equal status between men and women lies in the fact that the marriage contract is concluded between the groom and the bride's guardian, not the wife herself, albeit not without the bride's consent (Schneider 2019, 335). The husband is obliged to pay the woman the dower at the beginning of the marriage and maintenance during marriage in exchange for her obedience, especially with regard to marital sexuality. Thus, money and sexuality are tightly connected. The dower is normally divided into installments, one paid at the conclusion of the marriage contract and the rest on the death of the husband or after a possible divorce (Schneider 2019, 335). The dower is the property of the wife, and she can deny consummation of the marriage until she receives it. However, after having taken the first part of the dower, during marriage, and while receiving maintenance from the husband, the woman is obliged to obedience with regard to sex, and she needs the husband's permission to leave the house, go to work, etc. If she does not obey, the husband has the right to stop paying maintenance and this is what Nadia Sonneveld calls the "maintenance – obedience relation" (Sonneveld 2012, 15), which can perhaps be renamed more generally as the "money – obedience relation." Whereas the woman owns her dower and the husband has no claim to it, there is in classical law no community ownership of gains accrued during marriage, and after divorce or death, no division of the money earned by the husband (or wife) during the marriage.

Access to divorce is not equal, either. The normal divorce, *ṭalāq*, which can also be translated as "repudiation," is a man's sole prerogative and it requires no reason and no court procedure; the husband can pronounce it wherever and whenever he wishes, even if his wife is not present. After *ṭalāq*, however, the husband has to pay the full amount of dower to the wife, if he has not yet done so, so that the wife can make her living. A woman needs either the husband's consent, in what is called the divorce of redemption (*khul'*) in which she pays back her dower to the husband, or specific reasons like the non-payment of maintenance to her for a long period. There are also cases of "dispute and discord," in which the woman has to file a court claim to prove her dispute.

Despite substantial changes, especially in divorce law and the Supreme Judge's ruling with regard to the judicial *khul'*, the general money–obedience relation is untouched in the majority of modern family law codes in Muslim countries.[24] This is demonstrated in the present West Bank practice in which a couple who wants to marry and goes to the court in Ramallah is informed by the marriage officer about the woman's obligation of obedience and the husband-to-be's obligation of maintenance (see the video at the end of the article of Abū Ṭaʿīma 2013).

The 2010 Draft Law is reproduced in a collection of laws and draft laws of the Geneva Center for Security Sector Governance[25] (DCAF 2012, 156). It has the official form of a Draft Law under the heading "The Draft Consolidated Law of Personal Status No. () 2010" and is introduced as being "Based upon the Draft Law submitted by the Council of Ministers and following approval of the Legislative Council" (DCAF 2012, 156). The Draft Law of 2010 departs from both the legal tradition described earlier and the applicable JLPS of 1976 in the West Bank on several points.[26] It defines marriage as a "contract between a man and a woman . . . equal in rights and duties" (Article 3 of the 2010 Draft Law). Dower is mentioned in several articles but is not seen as an essential part of the contract (in contrast to JLPS 1976 Articles 25–43). Article 13 of the Draft Law of 2010 states that every person who has reached marriageable age can enter into a marriage contract by himself/herself. The 2010 Draft makes it optional for a person to have a legal guardian (Article 13 (2)), but the language is gender neutral, "the person" may choose a representative; so it would also be possible for a man to choose a guardian for the marriage. In the applicable law and especially in the tradition of the society, the (male) marriage guardian for the bride is omnipresent (JLPS 1976 Articles 9–13), and her right to sign her own marriage contract is contested.[27] Article 58 (1) of the Draft law says that marriage ends with death or divorce; the word used for divorce is *taṭlīq*, which is normally used in modern personal status codes for divorce in court; the classical Islamic term for repudiation (*ṭalāq*) does not appear in the document. Article 58 (2) adds that there is no divorce outside the court, in contrast to the JLPS, according to which *ṭalāq* can take place outside the court and is a prerogative of the husband (JLPS Articles 83–87). He simply has to inform the court within 15 days, and the court then informs the woman about her divorce (JLPS Article 101). Whereas in the 2010 Draft, both spouses can file for divorce (Article 58 (3)) and both, or their proxies, must be present (Article 58 (4)), women in the applicable law need reasons to file a petition for a divorce as, e.g., non-payment of maintenance or "dispute and discord," which they have to prove (JLPS Article 127, Article 132). Article 59 (6) introduces a new rubric called "violence in all forms," which does not exist in classical law or the applicable law. According to Article 15 of the Draft Law 2010, marriage with more than one woman is only allowed with court permission, making polygynous marriages more difficult, but not prohibiting them. In the applicable law, the JLPS of 1976, it is still the husband's right according to Article 28 in which it is stipulated that he cannot contract a fifth wife, and in Article 40 according to which he has to treat his wives "as equals." A new aspect of Islamic law, and a demand of the women's organizations,[28] is the community of accrued gains during marriage, as defined by Article 99 of the Draft Law of 2010. This would benefit women getting divorced by compensating them for their efforts in the marriage looking after the household and raising the children.

The Draft Law 2010 shows new approaches with regard to judicial divorce and equality in marriage. On the other hand, it has kept several pre-modern forms of divorce; it does not seem to do away with the dower – which is the basis of the maintenance – obedience model – and restricts but does not abolish polygyny. It thus bears all signs of a compromise.

The Communiqué

To discuss the Draft Law of 2010, the Sharia establishment held a meeting on 2 November 2013 on what they called a "study day" (Schneider 2021, 69–72). The result was a Communiqué published on the internet (al-Bayān al-khitāmī 2013)[29] that criticized the 2010 Draft Law without quoting its articles in detail. To consider how othering worked in this context, I will analyze the Communiqué according to the following questions:

1 What is the critique of the 2010 Draft Law?
2 Who is the other, and how is he/she defined?
3 How does the Sharia establishment talk about the other: directly, indirectly; with or without value judgment?
4 Where does the Sharia establishment draw the line between its own position and the position of the other?

The Dean of the Faculties of "Mission and Principles of Religion" and "Quran and Islamic Studies" of al-Quds-University/East Jerusalem, Dr. Ḥamza Dhīb, had invited this group of scholars and practitioners. According to the list given in the text, the group that met on 2 November 2013 was made up of state representatives, but only Sharia judges, not representatives of the ministries. Besides the Supreme Judge himself, Yūsuf Idʿīs, four other judges of the Sharia courts and the Sharia Appeal Court were present as well as 14 professors or lecturers, mainly from the al-Quds University/East Jerusalem where the meeting took place[30] but also from Hebron-University and Nablus-University, with one Sharia lawyer. All were men, not a single woman took part in the meeting to discuss women's rights and their position in the Sharia even though as of 2009, there have been three female Sharia judges[31] (Schneider 2021, 53, 98–100).

After a long discussion, the participants presented the following recommendations and comments – to the public as a result of their "study day," which I paraphrase with some quotations:

1 The group wishes to stress the importance of the functional jurisdiction of the Sharia judiciary for implementing its full competence and that the competent authority in proposing any law or claims to reform it in connection with the personal status law is the *Dīwān Qāḍī al-Quḍāt*/Office of the Supreme Judge. This is in accordance with the Basic Law, which affirms the necessity of respecting the judicial authority and confirms the principle of separation of powers.
2 The implementation of bodies for interfering with the work of the Sharia courts without competent authority is against the laws in force and therefore it was inappropriate for the committee [the NCLF, Ir. Schnei.] to submit the Draft of 2010.
3 The Draft infringes on Sharia in regulations and principles and has fallacies and conceptual confusions. For example, giving women financial competence is not necessary; this results in marriage contracts that are void, and scenarios incompatible with Sharia are given to end conjugal life.
4 The 2010 Draft does not address many main Sharia regulations that are connected with Islamic jurisprudence of the family and must be addressed.
5 The organizations and associations presenting the drafts and laws of Personal Status Law went beyond Sharia regulations in their claim to fight discrimination against women. They want "absolute equality" (*musāwāh muṭlaqa*) between man and woman. This appears to be an "unjust claim" (*iddiʿāʾ ẓālim*) since Islamic Sharia does "justice to women" (*anṣafat al-marʾa*), preserves their "rights" (*ḥuqūq*) and "dignity" (*karāma*), ensures security, "maintenance" (*nafaqa*), and "protection" (*riʿāya*), and guarantees rights in inheritance and other matters.
6 The Draft goes beyond Sharia in many articles and marginalizes the role of family in social relations. It ignores the role of guardians in marriage contracts and has a negative impact on the structure of the family, which has to be protected according to the laws.
7 The confirmation of the positive role of the organs of the Sharia judiciary for the family and the endowments is necessary.
8 The Draft submitted by the committee [the NCLF, Ir. Schnei.] is excessive, especially with the backdrop of a draft issued by the Supreme Judge Department.
9 There is a need to create a consultative Sharia body composed of Sharia professors of the Palestinian universities for the provision of scientific well-founded advice to inform the Sharia judiciary.

10 There should be a bar association for Sharia lawyers to support their efforts and guard their rights.
11 Media campaigns have to inform the people about the jurisdiction of family law based on Islamic rulings and to eliminate suspicions leveled against these rulings.

As this was an informal gathering of quite conservative representatives of the Sharia establishment, the recommendations are not an official statement, even if members of the SCHC were present. Despite this, the arguments of this Communiqué were influential enough to strengthen the Sharia establishment's position in the discourse about a new Palestinian family law and wiped the Draft Law of 2010 presented by the NCFL off the table, as will be outlined later.

The recommendations refer to three content-related issues: first, a critique of the Draft Law of 2010 from the point of view of Islamic law as interpreted by the scholars present at the study day – interestingly with no reference to the applicable law, the JLPS of 1976 and no explicit references to the text and to specific articles of the Draft Law of 2010, which is criticized (see 3, 4, 5, 6, and 8); second, the claim that only the SCHC in Palestine can draft family law explicitly denying this right to the NCFL (see 1 and 2); this claim ignores the fact that President Abbas created this committee and invited all its members (including representatives of the Sharia establishment) to discuss and develop a draft for a new Palestinian family law; third, the proposal of measures to realize this claim (see 7, 9, 10, and 11).

With regard to the first question, the critique of the Draft Law of 2010 refers to formal procedures as well as to the contest of the law: there is no "authority" (2) for the NCLF – it is referred to as a "body" – to develop and discuss a draft law, this authority is only with the SCHC (1). The 2010 Draft marginalizes, the scholars argue, the role of the family in society which has to be protected according to the law. This is an indirect but very serious accusation, often given by conservative Muslim scholars, according to which gender equality would destroy the social fabric and thus endanger the whole society and political system (Schneider 2016b; Schneider 2021, 155; see also Sonneveld 2012, 102). The 2010 Draft contains, they argue, infringements of Sharia in regulations and principles of Islamic Sharia, giving women competence in financial matters, which is not necessary. Here the Communiqué perhaps refers to the Draft Law's suggestion of community of accrued gains during marriage (Article 99) which are divided after divorce. Furthermore, rights in divorce are mentioned, which are, according to Sharia at least as the authors of the Communiqué define it, not acceptable. What is meant here is the stipulation of the Draft that men and women have equal rights to approach the court to get a divorce and that divorce is in the court only (Article 58). This would deny men the right they still have today in Palestine to extra-judicial repudiation (*ṭalāq*), which only has to be registered later. The authors of the Communiqué consider a reform of this classical right of repudiation as incompatible with Sharia (3).[32] Again, these "scenarios" are not described – or refuted – in detail. Another infringement consists in ignoring the role of guardians of marriage (Article 13).

The focus of the critique is gender equality, with the Sharia establishment insisting that the equality demanded by the women's organizations is unacceptable (5). Here the Communiqué seems to refer to the general definition of marriage in Article 3 of the Draft Law of 2010, according to which marriage is a "contract between a man and a woman . . . equal in rights and duties." This contradicts the classical Islamic definition of marriage as a contract between a man and a woman who is "allowed to him."[33] The Communiqué also objects to gender-equal access to divorce and the de-centering of the dower as a substantial and indispensable part of the marriage contract and the general demand for "absolute equality" (see 5).

The Communiqué makes very explicit its belief not only that Islamic law and nothing else is the basis for family law, but also that only the SCHC has the right to define gender relations according to Islam, to interpret the law, and to launch the only acceptable interpretation; to state what is right according to Islamic law and what is an infringement; and, on the institutional and organizational level, to deal with this issue, draw up and promote the draft. The SCHC therefore demands support, and the Supreme Judge's office has to be strengthened by a newly created consultative body of Sharia professors (9) as well as a Sharia bar association (10). A media campaign will put forward these claims and prerogatives to the Palestinian public (11).

With regard to the second question, it is obvious who the other is and how he/she is described. The state is not mentioned, and the other is or are the organizations and associations presenting the draft. But which organizations? There are no names given; there is no talk of the civil society or its representatives. In the whole text, the definition of the other remains vague, while in contrast to this vagueness, the "we" is clearly defined: it is the *Dīwān* of the Supreme Judge; the Sharia jurisdiction is also named. The Sharia establishment and the SCHC defend their alleged privilege of drawing up the draft law as well as their monopoly on the interpretation of Islamic law, especially family law. The description of their powerful and superior position, their rights and prerogatives, aims, and necessary measures, is detailed.

This leads to the third question: how does the Sharia establishment talk about the other here, especially the women's organizations? Paragraph 5 is revealing in this regard and deserves a closer look:

> The *organizations and associations* presenting drafts (*mashāriʿ*) and laws of Personal Status Law go beyond the Sharia regulations claiming to fight *discrimination against women*. They want *absolute equality* (*musāwāt muṭlaqa*) between man and woman. This appears to be *an unjust demand* (*iddiʿāʾ ẓālim*), because Islamic Sharia does *justice* to women (*anṣafat al-marʾa*) and preserves her *rights (ḥuqūq) and her dignity (karāma)* and ensures her security and the *maintenance (nafaqa) and keeping custody (riʿāya)* and guarantees her rights in inheritance and other rights.
>
> *[Italics Ir. Schnei.]*

Here men talk about women and women's rights – just as de Beauvoir described in her perceptive analysis of gender relations. It is all about men defining women's rights; men's superior rights are taken for granted. They need not be mentioned; they are a given, and there is no discussion about why this is the case and why women do not have equal rights. The organizations and their position remain vague, as explained earlier, but their shortcomings are outlined in detail: they are endangering society by marginalizing its core – family (see 6). This is a serious accusation in a society which values family and marriage highly. They commit infringements, fallacies, and conceptual confusions (see 3). Thus, they do not have the necessary knowledge to deal with this topic; they don't do it correctly, and the reason is that they are not able to do it correctly.

The scholars behind the Communiqué accuse the other of a destructiveness that is almost criminal, based as it is on ignorance and incapacity. They do not consider it necessary to refute the organizations' position in detail, instead limiting themselves to a shallow and general refutation of the Draft Law of 2010. Obviously, the representatives of the Sharia establishment did not consider the Draft worthy of in-depth discussion and refutation.

In addition, they, especially the women's organizations (5), are described as (only) claiming "to fight discrimination against women," a formulation that suggests the CEDAW, the "Convention on the Elimination of all Forms of Discrimination against Women" because the word "discrimination" is not part of the Islamic legal vocabulary. The other, i.e., the women's organizations, are said to be aiming not just at "equality" – meaning gender equality – but "absolute equality." "Equality" is at the heart of the debates about Islamic family law because it (the Arabic word used here is *musāwāh*) is the term used in Articles 2 and 16 of the Arabic version of CEDAW; Arabic being one of the official languages of the United Nations.[34] As I have argued elsewhere, legal debates often focus on the (re)interpretation of terminology and this is especially true with regard to what can be called the translation of international law into the national legislation of Muslim nation-states.

Equality, however, means different things in different contexts and to different actors: the Supreme Judge, Yūsuf Id'īs, used it in his lecture to students of Birzeit University (winter semester 2013), for example, for the new version of divorce, the judicial *khul'*, mentioned earlier.[35] He argued that he gave women agency and access to divorce (before consummation of the marriage!) and called this new version of divorce "equality" (*musāwāh*). Ultimately, it can be said, women did gain broader access to divorce but they did not gain equality, as the right to unrestrained repudiation (*ṭalāq*) has remained the prerogative of men.

There is no mention of "absolute equality" in either CEDAW or the Draft Law of 2010. The Sharia establishment in the Communiqué hyperbolically rephrases "equality" as "absolute equality" to characterize the supposed demand for "absolute equality" not only as wrong, a fault, and a confusion, but, more importantly, as an "unjust demand." The Arabic word used for "unjust" (*ẓālim*) is religiously very loaded. In medieval state law, *maẓālim*, the institution charged with dealing with *ẓulm*, injustice, was an important pillar of the ruler's authority and his power to correct wrongdoings, reflecting his obligation to a just rule (Schneider 2006, 30–38). The Sharia establishment draws the boundaries between their own position, which they consider correct, and the position of the women's organizations, as reflected in the 2010 Draft Law, which is labeled as wrong. To want "absolute equality" is an "unjust demand" since Islamic Sharia already does justice to women and gives women their rights. This is why the others, i.e., the women's organizations, only claim to fight discrimination, but, in reality, cannot do this. It is an interesting linguistic ploy that diverts the debate toward another topic that is now no longer equality but justice. Equality is replaced by justice.

However, this newly introduced concept of justice is no gender justice but is defined as the traditional patriarchal form of gender hierarchy: Islamic law "preserves her rights (*ḥuqūq*) and her dignity (*karāma*) and ensures her security and the maintenance (*nafaqa*) and keeping custody (*ri'āya*)." "Keeping custody" (*ri'āya*) refers to the male position as head of the family. The language is using specific terms that appear in Islamic law and the Quranic verse, not quoted explicitly but obviously implied, is again 4:34: men standing above women. Islamic justice and the preservation of women's dignity are defined as contained in women's right to maintenance (*nafaqa*) and their submission to (needless to say: male) "custody" (*ri'āya*). The "maintenance/money – obedience model," with maintenance and the wife's obedience to the husband as pillars of the Islamic family system, is here confirmed not only as the only interpretation that conforms with Islamic law but also as just. The women's organizations' demand for equality, hyperbolized here as "absolute equality," is simply unjust and thus would lead to absurdity.

The Communiqué must be read as an indirect but firm rejection of international law that is supported by the other, here "the organizations and associations," i.e., the women's organizations, which was introduced and has been discussed since the establishment of the Palestinian Authority (Welchman 2004). It rejects the opportunity to deal with "equality," the term used in CEDAW Articles 2 and 16, and translate it into the Palestinian legal context or harmonize it with the Palestinian legislation. The Sharia establishment's very traditional interpretation is presented as being the right one, in accordance with Islam, and no other more modern interpretation presented by the women's organizations or other players in the Palestinian society such as Mutaz Qafisheh (2018), professor of Hebron University, is considered acceptable. There is a clear line between right and wrong, and they are wrong because they endanger society and want, in fact, to destroy it with their infringements, fallacies, and confusions. No room is left to debate the law with the other actors in Palestinian society or to search for compromise. Real justice and the proper actions against discrimination are only in Islam – more precisely, in the conservative interpretation of Islamic legal concepts represented by the scholars and judges present at the meeting at al-Quds University.

The representatives of the Sharia establishment at al-Quds-University ignored that different interpretations of Islamic law, what Shaheen Ali calls the "Operational Islamic Law" (Ali 2000, 7–8; Schneider 2014, 63–75), exist in the legislation of several Muslim states. For example, in 2000, Egypt reformed the divorce law with regard to *khul'*, redemption, giving a Prophetic word a new meaning after 1,400 years and giving women *before and after* consummation of the marriage the right to divorce against the wish of the husband (Denker 2004, 137–39). This ignorance is surprising, as the Supreme Judge, Yūsuf Id'īs, took part in the meeting and, as outlined earlier, authored the new ruling regarding the so-called redemption divorce in 2012. His ruling of 2012 can be considered at least one step forward toward more gender equality in the West Bank and has been applauded by women's organizations in the West Bank. Despite this, the Communiqué implies that there is only one decisive interpretation, that of the Sharia establishment.[36]

The Communiqué can thus be seen as a final statement against which no objection is possible. The discussion is finished, as the other cannot discuss these topics, which are the preserve of the (male-dominated and, in this case, very conservative) Sharia establishment. The other, i.e., civil society, is out of the game: women have no say in defining their rights. The male Sharia establishment acts exactly as de Beauvoir outlined: men are present; they set the rules; functionally, they even are the rules and thus are not required to have to justify them. They are the subject, the absolute; women are the object, the other, the one who is talked about but has no voice (de Beauvoir 2011, 26).

All of this comes despite the fact not only that – as mentioned earlier – there are different possible interpretations of Islamic family law that allow for more-or-less gender-equal regulations but also that President Abbas gave the NCFL committee the task of drawing up the draft law. The Communiqué also contradicts Article 9 of the Basic Law, according to which all Palestinians shall be equal before the law. All the dimensions of othering that Spivak developed can be found in this text, along with a "powerful producing of the other as subordinate" (Jensen 2011, 64). The women's organizations are shown "who they are subject to" (Spivak 1985, 254). The other is both constructed as such against an own identity – laid out in detail by the Sharia establishment – and labeled as inferior against the superior self of the Sharia establishment. Women's organizations are what Spivak called "pathological and morally inferior" (Spivak 1985, 254–55; Jensen 2011, 65), as they want to marginalize the family and thus endanger the whole society. They cannot design a draft law that is in accordance with (correct) Islamic legal thinking; what they have produced is full of fallacies and confusions. It is not just that women have lesser rights; they also have to be excluded from the discourse, because, in accordance with Spivak's observation, the Sharia establishment is "the master" and thus "the subject of science or knowledge" (Spivak 1985, 256). Obviously, this knowledge is seen as inaccessible to the women's organizations.

Concluding Remarks

The end of the story is quickly told: in the next meeting of the NCLF scheduled in the President's Bureau in Ramallah on 20 November 2013, i.e., only two weeks later, under the supervision of Ḥasan al-ʿŪrī's assistant, Muḥammad Hindāwī, the women's organizations were confronted with a new Draft Law, prepared by the Supreme Judge's Office, the Draft of 2013.[37] The civil society was taken by surprise, as Nihāya Muḥammad, vice president of GUPW, told me. She complained bitterly about the Presidential Bureau's decision.[38] She pointed to the difference whether a draft based on international law or one based on a conservative interpretation of Islamic law should serve as a point of reference and as a starting point of the debates and criticized harshly the traditional definition of marriage in the 2013 Draft, which she considered the core and kernel of the problem: not equal partners, but the woman being "allowed" to the man.

I was present for some time of this meeting and heard a heated and controversial, and at times very emotional, debate. As the discussion started with the first three Articles of the Supreme Judge's Draft Law of 2013, the debate was about the regulation of engagement. But even with this topic – a topic where there is normally no difference between the Islamic law and civil law – the severe split between representatives of the Sharia establishment and women's organizations became evident. There was no final agreement, and there has not been another session since.[39]

As of today, there is not only no Palestinian family law in sight, but also there is not, to the best of my knowledge, even a draft law in preparation. Debates in Palestine became more intense when Palestine signed CEDAW in 2014.[40] The signing gave women's organizations some foundation, and they delivered extra reports to the CEDAW committee in 2018 pointing to the state's weak position and the many changes that would have to be made to achieve harmony of the applicable laws with both CEDAW and the provision of equality in the Basic Law (CEDAW, July 11, 2018). However, since 2014, the SCHC has been led by Maḥmūd Habbāsh who has fought hard against the influence of international law, gender equality, and a more modern interpretation of Islamic family law (Schneider 2021, 272).

To come to the final question: is othering a useful concept the way it was used here: analyzing its linguistic aspects in detail and relating them to the social and political context? I would answer this question with yes because after carefully analyzing the Communiqué the strategy of this process of othering becomes obvious. It consists in attacking the other on the linguistic level; delegitimizing him or her while remaining deliberately vague in terms of details; labeling the other as inferior and accusing him or, in this case, her, of faults; claiming the right to define the topic; and claiming to be the only one with the necessary knowledge to speak. In the end, this strategy was successful and had the effect of excluding the other from further debate. We don't know exactly what happened behind the scenes and how the Sharia establishment succeeded in pushing the Draft of 2010 aside and putting its version on the table in the meeting of 20 November 2013. But we know that their strategy was successful.

Of course, the strategy of othering is not confined to the Sharia establishment. It would be interesting to look at the way women's organizations express themselves. In general, though, the civil society and women's organizations have never claimed an exclusive right to draft a family law. Their argument, as outlined earlier, has always entailed having both civil and religious law and was thus defensive. Even between 2014 and 2018, when there was wide debate about international law and human rights in connection with President Abbas signing CEDAW in 2014 and the first Palestinian report on women's rights being due in 2018, women's organizations could not dominate the discourse (see Schneider 2021, 344). In the end, neither side succeeded, and the lack of a new Palestinian family law leaves women trapped in court when they try to get a divorce against their husband's will, with daily problems in child care, and forced to marry with a marriage guardian. Not only women, and their more secular representatives, but also women in the Sharia establishment (Damiri 2018; Schneider 2021, 342) have a powerful voice. But not powerful enough to win the game, and the Palestinian state seems too weak to support them outright.

In the context of this research, and in connection with what Thomas-Olalde/Velho call important for the analysis of subject formation, political formation, and the recognition of dominant discourses, it turned out that the concept of othering offered an important additional insight into how the power struggle is fought. It turned out to be a useful tactic and thus part of discursive strategies in the political game, refining, as Thomas-Olalde/Velho argue (2012, 47), the analysis of power relations.

Notes

1 The saying attributed to Arafat was quoted on the television program *Ḥārisāt Nārinā* (9 April 2017) by the host.
2 This means not only representatives of the Sharia court system but also Sharia scholars of the universities of Palestine.
3 There is a substantial debate about the definitions of "secularism" and "secularity" in Muslim countries which I will, however, not touch upon here. I will outline my understanding of the secular later.
4 See Qafisheh (2018) and Damiri (2018).
5 See different translations: www.islamawakened.com/quran/4/34/default.htm, accessed 14 June 2019. Arberry translates it as "men are managers of the affairs of women." The original wording is *al-rijāl qawwamūna ʿalā al-nisāʾ*, which can be translated literally as "men are standing above women" (see Schneider 2014, 46–57). 4:34 is a difficult verse which has challenged contemporary feminist Quran exegesis, and there are also verses that seem to imply gender equality (see Schneider 2014, 36–42). For the struggle for a modern gender equal interpretation, see Schneider (2020).
6 By "Palestine" or "State of Palestine," I refer to the area of the West Bank with Ramallah as its administrative and political center, and Gaza with Gaza city and East Jerusalem which is according to international law seen as the future capital of a Palestinian state. I am well aware that the statehood of Palestine is contested and that Palestine is still struggling for its political and legal independency. However, in using this label, I refer to the use of the UN which speaks in the official documents since 2012 of the "State of Palestine" (Gharib 2012).
7 See www.palestinianbasiclaw.org/basic-law/2003-amended-basic-law, accessed 29 April 2020.
8 The applicable JLPS of 1976 and the EFRL of 1954 are not in accordance with this because many of their articles contradict gender equality (see in detail Qafisheh 2018).
9 See https://tbinternet.ohchr.org/_layouts/15/TreatyBodyExternal/Treaty.aspx?CountryID=217&Lang=en, accessed 18 April 2020.
10 See the database of the faculty of law of the University of Birzeit: al-muqtafi: http://muqtafi.birzeit.edu/en/, accessed 7 April 2020.
11 A corresponding institution exists in Gaza, too. See Schneider (2018); Schneider forthcoming.

12 For detailed information, see my forthcoming book *Debating the Law, Creating Gender*.
13 For the EFRL of 1954, applicable in Gaza, see Schneider (2018). The legislation in Palestine is available through al-Muqtafi, see fn. 10.
14 See Schneider (2016a). In what follows, I will concentrate on the development in the West Bank; for Gaza, see Brown (2012) and Schneider (2018 2021, Chapter 9).
15 For the terminology of translation of international law into national law, see Schneider (2015, 2020).
16 See Randa al-Sinyūra, Head of WCLAC, in an interview with me on 27 November 2017. For WCLAC, see *Markaz al-Mar'a li-l-Irshād al-qānūnī wa-l-Ijtimā'ī*, www.wclac.org/, accessed 14 March 2019. According to the website, WCLAC "is an independent Palestinian, not-for-profit, non-governmental organization that seeks to develop a democratic Palestinian society based on the principles of gender equality and social justice."
17 Surayda Ḥusayn, General Director of WATC, in an interview with me on 7 December 2017. No website found, see Swissinfo (4 February 2018) for a report that the Swiss government cut funding of WATC because of "suspected violent links."
18 *Al-Ittiḥād al-'Āmm li-l-Mar'a al-Filasṭīniyya* is part of the PLO and therefore not a civil society organization in the narrow sense of the definition, see http://gupw-lb.org/, accessed 14 March 2019, for the Lebanon branch. I could not find a link for the West Bank branch; however, GUPW is active on Facebook (see www.facebook.com/pg/gupw.palestine/about/?ref=page_internal, accessed 14 March 2019).
19 See fn. 1, referring to one of the TV programs in which one of these highly revealing debates took place.
20 For an overview, see the PNGO (Palestinian Non-Governmental Organizations) Network/shabakat al-munaẓẓamāt al-ahliyya al-filasṭīniyya, see English: www.pngo.net/; Arabic: www.pngo.net/?lang=ar, accessed 15 September 2018.
21 The Charter is available here: www.pal-tahrir.info/audio/files/law.pdf, accessed 18 September 2018.
22 This is what my interviewees told me but no specific date for the creation of the NCLF was mentioned.
23 Ḥasan al-'Ūrī, interview on 13 October 2014. For further information, see Schneider (2020).
24 For a comparison between the classical pre-modern law and the developments in modern times, see Schneider (2014, 63–75).
25 DCAF, see: www.dcaf.ch/, accessed 27 March 2020. For the text, see www.dcaf.ch/sites/default/files/publications/documents/Legal_Collection_Women_EN.pdf, accessed 18 April 2020. I was given my own copy in Arabic during my stay as a visiting scholar at Birzeit University, which I have not found on the internet or in the normally very useful database al-Muqtafi of Birzeit University/Birzeit.
26 Due to lack of space only, some important points can be picked out. I have chosen those to which the Communiqué of the Sharia establishment, dealt with later, seems to refer. However, as I will outline, the Communiqué does not refer to the articles of the 2010 Draft directly and only touches upon its content very generally.
27 Welchman (2000, 155) quotes different interpretations of these articles of the JLPS 1976 as to whether a marriage guardian is an obligation for an adult woman or not. The legal text is not clear, as Article 13 only exempts a woman who has been married before from the obligation to have a marriage guardian.
28 Mahā Abū Dayyah, Head of WCLAC at that time, interviewed on 30 November 2013.
29 The title was "Communiqué of the special 'day of study' for the discussion of the draft of the personal status law proposed by the 'National Committee for the Family Law (NCFL)'" (*Al-Bayān al-khitāmī, bayān al-yawm al-dirāsī al- mukhaṣṣaṣ li-munāqashat mashrū' qānūn al-aḥwāl al-shakhṣiyya al-muqtaraḥ min'al-lajna al-waṭaniyya li-qānūn al-usra*).
30 See www.alquds.edu/en, accessed 23 April 2020.

31 At the time, as far as I can see, all professors at Palestinian universities in the faculties of Sharia were men.
32 Several Muslim countries have connected all forms of divorce including repudiation to the court, see Welchman (2007, 107–32).
33 The vice-president of GUPW, Nihāya Muḥammad, explained to me in an interview on 24 November 2013, that the principal difference for her and for the representatives of the civil society was in this definition of marriage as a contract between equal partners.
34 See www.un.org/womenwatch/daw/cedaw/, accessed 21 January 2019.
35 See Schneider (2015) and for Palestine, see Schneider (2021, 163).
36 For a different voice from the Sharia establishment, see Judge al-Ḍamīri (Damiri 2018).
37 For a detailed analysis of this very conservative Draft Law, see Goudarzi-Gereke (2018).
38 Interview with Nihāya Muḥammad, 24 November 2013.
39 Interview with Ḥasan al-ʿŪrī, 28 November 2017.
40 CEDAW was not signed until 2014, but it was of course debated earlier in Palestine and women's organizations demanded the signature vehemently.

References

Abu Hayyeh, Ashraf. 2011. *The Experience of Personal Status Law Reform in the Occupied Palestinian Territory*. Ramallah: WCLAC.

Abū Ṭaʿīma, Nāhid. 2013. "Taḥqīq ṣuḥufī – ʿabāʾa al-raʾīs wa-l-maḥākim al-sharʿiyya," *Maannews [Maʿan]*, June 23, 2013. Accessed September 9, 2017. http://maannews.net/Content.aspx?id=607478.

Abusada, Mkhaimar. 2010. "Islam Versus Secularism in Palestine: Hamas vs. Fatah." Conference Paper, prepared for The Transformation of Palestine: Palestine and the Palestinians 60 Years after the 'Nakba,' Heinrich Böll Stiftung, Berlin, March 2010. www.boell.de/en/2010/03/12/islam-versus-secularism-palestine-hamas-vs-fatah.

Al-ʿAzm, Sadiq Jalal. 1981. "Orientalism and Orientalism in Reverse." *Khamsin: revue des socialistes révolutionnaires du Proche-Orient* 8: 5–26.

Ali, Shaheen S. 2000. *Gender and Human Rights in Islam and International Law*. The Hague: Kluwer Law International.

Ashcroft, Bill, Gareth Griffith, and Helen Tiffin. 2000. "Othering." In *Post-colonial Studies. The Key Concepts*, 2nd ed., 156–58. London and New York: Routledge.

Baumgarten, Helga. 2005. "The Three Faces/Phases of Palestinian Nationalism, 1948–2005." *Journal of Palestine Studies* 34 (4): 25–48.

Bayān al-khitāmī, al-. 2013. "ʿUqida fī Kulliyyat al-daʿwā wa-uṣūl al-dīn fī Jāmiʿat al-Quds, yawm dirāsī li-munāqasha miswaddat mashrūʿ qānūn al-aḥwāl al-shakhṣiyya al-muqtaraḥ min al-lajna al-waṭaniyya li-qānūn al-usra (Dhū l-ḥijja 28 1434/Tashrīn al-thānī 2, 2013)." *feqhweb.com*, November 2, 2013. Accessed September 8, 2017. www.feqhweb.com/vb/t17803.html.

Beauvoir, Simone de. 2011. *The Second Sex*. Translated by Constance Borde and Sheila Malovany-Chevallier. New York: Vintage Books.

Brown, Nathan J. 2012. *Gaza Five Years on: Hamas Settles in*. Washington, DC: The Carnegie Endowment for International Peace.

Buskens, Leon. 2003. "Recent Debates on Family Law Reform in Morocco: Islamic Law as Politics in an Emerging Public Sphere." *Islamic Law and Society* 10: 70–131.

———. 2018. "Info From Civil Society Organizations." July 11, 2018. Accessed January 7, 2019. https://tbinternet.ohchr.org/_layouts/treatybodyexternal/SessionDetails1.aspx?SessionID=1171&Lang=en.

Communiqué of the Special "Day of Study" for the Discussion of the Draft of the Personal Status Law Proposed by the National Committee for the Family Law (NCFL) see: Bayān al-khitāmī, al-

Damiri, Somoud [Al-Ḍamīrī, Ṣumūd]. 2018. "'A Female *Sharīʿa* Judge in Palestine between *Sharīʿa* and Law': Personal Experience." In *Uses of the Past: Sharīʿa and Gender in Legal Theory and Practice in Palestine and Israel*, edited by Nijmi Edres and Irene Schneider, 97–117. Wiesbaden: Harrassowitz.

DCAF (The Geneva Center for the Democratic Control of Armed Forces). 2012. *Palestinian Women and Security: A Legal Collection (2012)*. Geneva: Geneva Center for the Control of the Armed Forces. Accessed September 23, 2019. www.dcaf.ch/sites/default/files/publications/documents/Legal_Collection_Women_EN.pdf.

Denker, Hendrik. 2004. "Die Wiedereinführung des *ḫulʿ* und die Stärkung der Frauenrechte. Eine Studie zur Reform des Personalstatusrechts im islamischen Rechtskreis am Beispiel des ägyptischen Gesetzes Nr. 1 von 2000." In *Beiträge zum Islamischen Recht IV*, edited by Silvia Tellenbach and Thoralf Hanstein, 125–209. Frankfurt am Main: Lang.

Engelcke, Dörthe. 2017. "Law-making in Jordan: Family Law Reform and the Supreme Justice Department." *Islamic Law and Society* 24: 1–35.

Gelvin, James L. 2014. *The Israel–Palestine Conflict. One Hundred Years of War*, 3rd ed. Cambridge: Cambridge University Press.

Gharib, Ali. 2012. "UN Adds New Name 'State of Palestine'." *The Daily Beast*, December 20, 2012. Accessed September 10, 2018. www.thedailybeast.com/un-adds-new-name-state-of-palestine.

Goudarzi-Gereke, Lara-Lauren. 2018. "Perspectives on Palestinian Family Law: Divorce Regulations in the Qāḍī al-Quḍāt's Draft Law of 2013 in the Context of Current Legislation and Demanded Reforms." In *Uses of the Past: Sharīʿa and Gender in Legal Theory and Practice in Palestine and Israel*, edited by Nijmi Edres and Irene Schneider, 47–67. Wiesbaden: Harrassowitz.

Hammami, Rema. 2004. "Attitudes towards Legal Reform of Personal Status Law in Palestine." In *Women's Rights & Islamic Family Law*, edited by Lynn Welchman, 125–43. London: Zed Books.

Ḥārisāt nārinā. 2017. "Ḥārisāt nārinā: Qānūn al-aḥkām al-shakhṣiyya, Rāniyā Alḥamdulillāh," *Talfazyūn Filasṭīn/Palestine TV*, April 9, 2017. Accessed January 13, 2018. www.youtube.com/watch?v=rChZeOOJpe0.

Hélie-Lucas, Marie-Aimée. 1994. "The Preferential Symbol for Islamic Identity: Women in Muslim Personal Laws." In *Identity Politics and Women*, edited by Valentine M. Moghadam, 391–407. Boulder, CO: Westview Press.

International Center for Not-For-Profit-Law (ICNL). 2017. "Civic Freedom Monitor: Palestine." July 12, 2017. Accessed January 31, 2017. http://www.icnl.org/research/monitor/palestine.html.

Jensen, Sune Qvotrup. 2011. "Othering, Identity Formation and Agency." *Qualitative Studies* 2: 63–78.

Khalil, Asem. 2009. "Constitutional Framework of the Future Palestinian State." Working Paper presented within the context of the Project: "The Contours of a Future State": A Multi-part Compendium of Palestinian Thinking Commissioned by the Institute of Law – Birzeit University.

Løvlie: Frode. 2014. "Questioning the Secular-Religious Cleavage in Politics: Comparing Fatah and Hamas." *Politics and Religion* 7: 100–21. Accessed March 27, 2020. www.cmi.no/publications/file/4875-questioning-the-secularreligious-cleavage-in.pdf.

Masud, Muhammad Khalid. 2005. "Communicative Action and the Social Construction of Shari'a in Pakistan." In *Religion, Social Practice, and Contested Hegemonies. Reconstructing the Public Sphere in Muslim Majority Societies,* edited by Armando Salvatore and Mark LeVine, 155–79. New York: Palgrave Macmillan.
Moors, Annelies. 2003. "Introduction: Public Debates on Family Law Reform: Participants, Positions, and Styles of Argumentation in the 1990s." *Islamic Law and Society* 10: 1–11.
Qafisheh, Mutaz. 2018. "Without Reservation: Reforming Palestinian Family Laws in Light of CEDAW." In *Uses of the Past: Sharī'a and Gender in Legal Theory and Practice in Palestine and Israel,* edited by Nijmi Edres and Irene Schneider, 29–46. Wiesbaden: Harrassowitz.
Said, Edward. 1994. *Orientalism*, 25th ed. New York: Vintage.
Scharff, Christina. 2011. "Disarticulating Feminism: Individualization, Neoliberalism and the Othering of 'Muslim Women'." *European Journal of Women's Studies* 18 (2): 119–34.
Schneider, Irene. 2006. *The Petitioning System in Iran: State, Society and Power Relations in the Late 14th/19th Century*. Wiesbaden: Harrassowitz.
———. 2014. *Women in the Islamic World.* Princeton, NJ: Markus Wiener Publishers.
———. 2015. "Translational Turn and CEDAW: Current Gender Discourses in the Islamic Republic of Iran." In *Indonesian and German Views on the Islamic Legal Discourse on Gender and Civil Rights,* edited by Fritz Schulze and Noorhaidi Hasan, 133–65. Wiesbaden: Harrassowitz.
———. 2016a. "Recht und Geschlechterordnung: Gesellschaftliche Debatten um die ḫul'-Scheidung in Palästina 2012–2014." In *Beiträge zum Islamischen Recht XI,* edited by Thoralf Hanstein and Irene Schneider, 45–69. Frankfurt am Main: Lang.
———. 2016b. "Polygamy and Legislation in Contemporary Iran: An Analysis of the Public Legal Discourse." *Iranian Studies* 49: 657–76.
———. 2018. "Divorce Gaza Style: Regulations and Discussions in Gaza and the West Bank (2013–2017)." In *Islamisches Recht in Wissenschaft und Praxis,* edited by Hatem Elliesie, Beate Anam, and Thoralf Hanstein, 177–205. Wiesbaden: Harrassowitz.
———. 2019. "Family Law and Succession." In *Routledge Handbook of Islamic Law,* edited by Khaled Abou El Fadl, Ahmad Atif Ahmad, and Said Fares Hassan, 324–39. London: Routledge.
———. 2020. "Gender Equal Islamic Theology in Germany." In *Muslim Women and Gender Justice,* edited by Dina El Omari, Juliane Hammer, and Mouhanad Khorchide, 62–85. London: Routledge.
———. 2021. *Debating the Law, Creating Gender: Sharia and Lawmaking in Palestine, 2012–2018.* Brill: Leiden.
Sha'bān, 'Umar. 2016. "Sharākat al-sulṭa ma'a l-mujtama' al-madanī . . . al-intikhābāt al-baladiyya namūdhajan." *Palthink*, August 16, 2016. Accessed October 5, 2017. http://palthink.org/ar/?p=1319.
Sonneveld, Nadia. 2012. *Khul' Divorce in Egypt: Public Debates, Judicial Practices, and Everyday Life.* Cairo: The American University in Cairo Press.
Spivak, Gayatri. 1985. "The Rani of Simur. An Essay on Reading the Archives." *History and Theory* 24: 247–72.
Thomas-Olalde, Oskar, and Astride Velho. 2012. "Othering and Its Effects – Exploring the Concept." In *Writing Postcolonial Histories of Intercultural Education,* edited by Heike Niedrig and Christian Ydesen, 27–51. Frankfurt am Main: Lang.
Welchman, Lynn. 2000. *Beyond the Code.* The Hague: Kluwer Law International.
———. 2004. "Legal Context: *Shari'a* Courts and Muslim Family Law in the Transitional Period." In *Women's Rights and Islamic Family Law,* edited by Lynn Welchman, 99–111. London: Zed Books.
———. 2007. *Women and Muslim Family Laws in Arab States.* Amsterdam: Amsterdam University Press.

10

DISRUPTED LOYALTIES? 21ST-CENTURY SINICIZATION OF THE CATHOLIC OTHER

Christoph Zimmer

Introduction

Religious believers may find themselves torn between the demand for loyalty toward their nation and the religious institutions they belong to. In this article, I want to draw attention to how the phenomenon of religious othering can emerge and persist as a result of this underlying conflict over loyalty. I will argue that the intent of de-othering as reconciliation between the demands posed by state and religion will get distorted if the underlying loyalty conflict remains unsolved and continues to dominate the discourses of rapprochement.

One recent and striking example of a striving for this kind of de-othering can be found in the Sino-Vatican relations. On 22 September 2018, after a long period of tension, the Vatican press office announced that representatives of the Holy See and the People's Republic of China (PRC) had signed a provisional agreement on the appointment of bishops to "help to heal the wounds of the past, restore full communion among all Chinese Catholics, and lead to a phase of greater fraternal cooperation, in order to renew our commitment to the mission of proclaiming the Gospel" (Pope Francis 2018). Despite this rhetoric of de-othering, the rapprochement immediately incited sharp critique. Some bishops like the Hong Kong-based Cardinal Joseph Zen Ze-kiun regarded the agreement as a betrayal of Catholic believers who for decades were persecuted and forced underground by the Chinese government, and journalists and critics asked whether the agreement was "a deal with the devil" (Sherwood 2018; Harlan 2018; Horowitz and Johnson 2018).

I will present my argument in five sections. In the first section, I trace back the transition of the Catholic Other into a loyalty conflict between the Pope and the Chinese state in the years after the founding of the People's Republic. In the second section, amid the growing numbers of Christian communities in China, I give reasons why the Chinese leadership may perceive the Christian Other as a threat.

DOI: 10.4324/b22926-11

In the third section, I examine how the Chinese leadership currently deals with the dangers they perceive from Catholics and how they seek to keep the Religious Other under tight institutional control. In the fourth section, I focus on the primary means, which I term "guidance" and "Sinicization," by which the loyalty of the Catholic Other has been ensured. In the fifth section, I discuss the renegotiation of loyalties in the context of the 2018 Sino-Vatican agreement. Finally, I will put this case study into a larger historical perspective.

The Historical Emergence of the Catholic Other

Soon after Eugenio Pacelli (1876–1958) became Pope Pius XII in 1939, he ended the centuries-long Rites Controversy regarding Confucian ancestor veneration that had been a major obstacle to Catholic evangelizing in China (Pope Pius XII 1940). He was eager to set up a Chinese ecclesiastical hierarchy and appoint indigenous Chinese bishops. However, after the Chinese Communist Party (CCP) took over China and proclaimed the PRC in 1949, tensions between the Vatican and the new Chinese government rose again due to the CCP's attempts to insulate Catholic communities from foreign influences.

In two encyclicals, written in 1951 and 1954, the Pontifex addressed this issue, repeatedly condemning the expulsion of western missionaries and the attempt to divide the Catholic communities from Rome under the pretense that patriotism and loyalty to the Chinese State required such separation (Pope Pius XII 1951). He rejected the government's claim that the church was "an enemy of the people" (Pope Pius XII 1952) and emphasized that "the Chinese Catholics are second to no one in their ardent love and ready loyalty to their most noble fatherland" (Pope Pius XII 1955, 1958). But as hostility toward the Catholic communities in China grew, the Pope began praising believers "who, suffering severe difficulties, have been outstanding in their loyalty to God and to the Catholic Church, and so have been 'counted worthy to suffer disgrace for the name of Jesus' (Acts 5.41)" (Pope Pius XII 1955).

The perceived loyalty conflict seemed intractable, and despite all efforts to prevent a schism, in 1957, the Chinese government established the Chinese Catholic Patriotic Association (CCPA). Soon afterward, the first two Chinese bishops were ordained without papal approval. Pius XII reacted with a further encyclical *Ad Apostolorum Principis* (1958), in which he was more explicit about what he regarded as the true intentions of the CCPA:

> This association – as has often been proclaimed – was formed ostensibly to join the clergy and the faithful in love of their religion and their country, with these objectives in view: that they might foster patriotic sentiments; that they might advance the cause of international peace; that they might accept that species of socialism which has been introduced among you and, having accepted it, support and spread it; that, finally, they might actively cooperate with civil authorities in defending what they describe as political

> and religious freedom. And yet – despite these sweeping generalizations about defense of peace and the fatherland, which can certainly deceive the unsuspecting – it is perfectly clear that this association is simply an attempt to execute certain well-defined and ruinous policies.
>
> *(Pope Pius XII 1958)*

During the next half century, Chinese Catholics, both clergy and laypeople, who remained loyal to Rome and refused to join the CCPA, suffered persecution and were forced underground, forming an entity usually referred to as "Underground Church" (dìxià jiàohuì) or "Loyal and Steadfast Church" (zhōngzhēn jiàohuì) (Leung Kit Fun 1992; Bush 1970; Chan Kim-Kwong 1949). While Catholics loyal to Rome were suspected of treason and branded as counterrevolutionaries, imperialists, and feudalists by Chinese Communists, those who joined the CCPA were suspected of schism, sometimes even heresy by the Roman Church. In 1978, when Rome allowed surviving underground bishops to ordain priests and appoint successors – which led to the establishment of the underground Bishops' Conference in Mainland China in 1989 – Beijing quickly responded by founding its own official Catholic hierarchy, the Bishops' Conference of the Catholic Church in China (BCCCC) in 1980.

In the meantime, Rome maintained its undivided influence on Catholic communities in the British Crown Colony of Hong Kong, Portuguese Macau, and the Republic of China in Taiwan by running parishes, seminaries, hospitals, schools, and universities. The transfer of sovereignty of Hong Kong in 1997 and Macao in 1999 to the PRC, however, created a complex situation in which the Roman Catholic Church could legally operate in the special administrative regions but was officially banned from Mainland China. The ongoing persecution of underground Catholics unwilling to cut their affiliation with Rome provoked Pope Benedict XVI (r. 2005–2013) to write to the Church in China in 2007. He renewed his predecessor's critique of the Chinese state appointing bishops for the CCPA and emphasized the Petrine and episcopal ministries as "essential and integral elements of Catholic doctrine on the sacramental structure of the Church" (Pope Pius XII 1958), leaving little room for any rapprochement. On the contrary, he once more expressed his confidence that believers' "sufferings past and present for the Holy Name of Jesus and [their] intrepid loyalty to his Vicar on earth will be rewarded" (Pope Benedict XVI 2007a).

Against this backdrop of othering, the Holy See under Pope Francis (r. since 2013) announced on 22 September 2018 a provisional agreement on the appointment of bishops (Benedict XVI 2007a) and readmitted to full ecclesial communion eight Chinese bishops who previously had been ordained by the Chinese state without Papal mandate. Eventually, two underground bishops were replaced by their official counterparts. Regarding future appointments, it was agreed that Beijing would provide a list of candidates from which Rome would choose future bishops (Holy See Press Office 2018a). The Pope, however, admitted that this change of course might cause that believers who had stayed loyal to Rome during the last decades now "sense themselves somehow abandoned by the Holy See and anxiously question the value of their sufferings endured out of fidelity to the Successor of Peter" (Pope Francis 2018).

The Appeal of Catholic Otherness

How many religious believers are in China, and why have they been willing to suffer persecution at all? According to a white paper released by the Chinese Government in April 2018, the official number of religious believers is 200 million or approximately 14.2% of the total population; 38 million people are said to adhere to the Protestant Church (2.71% of the population), while 6 million believers are said to adhere to Catholicism (0.42% of the total population) with ca. 6,000 churches and places of assembly in 98 dioceses; 20 million people profess to Islam (1.42% of the population), and 136 million people practice religions like Daoism and Buddhism (The State Council Information Office of PRC 2016). In comparison, the CCP claims to have approximately 90 million members. These numbers reflect only those belonging to officially registered religious institutions; independent organizations in 2015 pointed to a far higher number of Christians, estimating there may be some 83 million Protestant Christians (6% of the total population), and 13 million Catholics (1% of the population). Around 70% of Christians are reported to live in rural areas and often belong to ethnic minorities. In places where the population is heavily shaped by ethnic minorities, there can be a Christian majority of up to 80% (Wenzel-Teuber 2018, 2020). However, the appeal of Christianity is by no means limited to rural areas or ethnic minorities. Until recently, Christian churches were both a common and frequent sight in the large modern cities of the PRC, attracting especially the young, ambitious, and urban middle class. Some models estimate that by 2050, the number of Christians in China will range between 71 and 450 million out of a population between 1.3 and 1.4 billion people (Hackett 2015).

The increasing number of Christians reflects a steady and growing appeal of Christianity that can be explained from different perspectives. As Humanistic Psychology and its most prominent exponent Abraham Maslow (1908–1970) point out, people strive to satisfy their higher needs for morality, self-actualization, and transcendence once more basic physiological, safety, and social needs are met (Maslow 1943, 1954). This explanation might be especially valid for the rising urban middle class in China that now enjoys greater material well-being. In addition, China is experiencing a large internal migration of laborers from the countryside to the growing metropolises and their surrounding satellite cities (Murphy 2008; Shen 2018); these migrants have brought their religious beliefs to the cities, fostering their spread. Non-Christian migrants who leave their hometowns are uprooted from their traditional social support networks (guānxì) and often experience isolation and insecurity. This makes them the preferred targets of Christian mission activities, as they offer networks of trust and mutual aid (McCarthy 2013).

Christianity's emphasis on charity might also seem attractive amid a yet not fully developed public welfare system.

Another reason for the appeal of Christianity is that, despite its role during colonial times, Christianity is still associated with what its admirers call a western way of life that promises not only a path to eternal bliss but also earthly well-being and individual dignity. In this context, some scholars point to the broad reception of Max Weber and his writings in current Chinese academia. Weber traces the origins of capitalism back to the Protestant work ethic, and some people might therefore conclude that being a Christian helps one succeed in a capitalist environment (Aikman 2003). Finally, for some, Christianity serves as an expression of protest against an increasingly materialistic culture, the moral void after the Cultural Revolution, and recent political campaigns that are demanding Chinese cultural self-confidence (wénhuà zìxìn).

The conversion to Christianity and Catholicism in the Chinese context potentially alienates believers from predominant values and state ideologies. This process of self-othering can go alongside the establishment of new loyalty ties apart from state and party. The total number of religious believers in general and the increasing number of Christians in particular potentially undermine loyalty to the Chinese leadership. This is especially the case when religious communities like the Catholic Church are closely affiliated with foreign entities that remain outside the reach and control of the Chinese state and Communist Party.

Handling the Catholic Other

On 28 August 2017, the State Council of the PRC crafted a new version of the "Regulation of Religious Affairs" (State Council of the People's Republic of China 2017), which came into force in February 2018. The new regulation provided a legal instrument to hold individuals accountable and penalize religious officials, who

> (1) preach, support and fund religious extremism, undermine national unity, divide the country, conduct terrorism or participate in related activities, (2) accept foreign control, accept unauthorized appointments by foreign religious groups or institutions and violate the principles of independence, autonomy and self-administration, (3) accept domestic and foreign donation by violating related national regulations, (4) organize or preside over unauthorized religious activities outside of venues of religious worship, (5) other behavior that violates law, regulations or rules.
>
> *(State Council of the People's Republic of China 2017)*

Accordingly, soon after the signing of the provisional agreement between the Holy See and the Chinese government in September 2018, state authorities increased efforts to register formerly underground Catholic clergy and force them to sign documents accepting the principles of independence, autonomy, and self-administration of the Church in China, i.e., adherence to the fundamental principles of the CCPA (Holy See Press Office 2019). Bishops and priests who refused to sign – including prominent clergy like Bishop Guo Xijin (b. 1958) and Bishop Cui Tai (b. 1950) – remained under house arrest or were put under it. Unregistered Catholic churches have reportedly been demolished, crosses removed, and holy paintings replaced by party slogans (Congressional-executive Commission on China 2018). Simultaneously, the Chinese state-controlled news agency Xinhua has reported that hundreds of districts have launched campaigns to battle "Evil Cults" and are targeting unauthorized Christian communities.[1] Exercising the right to religious freedom guaranteed by the Chinese constitution is henceforth only possible within the narrow framework of officially recognized and controlled religious associations.

State and Party Administration of Religious Affairs

With the purpose to control China's seven official national religious associations, the Administration of Religious Affairs was established in 1954. Until 2018, it used to be a department under the State Council, the formal government of the PRC (The State Council Information Office of the PRC 2016). Along with associations for Buddhism, Daoism, and Islam, there are four organizations that head the Christian communities, two of which oversee Catholic communities. One is the Chinese Catholic Patriotic Association (CCPA), and the other is the Bishops' Conference of the Catholic Church in China (BCCCC). Alike, the Protestant Church in China is characterized by a dual organizational structure, often referred to as "The Two Assemblies" (liǎnghuì).

In 2018, the Administration of Religious Affairs was moved under the supervision of the CCP's United Front Work Department. This agency's purpose is to protect CCP rule, manage potential opposition, and influence relevant individuals and groups inside and outside of China. The agency reports directly to the Central Committee, the party's highest organ. The shift of the department from a state institution to a party organ indicates narrower ideological boundaries and efforts to assure more compliance with the party's policies regarding religion. It further helps to frame religious affairs as a primarily domestic matter. However, despite the transfer, the leadership of the Administration of Religious Affairs remains constant.

The Revised Statutes of the Catholic Church in China

As officially recognized by the Administration of Religious Affairs, the Catholic Church in China as has a dual organizational structure. The CCPA is led by Bishop John Fang Xingyao (b. 1953), who since 2008 has been a member of the Chinese People's Political Consultative Conference, a high-ranking political advisory body of the People's Republic. The BCCCC is led by Bishop Joseph Ma Yinglin (b. 1965). He was a delegate of the 10th National People's Congress (2003–2008), and since 2008, he has also been a member of the Chinese People's Political

Consultative Conference.[2] The participation of both bishops in high-ranking state organs underlines their commitment and loyalty to the PRC and its ruling CCP.

In the framework of the Chinese political system, the double structure should reflect what the CCP calls the democratic leadership of the Catholic Church in China, consisting of both a top-down ecclesiastical hierarchy and a bottom-up administrative system. The competencies of the two institutions are not clearly distinct from each other and representatives of each institution take also positions in the other. Yet the structural division grants greater mutual control and therefore more compliance with the party's leadership.

In December 2016, both organizations revised their statutes.[3] They described their purpose in similar words:

> To uphold the principles of sovereignty, autonomy and the church's self-administration in the fields of politics, economy and church affairs, to protect the national sovereignty and the right to autonomy of the church. To adhere to the direction towards Sinicization and the adaption to the socialist system. To unite and guide nationwide clergy and laity in order to respect the national constitution, the law, regulation and policies and to play a positive role in social-economic development. To make contribution to protect the unity of the fatherland, the harmony of the society, peaceful relation between the religions, world peace.[4]

However, the revised Statutes of the CCPA (Chinese Catholic Patriotic Association 2017) add: "to protect the leadership of the Communist Party and the Socialist System . . . , to uphold the banner of patriotism. . . . To dedicate its powers to realize the dream of the great rejuvenation of the Chinese Nation."[5] Meanwhile, the statutes of the BCCCC (Bishops' Conference of Catholic Church in China 2017) emphasize that its purpose is "To promote the greater welfare of the nation, the society and humanity," and therefore have a slightly more international orientation. Despite reference to what one may call "greater causes" like the welfare of humanity, the statutes of the CCPA and BCCCC clearly reflect the primary intent to ensure Catholic believers' loyalty toward China's socialist leadership.

However, for the first time, the BCCCC's revised statutes refer to the Chinese bishops' common bond with the Roman Pope. The Pope's authority is acknowledged as far it is concerned with church doctrine. The new statutes therefore opened the door for rapprochements with Rome. Yet, to prevent any doubts where loyalty is due, the very same paragraph highlights that the BCCCC as an organizational structure is accountable only to the National Convention of the Catholic Church in China, a joint commission consisting of representatives of both the BCCCC and the CCPA.[6]

The most striking element of the statues is the appearance of two concepts: the CCPA refers to different forms of "guiding" (dǎo) more than ten times, while the BCCCC's statutes do so nine times.[7] Moreover, a "direction towards Sinicization" (Zhōngguóhuà fāngxiàng) is mentioned twice in the statutes of the CCPA (in contrast, God, Jesus Christ, and the Holy Spirit aren't mentioned at all) and twice in the BCCCC's statutes. The introduction of "Sinicization" – a term that started appearing in official speeches and documents around 2015[8] – is a major innovation in comparison to previous CCPA and BCCCC statutes.

Means for Ensuring the Catholic Other's Loyalty

The concepts of guidance and Sinicization, which are promoted in the statutes, are intended to play a key role in the process of ensuring the Catholic Other's loyalty toward the PRC and CCP rule. What do guidance and Sinicization in the context of the PRC's religious policies mean?

Guidance

Compared with the previous version, the new "Regulation of Religious Affairs" (2017) strongly emphasizes the State's role in guiding religions to adapt to a socialist society.[9]In concrete terms, places of worship must "accept guidance, control and inspection of local authorities,"[10] and local authorities are prompted to exercise their mandated right to regulate religious bodies.[11] The new Regulation broadly reflects the views of Wang Zuo'an (b. 1958), who has directed the Administration of Religious Affairs since 2009 and has served as vice-director of the United Front Work Department since 2018 (United Work Front Department of the CCP Central Committee 2020). Besides Wang's 2010 Chinese monograph, *The Problem of Religion in China and Religious Policies* (Wang Zuo'an 2010), his basic ideas and concepts are outlined in several articles and are often quoted word for word by high-ranking state and party officials. With his predecessor in the office as head of the Administration of Religious Affairs Ye Xiaowen (b. 1950), he can be considered the main architect of the PRC's religious policies.

In 2016, he published an article in *Xuexi Shibao*, the official mouthpiece of China's Central Party School. Entitled "Guidance is the Key of Religious Work" (Wang Zuo'an 2016), the article defines "guiding" by contrasting it to two other ways of dealing with religious matters, i.e., neglection and prohibition (Wang Zuo'an 2016). Wang declares himself in favor of guiding since it is the only one that takes three important features of religion into account, namely, its complexity, long-term character, and transformation: according to Wang, the complexity of religion consists in its entanglement with economic, political, social, cultural, and ethnic matters. Although he regards religion predominantly as a domestic issue, he warns that "Western countries – in the name of religious freedom – distort the religious situation in China and defame the national policy toward religion. Foreign powers using religion to infiltrate China and try to alter the ideology and the political system" (Wang Zuo'an 2016). He then connects the threat of foreign infiltration via religion with the so-called "Three evils," a term used to refer to terrorism, separatism, and religious extremism (Li 2019). Wang explains that China is still at the first stage of socialism and thus far from the material and cultural conditions that allow for an eradication of religion's origins. The complete prohibition of religion by force, he warns, might lead to the "error of pathological haste" alluding to the disastrous effects of the Cultural Revolution (Wang Zuo'an 2016).

Wang admits that, while in the past, religion attracted "elderly, women, rural people, people of low income and low backgrounds," it now increasingly attracts "middle aged people, urban dwellers, high-income people and those of higher education records."[12] Only the active guiding of religion meets the challenges posed by religion. But where should religion be guided to? Wang declares that the direction and ultimate objective of guidance are to "accommodate religion actively to the socialist society." More concretely, clergymen and the faithful

> are to be guided to ardently love the motherland, support the leader of the Chinese Communist Party, support the socialist system, to persevere on the road of Socialism with Chinese characteristics. They are to be guided to protect the unity of the motherland, the ethnic solidarity and social stability, obey and serve the greatest interest of the state and the common benefit of the Chinese Nation. The direction toward Sinicization is to be carried on; one has efficiently to guard against falling away from Sinicization and withstand foreign powers instrumentalizing religion to conduct infiltration.
>
> *(Wang Zuo'an 2016)*

He adds that this requires a high commitment of the Party and the State, which "have to do well at guiding, should not use compulsory methods, neither launch campaigns nor act indecisively" (Wang Zuo'an 2016). The emphasis on guiding and its praise as a golden key to religious matters is repeated in many other official and semi-official publications.

Sinicization

The 2016 revised statutes of the BCCCC and the CCPA both mention for the first time the "adherence to the direction toward Sinicization" as one of their purposes.[13] Two years later, on 8 October 2018, the BCCCC and the CCPA jointly issued a document entitled "Carrying on the Direction of Chinese Catholicism's Sinicization – A Five Year Plan 2018–2022" (Catholic Church in China 2018). The plan makes reference to speeches delivered by President Xi Jinping (b. 1953) advocating Sinicization.

The first of the plan's six features is a demand for the political, legal, and social identification of clergy and laypeople with the Chinese State, the Communist Party, and the Socialist System. Believers must be educated toward "Socialism with Chinese Characteristics" including "Xi Jinping Thought" and the nationally promoted 12 Chinese Core Socialist Values. Believers are further encouraged to stick to the principles of independence, autonomy, and self-administration of the Catholic Church in China. They should be educated toward the CCP's understanding of a rule of law and contribute to the economic and social development of China.

The second demand is that Chinese cultural consciousness and confidence should be increased within the church by organically connecting faith to elements of traditional Chinese culture. The Christian faith should be enriched by the Chinese humanistic tradition, while the history of Catholicism in China should be rewritten from the perspective of the Chinese Church under the aspect of Sinicization.

Third, the plan outlines the development of a theological framework with Chinese characteristics, summarizing past experiences of Sinicization, searching for examples of inculturation of the Catholic Church in other countries that shaped Chinese Catholic theology, and offering platforms for this research. The document mentions Chinese ethics, ideas of nature, and the concept of the unity of earth and heaven as examples of possible links between Christianity and Chinese philosophical thinking.

Fourth, the documents encourage believers to deepen their knowledge and understanding of the unique administration of the Chinese Church in China and its dual organizational structure. Fifth, Sinicization focuses on a liturgical reform that makes special efforts to embody traditional Chinese ritual practice based on experiences of past reforms and scientific research. A Chinese liturgy should adapt to local circumstances and pay attention to the ritual culture of ethnic minorities. New liturgical expressions should be tested in pilot projects.

The sixth proposition focuses on church architecture, painting, and sacral music, which should be in accordance with traditional Chinese aesthetics. Believers are to be encouraged to change their views that church art must be "western." A catalog of good examples should be compiled, artists with theological expertise should be trained, and the resulting efforts should be promoted.

The Direction toward Sinicization thus covers a wide range of political, sociocultural, theological, administrative, liturgical, and artistic aspects. Remarkably, it tries to justify certain features of Sinicization by seven references to official documents of the Second Vatican Council and their call for inculturation. At the first glance, it therefore appears to strive for a process of de-othering, marking a common ground between the Roman Catholic Church's authority and the Chinese government's efforts to ensure Catholic believers' integration into the socialist society.

Unfortunately, the five-year plan remains very vague and often tautological, proposing research and analysis of past examples of Sinicization without defining the concept. The broad allusions to a homogenous "Chinese culture" are unspecific, and terms like "Chinese ethics," "Chinese aesthetics," or "Chinese ritual culture" are themselves subject to debate, especially, if people strive for more than a folkloristic façade. But this is not the main problem; the real issue is that Sinicization in the five-year plan is primarily associated with current political ideologies and thus becomes synonymous with a process of bringing Catholic communities in line with Chinese Socialism. As "guiding" represents an extrinsic approach by which the loyalty of religious communities toward the PRC and CCP rule shall be ensured, Sinicization seems to aim at these communities' intrinsic adherence to the Chinese leadership.

Reasons for Renegotiating the Catholic Other's Loyalties

The 2018 agreement between the Vatican and the PRC is an attempt by both sides to renegotiate disrupted loyalties. On the one hand, the CCPA and BCCCC are acknowledged and thus reincorporated into the Universal Roman Church. On the other hand, Chinese citizens of Catholic faith are reintegrated into the socialist framework of the Chinese State. Although both sides share a rhetoric of de-othering and reconciliation, a further examination of the motifs behind the agreement unfolds the ongoing struggle of conflicting loyalties.

Benefits for the PRC

Domestically, the 2018 agreement not only increases the authority of the CCPA and the BCCCC over their members but also, due to the desired unification with the underground church, extends these institutions' influence over all Catholic communities in China. The principles of guiding and Sinicization can thus be implemented with the implicit approval of the Holy See. Paradoxically, the rapprochement with Rome gives the State and Party *more* influence and control. The fusion of the CCPA and BCCCC with the Catholic underground church means that its records, registers, and places of worship must be handed over to the official Chinese institutions. Former members of the underground church may face repression at their schools, universities, and workplaces. In the future, believers' known participation in church activities could presumably impact their score in the Social Credit System, a digital reputation system currently introduced in many parts of the People's Republic. Structures that might be suspected as a source of possible opposition to Chinese policies can be easier detected and eradicated. Sinicization as a vehicle for the official ideology that is primarily dominated by the Chinese Han majority can also take advantage of religious institutions to oppress Chinese ethnic minorities and ensure their loyalty to the CCP leadership. The rapprochement with the Holy See can be instrumentalized for the CCP's battle against so-called "evil cults" and thus to legitimate the persecution of other religious groups. Already in 2018, the Chinese Anti-Cult Association (CACA) – a platform for various social, religious, and legal institutions – referred to the Pope, quoting his critique of the "Church of the Almighty" from 2013, where he warned about "moral and physical violence, such as torture, kidnapping, poisoning and murder" (Su 2018). The rapprochement between the Chinese state and the Roman Catholic Church thus alienates Catholic communities from other religious groups that are not officially recognized.

Internationally, the recognition of the CCPA and the BCCCC as affiliates of the Universal Roman Catholic Church by the Holy See gives the Chinese government an opportunity to demonstrate its alleged commitment to religious freedom on the world stage. By means of the state-controlled institutions representing the Catholic Church in China, especially the BCCCC, the Chinese State is further enabled to exert influence on the Universal Roman Church and strengthen its global soft power. Finally, the agreement acknowledges Beijing's claim to have a say in the appointment and ordination of Catholic bishops, which means the Chinese government becomes a decisive factor in deciding the line of apostolic succession. This could serve as a blueprint for the Chinese state in similar religious controversies over the correct preservation of religious lineages, for instance in the appointments of Tibetan Lamas. Rome's concession to Beijing's role and say in religious matters can therefore be regarded as a huge symbolic victory for Beijing.

Benefits for the Holy See

Four days after the announcement of the agreement with China, the Holy See published a letter to the Catholics of China (Pope Francis 2018). In it, Pope Francis not only invites all "Chinese Catholics to work toward reconciliation" (Pope Francis 2018) but also states that "All Christians, none excluded, must now offer gestures of reconciliation and communion" (Pope Francis 2018). This striving for reconciliation reflects the encyclical *Evangelii Gaudium* (2013), which Pope Francis issued eight months after his election and which outlines a program for his pontificate. The document offers guiding principles in dealing with the secular society. Two of these originate in his conviction that "unity prevails over conflict" (Pope Francis 2013) and that "realities are more important than ideas" (Pope Francis 2013). This drive toward unity and the acknowledgment of realities echoes in his message to the Catholics of China: Pope Francis expresses his intentions "to support and advance the preaching of the Gospel, and to reestablish and preserve the full and visible unity of the Catholic community in China" (Pope Francis 2018). He calls on the Catholic community in China to unite and overcome the divisions of the past, which is marked by "deep and painful tensions, hurts and divisions, centered especially on the figure of the bishop as the guardian of the authenticity of the faith and as guarantor of ecclesial communion" (Pope Francis 2018). He explains the existence of the underground church as a result of an exceptional historical condition:

> When, in the past, it was presumed to determine the internal life of the Catholic communities, imposing direct control above and beyond the legitimate competence of the state, the phenomenon of clandestinity arose in the Church in China. This experience – it must be emphasized – is not a normal part of the life of the Church and "history shows that pastors and faithful have recourse to it only amid suffering, in the desire to maintain the integrity of their faith."
>
> *(Pope Francis 2018)*

Pope Francis then turns to the question of loyalty, writing that "[o]n the civil and political level, Chinese Catholics must be good citizens, loving their homeland and serving their country with diligence and honesty, to the best of their ability" (Pope Francis 2018). By highlighting the Catholic faith's demand for loyalty toward the country, Pope Francis is in strong accordance with traditional Catholic doctrine (USCCB 2000).

However, Pope Francis follows this by specifying these obligations and setting limits on citizens' loyalty toward their government, which resemble the Second Vatican Council (1962–1965) and its pastoral constitution *Gaudium et Spes* (Vatican Council 1966):

> On the ethical level, they should be aware that many of their fellow citizens expect from them a greater commitment to the service of the common good and the harmonious growth of society as a whole. In particular, Catholics ought to make a prophetic and constructive contribution born of their faith in the kingdom of God. At times, this may also require of them the effort to offer a word of criticism, not out of sterile opposition, but for the sake of building a society that is more just, humane and respectful of the dignity of each person.
>
> *(Pope Francis 2018)*

Although Pope Francis doesn't reference to the efforts described as Sinicization, the term finds its counterpart in the Church's concept of inculturation. Rooted in the Vatican Council's decree on missionary activity *Ad Gentes*, "inculturation" became a popular concept to describe: "the intimate transformation of authentic cultural values through their integration in Christianity and the insertion of Christianity in the various human cultures" (Paul II 1991). The concept allows a larger range of concessions to the local demands of Catholic communities while assuring close relations with the Universal Church represented by Rome. Furthermore, Pope Francis repeatedly stated that pastoral concern led to the 2018's provisional agreement (Pope Francis 2018). Half of the Chinese dioceses were without a bishop, and Chinese state officials used these vacancies as an argument to justify increased Chinese state intervention (Wenzel-Teuber 2017).

Eventually, a more subtle motive for the 2018 agreement may be the wish to protect Catholics from crackdowns like those other religious groups – Muslims Uighurs, Protestant Christians, Tibetan Buddhists, and adherents of so-called "evil cults" – currently suffer. Pope Pius XII's decision to expose millions of Catholic believers to persecution, discrimination, torture, and death due to his resistance to the CCP's interference with church matters might seem questionable in the context of today's ideas and Pope Francis's principle that "realities are more important than ideas." Rome's loyalty to Catholic believers in China could then be regarded as efforts to protect them from further othering and discrimination. However, this might raise questions about whether the Roman Catholic Church ought to show greater solidarity to those groups that cannot count on strong foreign protection.

Conclusion: Anything but New

From a historical perspective, the disputes between the Holy See and the state about the question of who is ultimately responsible to appoint clergy is anything but new. It reflects the centuries-old struggle between secular and spiritual powers and the question of to whom believers owe loyalty. Theologically, it finds its expression in the doctrine of two swords. Historically, the most famous example might be the Investiture Controversy in the late 11th and early 12th centuries, when the question of who has the ultimate right to appoint bishops turned into the election of an antipope, a Church schism, insurrection, and civil war. The historic controversy was settled by the Concordat of Worms (1122) granting Rome the exclusive right to appoint bishops while allowing the king's presence during their election, thus giving him an opportunity to protect his secular interests (Zey 2017). When the agreement between Pope and King was announced, it was – not different from today – accompanied by loud protest, and the concessions to the King were perceived as a betrayal of the Freedom of the Church (Schatz 2008). However, some European states like Germany still retain rights to confirm or reject the appointment of a bishop by Rome and due to concordats, some bishops still owe oaths of loyalty to the state or its constitution.

Similarly, confronted with critics arguing that Pope Francis sold the church out to Beijing, the Pontifex referred to historical examples like the Austro-Hungarian Empire, Portugal, and Spain whose emperors and kings once were also responsible for the election of bishops.[14] Above all, he emphasized that the provisional agreement is about a "dialogue about eventual candidates" and by no means a renunciation of Rome's right to appoint bishops (Burke 2018). However, in the Chinese case, the recent policies regarding religion, and the principles of guidance and Sinicization make the underlying loyalty conflict seem far from being solved. Despite an occasional rhetoric of de-othering in the context of the 2018 provisional agreement, all documents show strong efforts to transfer and ensure loyalty to the PRC and CCP rule. The underlying loyalty conflict might therefore even result in a new period of divisions among Catholic communities and enter a new cycle of othering.

Notes

1 The notion of "Evil Cults" has a long history in China (see Palmer 2008).
2 See Catholic Church in China (2017).
3 These statutes are: Bishops' Conference of Catholic Church in China (BCCCC), "Zhōngguó tiānzhǔjiào zhǔjiào tuán zhāngchéng [Statutes of the BCCCC]," further quoted as "BCCCC's Statutes"; and Chinese Catholic Patriotic Association (CCPA), "Zhōngguó tiānzhǔjiào àiguó huì zhāngchéng [Statutes of the CCPA]," Catholic Church in China (2017).
4 CCPA's Statutes, §3. See also BCCC's Statutes, §3.
5 CCPA's Statutes, §3 CCPA.
6 See CCPA's Statutes, §9; see also BCCCC's Statutes §9.
7 CCPA's Statutes §3, §4, §6, §12, §21, §22, §26, §41; BCCCC's Statutes §2, §3, §4, §6, §12, §26.
8 CCPA §3, §6. BCCCC §3, §6.
9 Religious Affairs Regulation, §4.
10 Religious Affairs Regulation, §26. The triptych of "guidance," "control," and "inspection" is sad to be a responsibility of "party member of all levels," see also Wang (2018).
11 Religious Affairs Regulation, §42.
12 Wang Zuo'an (2016). The conception of the phenomenon of religion around five characteristics – namely, its *long-term character*, its *mass character*, its *national character*, its *international character*, and its *complex character* – goes back to Ye Ziaowen, who was the *Director*

of the Bureau of Religious Affairs of the State Council from 1995 until 2009, when he was appointed Party Secretary of the *Central Institute of Socialism*. See also Ye (1996, 2000).

13 BCCCC's Statutes §3; ACPA Statutes §3.

14 He refers to the Spanish *Patronato real* and the Portuguese *Padroado* founded on provisions fixed in the Papal bulls *Inter Cetera* (1493), *Eximiae devotionis* (1493), *Eximiae devotionis* (1501), *Ullius fulcite praesidio* (1504), and *Universalis ecclesiae* (1508).

References

Aikman, David. 2003. *Jesus in Beijing. How Christianity Is Transforming China and Changing the Global Balance of Power*. Washington, DC: Regnery.

Benedict XVI. 2007a. "Ai Vescovi, ai presbiteri, alle persone consacrate e ai fedeli laici della Chiesa cattolica nella Repubblica Popolare Cinese'Acta Apostolicae Sedis (ASS)." 99 (7): 553–81.

———. 2007b. "Letter to the Bishops, Priests, Consecrated Persons and Lay Faithful of the Catholic Church in the People's Republic of China (May 27, 2007)." *The Holy See*, Rome, Italy, Libreria Editrice Vaticana. Accessed August 16, 2020. www.vatican.va/content/benedict-xvi/en/letters/2007/documents/hf_ben-xvi_let_20070527_china.pdf.

Bishops' Conference of Catholic Church in China (BCCCC). 2017. "Zhōngguó tiānzhǔjiào zhǔjiào tuán zhāngchéng [Statutes of the BCCCC]." *Catholic Church in China*, Beijing, February 2017. Accessed August 16, 2020. www.chinacatholic.cn/html/report/17020785-1.htm.

Burke, Greg. 2018. "Full Text of Pope Francis' in-Flight Press Conference from Estonia." *Catholic News Agency (CAN)*, September 2018, Denver, CO. Accessed July 24, 2020. www.catholicnewsagency.com/news/full-text-of-pope-francis-in-flight-press-conference-from-estonia-33293.

Bush, Richard C. 1970. *Religion in Communist China*. Nashville: Abingdon.

Catholic Church in China. 2017. "Zhujiaotuan Fuzeren Jianli [Short Biography of the Officials of the Bishops' Conference]." *Catholic Church in China*, Beijing. Accessed August 16, 2020. www.chinacatholic.cn/html/report/14060010-1.htm.

———. 2018. "Tuījìn wǒguó tiānzhǔjiào jiānchí zhōngguó huà fāngxiàng wǔ nián gōngzuò guīhuà 2018–2022 [Carrying on the Direction of Chinese Catholicism's Sinicization – A Five Year Plan 2018–2022]." *Catholic Church in China*, Beijing, August 2018. Accessed August 16, 2020. www.chinacatholic.cn/html/report/18100224-1.htm.

Chan Kim-Kwong. 1992. *Struggling for Survival: The Catholic Church in China From 1949 to 1970*. Hong Kong: Christian Study Centre on Chinese Religion and Culture.

Chinese Catholic Patriotic Association (CCPA). 2017. "Zhōngguó tiānzhǔjiào àiguó huì zhāngchéng [Statutes of the CCPA]." *Catholic Church in China*, Beijing, February 2017. Accessed August 16, 2020. www.chinacatholic.cn/html/report/17020785-1.htm.

Congressional-executive Commission on China. 2018. *Annual Report 2019*. Washington: U.S. Government Publishing Office.

Francis. 2013. "Evangelii Gaudium." *Acta Apostolicae Sedis (ASS)* 105 (12): 1019–137.

———. 2018. "Message of his Holiness Pope Francis to the Catholics of China and to the Universal Church." *Holy See*, Rome, Italy, Libreria Editrice Vaticana, September 26, 2018. Accessed August 16, 2020. www.vatican.va/content/francesco/en/messages/pont-messages/2018/documents/papa-francesco_20180926_messaggio-cattolici-cinesi.html.

Hackett, Conrad et al., 2015. "The Future of World Religions: Population Growth Projections, 2010–2050." *Pew Research Center*. Accessed August 16, 2020. https://assets.pewresearch.org/wp-content/uploads/sites/11/2015/03/PF_15.04.02_ProjectionsFullReport.pdf.

Harlan, Chico. "Vatican and China Reach 'Provisional' Deal on Appointment of Bishops." *The Washington Post*, Washington DC. Accessed August 16, 2020. www.washingtonpost.com/world/vatican-and-china-reach-provisional-deal-on-the-appointment-of-bishops/2018/09/22/8e2054e6-be59-11e8-8792-78719177250f_story.html.

Holy See Press Office. 2018a. "Briefing Note About the Catholic Church in China." *The Holy See*, Italy, Stampa della Santa Sede. Accessed August 16, 2020. http://press.vatican.va/content/salastampa/en/bollettino/pubblico/2018/09/22/180922g.pdf.

———. 2018b. "Communiqué concerning the signing of a Provisional Agreement between the Holy See and the People's Republic of China on the appointment of Bishops." *The Holy See*, Rome, Italy, Stampa della Santa Sede. Accessed August 16, 2020. https://press.vatican.va/content/salastampa/en/bollettino/pubblico/2018/09/22/180922d.pdf.

———. 2019. "Orientamenti pastorali della Santa Sede circa la registrazione civile del Clero in Cina." *The Holy See*, Italy, Stampa della Santa Sede, June 28, 2019. Accessed August 16, 2020. http://press.vatican.va/content/salastampa/it/bollettino/pubblico/2019/06/28/0554/01160.html#en.

Horowitz, Jason, and Ian Johnson. 2018. "China and Vatican Reach Deal on Appointment of Bishops." *The New York Time*, New York. Accessed August 16, 2020. www.nytimes.com/2018/09/22/world/asia/china-vatican-bishops.html.

Vatican Council. 1966. "Gaudium et Spes." *Acta Apostolicae Sedis (ASS)* 58: 1025–115.

Leung Kit Fun, Beatrice. 1992. *Sino-Vatican Relations. Problems in Conflicting Authority 1976–1986*. Cambridge: Cambridge University Press.

Li, Enshen. 2019. "Fighting the 'Three Evils': A Structural Analysis of Counter-Terrorism Legal Architecture in China." *Emory International Law Review* 33 (3): 311–65.

Maslow, Abraham. 1943. "A Theory of Human Motivation." *Psychological Review* 50 (4): 370–96.

———. 1954. *Motivation and Personality*. New York: Harper.

———. 1971. *Farther Reaches of Human Nature*. New York: Viking Press.

McCarthy, Susan K. 2013. "Serving Society, Repurposing the State: Religious Charity and Resistance in China." *The China Journal* 70: 48–72.

Murphy, Rachel, ed. 2008. *Labour Migration and Social Development in Contemporary China*. London: Routledge.

Palmer, David A. 2008. "Heretical Doctrines, Reactionary Secret Societies, Evil Cults: Labelling Heterodoxy in 20th Century China." In *Chinese Religiosities: The Vicissitudes of Modernity and State Formation*. edited by Mayfair Yang, 113–34. Berkeley: University of California Press.

Paul II, John. 1991. "Redemptoris Missio." *Acta Apostolicae Sedis (ASS)* 83 (4): 249–340.

Pius XII. 1940. "Plane Compertum Est." *Acta Apostolicae Sedis (ASS)* 32 (1).

———. 1951. "Evangelii Praecones." *Acta Apostolicae Sedis (ASS)* 43 (11): 497–528.

———. 1952. "Cupimus Imprimis." *Acta Apostolicae Sedis (ASS)* 44 (3): 153–58.

———. 1955. "Ad Sinarum Gentem." *Acta Apostolicae Sedis (ASS)* 47 (1): 5–15.

———. 1958. "Ad Apostolorum Principis." *Acta Apostolicae Sedis (ASS)* 50 (13): 601–14.

Schatz, Klaus. 2008. *Allgemeine Konzilien – Brennpunkte der Kirchengeschichte*. Paderborn: Beck.

Shen, Anqi. 2018. *Internal Migration, Crime, and Punishment in Contemporary China*. Basel: Springer.

Sherwood, Harriet. 2018. "Vatican Signs Historic Deal with China – But Critics Denounce Sellout." *The Guardian*. Accessed August 16, 2020. www.theguardian.com/world/2018/sep/22/vatican-pope-francis-agreement-with-china-nominating-bishops.

State Council of the People's Republic of China. 2017. "Zōngjiào shìwù tiáolì' [Regulation of Religious Affairs]." *Zhōnghuá rénmín gònghéguó zhōngyāng rénmín zhèngfǔ* [The Central People's Government of the People's Republic of China], Beijing 2017. Accessed August 16, 2020. www.gov.cn/zhengce/content/2017-09/07/content_5223282.htm.

Su Jianan. 2018. "Luómǎ jiàotíng xiàng quánqiú tiānzhǔjiào tú fāchū fángbèi "quánnéng shén" jǐngshì [The Holy See issues a warning against "Almighty God" to Catholics around the world]." *Zhōngguó fǎn xiéjiào wǎng* [China Anti-cult Network], 2018. Accessed August 16, 2020. www.chinafxj.cn/c/2018-05-21/532909.shtml.

The State Council Information Office of the People's Republic of China. 2016. "China's Policies and Practices on Protecting Freedom of Religious Belief." In *The State Council Information Office of the People's Republic of China*. Beijing, China, June 2016. Accessed August 16, 2020. www.scio.gov.cn/zfbps/32832/Document/1626734/1626734.htm.

United States Conference of Catholic Bishops (USCCB). 2000. *Catechism of the Catholic Church* (CCC), 2nd ed. Vatican City: Libreria Editrice Vaticana.

United Work Front Department of the CCP Central Committee. 2020. "Wáng Zuò'ān jiǎnjiè [Short biography of Wang Zuo'an]." In *The United Work Front Department of the CCP Central Committee*. Beijing. Accessed August 16, 2020. www.zytzb.gov.cn/wza.jhtml.

Wang Zuo'an. 2010. *Zhōngguó de zōngjiào wèntí hé zōngjiào zhèngcè* [*The Problem of Religion in China and Religious Policies*]. Beijing: Zōngjiào wénhuà chūbǎn shè [Religious Culture Press].

———. 2016. "Zōngjiào gōngzuò guānjiàn zài 'dǎo' [Guidance Is the Key of Religious Work]." *Zhōngguó gòngchǎndǎng xīnwén wǎng* [CCP News Site], Beijing, September 2016. Accessed August 16, 2020. http://theory.people.com.cn/n1/2016/0808/c49150-28618337.html.

———. 2018. "Zhuólì tígāo xīn shídài zōngjiào gōngzuò shuǐpíng [Efforts to Improve the Level of Religious Work in the New Era]." *Qiushi* 16. Accessed August 16, 2020. www.qstheory.cn/dukan/qs/2018-08/17/c_1123284988.htm.

Wenzel-Teuber, Katharina. 2017. "Die 9. Nationalversammlung der Vertreter der katholischen Kirche Chinas und der sino-vatikanische Dialog." *China Heute* 36 (1): 4–7.

———. 2018. "Statistics on Religions and Churches in the People's Republic of China – Update for the Year 2017." *Religions & Christianity in Today's China* 8 (2): 26–51.

———. 2020. "Statistics on Religions and Churches in the People's Republic of China – Update for the Year 2019." *Religions & Christianity in Today's China* 10 (2): 21–41.

Ye Xiaowen. 2000. "China's Current Religious Question: Once Again, an Inquiry Into the Five Characteristics of Religion (March 22, 1996)." *Chinese Law and Government* 33 (2): 75–100.

Zey, Claudia. 2017. *Der Investiturstreit*. München: UTB.

11

RELIGIOUS OTHERING IN HINDI FILMS

Diana Dimitrova

This article explores the representation of Hinduism and non-Hindus in Bollywood Films of the late 1990s and early 2000s. It will deal with constructed notions of "otherness" as revealed in the representation of the "West" and of "India" in popular Hindi films, focusing on the discourse of difference as well as on issues of nationalism, diaspora, and globalization. It is characteristic of these films that they deal with aspects of modernity, westernization, and globalization in order to assert a modern Hindu-Indian identity that is different, "other," and often traditional and conservative.

Bollywood Film: History, Periodization, and Esthetic

"Bollywood Film" denotes the Hindi–Urdu popular cinema of India, which has its center in Mumbai (Bombay). It has been argued that the term "Bollywood" is not a perfect one, "as it implies that Hindi cinema is a derivation of Hollywood and thus an insulting term" (Dwyer 2005, 4). However, it is the dominant global term to refer to the prolific Hindi language film industry in Bombay and has also become part of the academic jargon appearing on the titles of many recent books on Hindi–Urdu popular cinema. Therefore, I have adopted it in this essay.

The beginnings of cinema in India go back to 1896 when the first cinematography show was presented at Watson's Hotel in Bombay. Dhundiraj Govind Phalke (Dadasaheb Phalke 1870–1944) is venerated nowadays as the "Father of Indian cinema." His first film *Raja Harischandra* made its debut in Bombay's Coronation Cinematograph Theatre in 1913 and is considered the first Hindi film. Sound and music arrived in Indian cinema in 1931. In the following two decades, several studios, organized along lines similar to Hollywood, made an important contribution to the further development of the Hindi film industry. Four important studios of this era were Imperial Films Company in Bombay, Prabhat Film Company in

DOI: 10.4324/b22926-12

Pune, New Theatres in Calcutta, and Bombay Talkies. During World War II, there were shortages of raw film stock and a thriving black market. The priority that was given to films supporting the war resulted in the production of numerous war movies. During and after Partition, the importance of the Bombay film industry grew, as the film industries located in Calcutta and Lahore lost personnel and audiences. The post-independence film industry was shaped by the histories of migration and displacement. Bombay became one of the few centers in India where the Urdu language was kept alive, as Hindi films continued to be made in Hindustani, building on a common Hindi–Urdu vocabulary, and not in the highly Sanskritized Hindi, promoted by the government. Moreover, Urdu poets and many Muslim stars, directors, lyricists, and screenwriters have enjoyed prominence and success in the film industry located in Bombay (Ganti 2004, 8–23).

Scholars have categorized Hindi film-making in post-Independence India in three main eras: Hindi cinema in the "nation-building" Nehruvian era in the 1950s, Hindi cinema during the crisis of the state in the 1970s, and Hindi cinema in the period of liberalization and satellite television after 1991 up to present day (Ganti 2004, 23–43).

The politics of Bollywood have been studied by scholars in terms of the ideology of class, gender, and sexuality and of the nation. M. Madhava Prasad's book on the *Ideology of the Hindi Film* elaborates on the historical construction of class and gender in film. Bollywood film is also seen as a medium for exploring the nation. An important study here is Sumita Chakravarty's *National Identity in Indian Popular Cinema 1947–1987*. Chakravarty deals with questions of identity, authenticity, citizenship, and collectivity. As the dominant media institution within India, the Bombay film industry plays an important role in constructing and defining the concepts of traditional and modern, global and local, and notions of "culture," "nation," and "Indian" (Ganti 2004, 3).

The sources and origins of the esthetic of Bollywood film are to be found in Indian music and dance, folk dramatic tradition, Urdu literature, classical Sanskrit drama, the epic narratives of the Mahābhārata and Rāmāyaṇa, Shakespeare, and European drama, especially as transmitted and rendered by the Parsi theater of the Colonial period, and of European and World Cinema. The importance of the Parsi theater cannot be emphasized enough. The Parsi theater groups provided the first writers and performers for the film industry, as most actors of the Parsi theater switched over to film acting. Assimilation of Shakespeare, Persian lyric poetry, Indian folk traditions and Sanskrit drama, operatic structure integrating songs into the narrative, use of the Urdu language, and dominance of the genres of the historical, mythological, and romantic melodrama are key features of the Parsi theater. Scholars therefore see the tradition of the Parsi theater as the immediate esthetic and cultural precursor of the esthetic of popular Hindi cinema (Radhyaksha and Willemen 1999; Ganti 2004, 8).

Important features of the classical Bollywood film are the use of melodrama to heighten emotional response, universal target audience, the understanding of cinema as mass entertainment and as a variety show, and the implementation of hybrid business models, in which cinema and music industries are closely coordinated. One of the most distinctive elements of Bollywood film that audiences unfamiliar with the genre notice immediately is the role that songs play. The centrality of music has its roots in older performance traditions, for instance, in classical Sanskrit drama, folk theater, and Parsi theater, which integrated music, dance, and song in the performance. In Hindi films, music and film define and propel the development of the plot. They also convey the heightening of emotion, typical of the melodramatic esthetic of Bollywood film, especially regarding love and romance. Thus, the development of romance in most films is played out in the song sequences.

Songs are also used to represent fantasy, desire, and passion that are inherent in the development of the love story. Similarly, allusions to eroticism, sexuality, and physical intimacy are conveyed in the songs. Sometimes the songs contribute to the characterization of the main roles, especially when they are used to introduce the leading actors in the film. Last but not least, songs are essential to the marketing of a popular Hindi film and to its commercial success. Tejaswini Ganti has made the observation that songs also operate as virtual tourism, as many songs are shot in exotic locations and abroad, for instance, in Europe, North America, and Australia. Songs, especially songs in exotic or foreign locations, are the critical element in a film's repeat value (Ganti 2004, 78–87). Ganti is right in observing that Hindi films circulate globally, so many governments use Bollywood films to promote tourism in their countries. On the other hand, the continuously growing interest in foreign locations may be the consequence of the increasing globalization in India and the need to address issues related to the global and the local, immigration, diaspora, and hybrid identities.

Most Indian films do not fit in the Western descriptions of film genres such as "musical," "comedy," "drama," "action," and "love story," since each Hindi film may contain all of these elements and more. Nevertheless, scholars have attempted to classify and organize Bollywood films under these rubrics. Thus, Subhash Jha distinguishes between "drama," "comedy," "war drama," "family drama," "thrillers and mysteries," "romance," "historical," "action," and "parallel cinema" (Jha 2005).

The phenomenal box-office success of the film *Ham āpke haiṃ kaun* ("Who Am I to You"), 1994, established the dominance of the genre of "family entertainers" in the films of the mid-1990s. These are love stories filled with songs and dances and elaborate cultural spectacles like weddings, set against the backdrop of extremely wealthy, extended, and frequently trans-national families. This film set the trend for filmmaking in the 1990s in terms of themes, visual style, music, and marketing (Ganti 2004, 39). What is remarkable about the films of the 1990s is the nearly complete erasure of class difference, caste affiliation, and the focus on wealth. The protagonists are incredibly rich, but these wealthy businessmen are not the symbol of exploitation and injustice but are depicted as loving fathers. Furthermore, in this type of film, there are no villains, and therefore the state and its representatives are absent, too. Additionally, there is a high level of conformism. Thus, in love stories depicted in earlier films, the young people rebelled against parental disapproval. In the films of the 1990s and 2000s, there is parental opposition and disapproval, too. However, the conflict is internalized as a conflict between individual desire and duty to one's family (Ganti 2004, 40). Dominant is the theme of compliant daughters and sons willing to sacrifice their love for the sake of family honor and harmony. This compliance with patriarchal norms illustrates the conservative outlook of many contemporary Indian films. It is linked to the deliberate presentation of a commodified Indian identity, which aims at the celebration of "family values" (represented by the stereotypical North Indian Hindu joint family) and an affirmation of "Indian tradition" in an increasingly globalized world.

Another trend is the upsurge of nationalism in films. Tejaswini Ganti argues that the nationalism of contemporary Bollywood films is different from the patriotism and nationalism of earlier films. She states that the focus and subject matter is not the West with its immoral and materialistic culture that is contrasted to the cultural superiority of India, but the figure of the terrorist. She concludes that nationalism is no longer depicted through a simple East–West dichotomy (Ganti 2004, 42). While the significance of films such as *Bombay*, *Dil se* ("From the Heart"), and *Roja* and their treatment of the evils of terrorism, communalism, and separatism would support this inference, I would argue that the dichotomy between India and the West and the global and the local remains a powerful tool for constructing national and cultural identity, affirming "Indian tradition" and "Indian" values in some of the most influential, successful, and trend-setting films of the 1990s and the 2000s.[1]

I will therefore discuss the construction of an Indian cultural identity by means of representing India and its religion, culture, and values as distinct, unique, and superior and at the same time marking India's difference from other cultures, notably from the West. The "West," as this "other" was incorporated into India's image of itself. This encounter with difference and the construction of "otherness" is analyzed in terms of the discourses of "self" and "otherness" through which India came to represent itself and imagine its difference from the West. The two films that I will discuss in this article are films that belong to the period of liberalization and satellite TV of the 1990s and 2000s. According to Jha's classification, they belong to two different genres: the historical: *Lagān* and the romance *Ham dil de cuke sanam* (*HDDCS*).

The Discourse of Otherism and the Construction of Difference

In his book *Orientalism*, Edward Said analyzed various discourses and institutions which constructed and produced the entity called "the Orient" as an object of knowledge. He calls this discourse "orientalism." Said refers mainly to the Middle East, and his main focus is French writing about the Middle East. However, by analogy, his methodology and findings can be used to analyze similar discourses about South Asia and India, as reflected in British colonial writing. The discursive practices of "orientalism" involve idealization, the projection of fantasies of desire and degradation, the use of stereotypes, the failure to recognize and respect difference, and the tendency to impose European categories and norms and to see the difference through the modes of perception and representation of the West (Hall et al. 2000, 215). As Said has argued, "the essence of Orientalism is the ineradicable distinction between Western superiority and Oriental inferiority" (Said 1979, 1985, 42).

In the era of post-colonialism, globalization, and the emergence of former colonized countries as independent and powerful nations who have become important global players, similar discourses about the "West" have originated in the "Orient." Thus, India has generated various discourses, which have produced and constructed the entity of "the West." The discursive practices are similar to that of "orientalism" – idealization, the projection of fantasies of desire and degradation, the use of stereotypes, the failure to recognize and respect difference, and the tendency to impose Indian categories and norms and to see the difference through Indian modes of perception and representation. For lack of a better term, we may call this discourse "occidentalism." As is typical of this type of discourse, difference and "otherness" are used to promote the idea of the superiority of India and Indian values. The mass media, and especially popular Hindi films, have contributed significantly to the formation and spread of this discourse.

I will use the term "otherism," which I have coined in my last book, to denote the universal discourse of "otherness and othering" (Dimitrova 2014, 1–19). Unlike Said's "orientalism" (Said 1979, 1985), otherism is a more inclusive term, as it reflects not only on race and ethnicity but also on gender and sexuality, and goes beyond the "West and the rest" dichotomy to include each religion's/nations's/culture's inner and outer "others." In the discourse of otherism, any religion/culture/gender/sexuality can be the "other" and be "othered," when stereotyped, viewed, and talked about from a certain dominant perspective, be it "orientalist," "occidentalist," etc.

It is the narrative of power that defines otherism: the owner of the discourse is the party who sees itself in the position of power to other the other party and marginalizes it by producing meanings about it as different or inferior. This could be the "West" othering the "Rest" or India othering the "West," or Hinduism othering its others who are non-Hindus and therefore do not share the same value system of caste and culture – in order to establish its own position of superiority – as revealed in the two films discussed here.

Hinduism and Its Others in the Films Lagān and HDDCS

Thus, in the film *Lagān*, it is the Indian villagers who are portrayed as morally superior and heroic, while the British rulers are stereotyped as arrogant, cruel, and superficial. British rule is exposed as unjust and oppressive. The film is set in a North Indian village, Champaner, which is part of a princely state, in 1893. The villagers have to pay a tax on land, *lagān*. The Rājā pleads with Captain Russel (Paul Blackthorne) to lower the tax, as there was no rain and the villagers would starve, but instead, he imposed twice the tax. Annoyed at the rebelliousness of the villagers and of Bhuvan's (Aamir Khan) daring comparison of British cricket to the villagers' game *gulli-daṇḍa*, Russel says that he will exempt them from paying tax for three years if they beat the British at cricket. If they lose, they will have to pay extra tax. Bhuvan succeeds in persuading the villagers to fight against British injustice. The villagers do not know the rules of cricket, but Russel's sister Elizabeth (Rachel Shelley) helps them to master the game. The film shows the villagers united in their fight against the enemy, across both caste lines and the lines of religious affiliation: Hindus with caste affiliation and untouchables, Muslims, and Sikhs all take part in the game and contribute to the victory of the villagers. In this way, the film not only constructs the moral superiority and heroism of the Indian villagers by contrasting them to the "otherness" of the British but also promotes the idea of national unity, Indian values, and "Indianness."

The *pūjā* in the temple and the prayer to Krishna before the decisive last game make the fight of the villagers "sacred." Thus, the villagers represent, to use Benedict Anderson's term, the "imagined community" of the Indian nation, which becomes a sacred collectivity. Émile Durkheim called the cultural beliefs, moral values, symbols, and ideas shared by any human group "collective representations." Representations create a symbolic world of meanings within which a cultural group lives (Hall 2000a, 157). Thus, the film *Lagān* constructs a powerful symbolic world of "Indianness": different from all evils of the West: heroic, just, morally superior, sacred, and universalistic Hindu. One cannot overlook the fact that even though the villagers are Hindu, Muslim, and Sikh, it is the Hindu pūjā and prayer to the Hindu god Krishna, in a Hindu temple, which makes their fight sacred.

The difference between "Indianness" and the "West" and the construction of "otherness" are reinforced by the introduction of the female characters. Elizabeth is an educated British woman, while Gauri (Gracy Singh) is a simple Indian village girl. They are both portrayed as being in love with Bhuvan. The love romance between Bhuvan and Gauri, and between Elizabeth and Bhuvan is conveyed in the songs, which present a beautiful mixture of British and Indian musical styles and dances. Elizabeth is depicted as full of admiration for India: she learns Hindi, willingly participates in the Hindu pūjā, and in her dreams, she sees herself dressed as an Indian woman living together with Bhuvan in an Indian village. Her love for Bhuvan is an expression of the desirability and attractiveness of India and Indians. By contrast, Bhuvan "chooses" Gauri, thus affirming the attractiveness and desirability of the Indian "self," not of the Western, foreign, British "Other."

It is interesting to note that the interpretation of the love triangle between Bhuvan, Gauri, and Elizabeth is based on the mythology of the Hindu god Krishna, his favorite *gopī* (cowherd girl) Radha, and the devotional woman-poet Mira who sees herself as wed to Krishna. The audiences quickly grasp that Bhuvan represents Krishna, Gauri stands for Radha, and Elizabeth signifies Mira. This interpretation, which is in line with Hindu mythology, is reinforced by the beautiful scene, in which Krishna and Gauri enact the rāsa-līlā (love-play) dance between Krishna and Radha, to the delight of their fellow villagers who watch Bhuvan and Gauri's performance, and to our own delight as the audience of the film.

Another film that deals with issues related to Hinduism and its others is the film *HDDCS* (I have given my heart away). Nandini (Aishwarya Rai) is the daughter of a teacher of classical Indian music. She lives in a vast *haveli*. The joint family in which she was raised lives according to Indian patriarchal tradition. Sameer Rossellini (Salman Khan), who is half-Italian, half-Indian, and who lives in Italy, comes to India to study music with Nandini's father. He and Nandini fall in love. However, she is promised in marriage to Vanraj (Ajay Devgan). Even though her parents realize that she loves Sameer, and not Vanraj, they do not consent to their marriage, as Sameer is "the Other:" a "foreigner," a Christian, and therefore outside the caste system. By contrast, Vanraj is Indian, a Hindu, and of appropriate caste; therefore, he is considered a suitable husband for Nandini. When Vanraj finds out that his wife loves someone else, he takes her to Italy to search for Sameer. On their journey, Nandini comes to appreciate Vanraj. When she finally meets Sameer, she decides to go back to her husband Vanraj.

Symbolically, Nandini decides not only for a life together with Vanraj but also to stay married, and to live in India and within the Hindu tradition. Had she chosen to stay with Sameer, she would have had to obtain a divorce first, live in Italy, in the West, and live among Christians, outside of the Hindu tradition. The film does not convey the message that this is an enviable option. When Vanraj and Sameer meet in Italy, they drink and sing together; both of them home-sick for India, its festivals, and rituals. Sameer who has grown up in Italy and is about to become a successful musician is presented as being lonely and longing to return to India. When Nandini leaves him, he cries and tells his mother that he does not want to live in Italy anymore. Thus, "Indianness" and Indian values and traditions are affirmed and reinforced by contrasting them with the difference and otherness of the West and of non-Indians like Sameer who long to "belong" to India, and not to the West.

It is interesting to note that Vanraj and Nandini come to know each other and become "friends" not in Vanraj's home in India, but in the not-so-traditional atmosphere of the West. Although they have not consummated their marriage, they share a room in the hotel, eat together, and spend the entire day together. They even experience physical intimacy when they embrace on the train in order to avoid the conductor and conceal the fact that they travel without tickets. It is when Nandini is injured and hospitalized that she comes to understand that she and Vanraj are one. As she is unable to do this herself, it is Vanraj who applies the vermilion in the parting of her hair. According to tradition, married Hindu women apply vermilion in the parting of their hair. This is a beautiful image of bonding and affection between husband and wife, which is laden with symbolic meaning for Hindu audiences. Once again, the "otherness" of the West and its culture create a strong sense of belonging and cultural identity.

Another intriguing circumstance is the presence of Christianity and the Christian church in the film. Throughout the film, Sameer often talks of his Bābā and asks for favors from him. It is not clear whether he refers to God the Father or to his own father who has died or to both. He and Vanraj meet accidentally in the church. When he realizes that Vanraj suffers and that a loved one of his suffers and is in pain, Sameer makes him pray in the church and prays with him that his wish be granted. At that time, Sameer does not know who Vanraj is and that he is praying for Nandini. At the end of the film, when Nandini decides to go back to Vanraj, he remembers that he and Vanraj prayed together for him and his loved one in the church. Therefore, Sameer believes that this is why things take the course they do. We may argue that Christianity and the "Christian" identity of Sameer are used as a marker of his difference and "otherness" and as a means to reinforce the Hindu identity of Nandini and Vanraj. On another level, we may also observe that even though the prayer in the church helps Nandini to recover and also helps Vanraj to get her back, it cannot make up for Sameer's loneliness in Italy and his longing to return to India and to belong there. Though Christian, Sameer is half-Indian. He looks Indian and feels Indian. Living away from India, in the diaspora, he lives in a culture of hybridity. He must learn to inhabit two identities, to speak two cultural languages, and to translate and negotiate between them. The film implies that this culture of hybridity is often linked to loneliness and marginality.

Conclusion

We may want to raise the question of whether the globalizing process with its tendency toward hybridization and "cultural homogenization" would undermine national forms of cultural identity. Since there is an uneven direction to the global flow, and since unequal relations of cultural power between the West and the rest of the world persist, globalization may appear to be essentially a western phenomenon. It is therefore not surprising that the trend toward "global homogenization" is matched by a powerful revival of "ethnicity." The reaffirmation of cultural roots and the return to tradition and orthodoxy has long been one of the most powerful sources of counter-identification in many post-colonial societies. Thus, alongside the tendency toward global homogenization, there is also fascination with difference, ethnicity, and "otherness." As my analysis showed, Bollywood film reverses the "orientalist" discourse in order to produce and construct a discourse of "occidentalism," in which the notions of "the self" and the "the other" are redefined. Through this discourse of difference and "otherness," a national cultural identity is constructed, which, in the films discussed, is presented as Hindu-Indian and in harmony with traditional values.

Note

1 This article was first published in the *Journal of Religion and Film* under the title "Hinduism and Its Others in Bollywood film of the 2000s." I would like to thank the editors of the *Journal* for granting permission to publish the article in the present volume.

References

Anderson, B. 1991. *Imagined Communities*. London and New York: Verso.

Bhabha, H. 1999. "DissemiNation: Time, Narrative, and the Margins of the Modern Nation." In *Nation and Narration*, edited by Homi Bhabha, 291–322. London and New York: Routledge.

———, ed. 1990, 1999. *Nation and Narration*. London and New York: Routledge.
———. 2002. "The World and the Home." In *Dangerous Liaisons: Gender, Nation and Postcolonial Perspectives*, edited by Anne McClintock, Aamir Mufti, and Ella Shohat, 445–55. Minneapolis and London: University of Minnesota Press.
Bhansali, S. L. (Director). 1999. *Ham dil de cuke sanam*. I Have Already Given My Heart Away.
Chakravarty, S. S. 1993. *National Identity in Indian Popular Cinema 1947–1987*. Austin: University of Texas Press.
Chatterjee, P. 1993. *The Nation and Its Fragments: Colonial and Postcolonial Histories*. Princeton: Princeton University Press.
Dimitrova, D., ed. 2014. *The Other in South Asian Religion, Literature and Film: Perspectives on Otherism and Otherness*. London and New York: Routledge.
Duara, P. 1996. "Historicizing National Identity, or Who Imagines What and When." In *Becoming a National: A Reader*, edited by Geoff Eley and Ronald Grigor Suny, 151–78. New York and Oxford: Oxford University Press.
During, S. 1999. "Literature-Nationalism's Other? The Case for Revision." In *Nation and Narration*, edited by Homi Bhabha, 138–53. London and New York: Routledge.
Dwyer, R. 2005. *100 Bollywood Films*. New Delhi: Roli Books.
———. 2006. *Filming the Gods: Religion and Indian Cinema*. London and New York: Routledge.
Dwyer, R., and D. Patel. 2002. *Cinema India: The Visual Culture of the Hindi Film*. New Brunswick: Rutgers University Press.
Eley, G., and R. G. Suny, eds. 1996. *Becoming a National: A Reader*. New York and Oxford: Oxford University Press.
Ganti, T. 2004. *Bollywood: A Guidebook to Popular Hindi Cinema*. New York and London: Routledge.
Gokulsingh, K. M., and W. Dissanayake, eds. 1998. *Indian Popular Cinema: A Narrative of Cultural Change*. New Delhi: Orient Longman.
Gowariker, A. (Director) 2001. *Lagān* (Rent on Land).
Gulzar, G. N., and S. Chatterjee, eds. 2003. *Encyclopaedia of Hindi Cinema*. New Delhi: Encyclopaedia Britannica (India) and Mumbai: Popular Prakashan.
Guha, R., and G. C. Spivak, eds. 1988. *Selected Subaltern Studies*. New York and Oxford: Oxford University Press.
Guneratne, A. R., and W. Dissanayake, eds. 2003. *Rethinking Third Cinema*. New York and London: Routledge.
Hall, S. 1996. "Ethnicity: Identity and Difference." In *Becoming a National: A Reader*, edited by Geoff Eley and Ronald Grigor Suny, 339–51. New York and Oxford: Oxford University Press.
———. 2000a. "The Question of Cultural Identity." In *Modernity: An Introduction to Modern Societies*, edited by Stuart Hall et al., 595–634. Oxford: Blackwell.
———. 2000b. "The West and the Rest: Discourse and Power." In *Modernity: An Introduction to Modern Societies*, edited by Stuart Hall et al., 184–228. Oxford: Blackwell.
———. 2002. "The Local and the Global: Globalization and Ethnicity." In *Dangerous Liaisons: Gender, Nation and Postcolonial Perspectives*, edited by Anne McClintock, Aamir Mufti, and Ella Shohat, 173–87. Minneapolis and London: University of Minnesota Press.
Hall, S., D. Held, D. Hubert, and K. Thompson, eds. 1996, 2000. *Modernity: An Introduction to Modern Societies*. Oxford: Blackwell.
Hobsbawm, E. 2003. "Introduction: Inventing Traditions." In *The Invention of Tradition*, edited by Eric Hobsbawm and Terence Ranger, 1–14. Cambridge: Cambridge University Press.

Hobsbawm, E., and T. Ranger, eds. 1983, 2003. *The Invention of Tradition*. Cambridge: Cambridge University Press.

Jha, S. K. 2005. *The Essential Guide to Bollywood*. New Delhi: Roli Books.

Kabir, N. M. 2001. *Bollywood: The Indian Cinema Story*. London: Channel 4 Books.

Kavoori, A. P., and A. Punathambekar, eds. 2008. *Global Bollywood*. New York and London: New York University Press.

Kazmi, F. 1999. *The Politics of India's Conventional Cinema: Imaging a Universe, Subverting a Multiverse*. New Delhi: SAGE.

Ludden, D. 2001a. "A Brief History of Subalternity." In *Reading Subaltern Studies: Critical History, Contested Meaning, and the Globalisation of South Asia*, edited by David Ludden. New Delhi: Permanent Black.

———, ed. 2001b. *Reading Subaltern Studies: Critical History, Contested Meaning, and the Globalisation of South Asia*. New Delhi: Permanent Black.

McClintock, A. 1996. "'No Longer in a Future Heaven': Nationalism, Gender and Race." In *Becoming a National: A Reader*, edited by Geoff Eley and Ronald Grigor Suny, 260–87. New York and Oxford: Oxford University Press.

McClintock, A., A. Mufti, and E. Shohat, eds. 2002. *Dangerous Liaisons: Gender, Nation and Postcolonial Perspectives*. Minneapolis and London: University of Minnesota Press.

McGrew, A. 2000. "A Global Society?" In *Modernity: An Introduction to Modern Societies*, edited by Stuart Hall et al., 466–503. Oxford: Blackwell.

Mishra, V. 2002. *Bollywood Cinema: Temples of Desire*. New York and London: Routledge.

Pauwels, Heidi R. M., ed. 2007. *Indian Literature and Popular Cinema: Recasting Classics*. London and New York: Routledge,

Pendakur, M. 2003. *Indian Popular Cinema: Industry, Ideology and Consciousness*. Cresskill, NJ: Hampton Press.

Prasad, M. M. 1998. *Ideology of the Hindi Film: A Historical Construction*. New Delhi: Oxford University Press.

Rajadhyaksha, A., and P. Willemen. 1995, 1999. *Encyclopaedia of Indian Cinema*. New Delhi: Oxford University Press.

Renan, E. 1996. "What is a Nation?" In *Becoming a National: A Reader*, edited by G. Eley and Ronald G. Suny, 42–56. New York and Oxford: Oxford University Press.

Said, E. 1979, 1985. *Orientalism*. New York: Vintage Books.

Spivak, G. C. 1988. "Subaltern Studies: Deconstructing Historiography." In *Selected Subaltern Studies*, edited by Ranajit Guha and Gayatri Chakravorty Spivak, 3–34. New York and Oxford: Oxford University Press.

Thompson, K. 2000. "Religion, Values, and Ideology." In *Modernity: An Introduction to Modern Societies*, edited by Stuart Hall et al., 395–422. Oxford: Blackwell.

Vasudevan, R. S., ed. 2000. *Making Meaning in Indian Cinema*. New Delhi: Oxford University Press.

INDEX

9781032280677